The UN and Transnational Corporations

United Nations Intellectual History Project

Ahead of the Curve? UN Ideas and Global Challenges
    Louis Emmerij, Richard Jolly, and Thomas G. Weiss

Unity and Diversity in Development Ideas: Perspectives from the UN Regional Commissions
    Edited by Yves Berthelot

Quantifying the World: UN Ideas and Statistics
    Michael Ward

The UN and Global Political Economy: Trade, Finance, and Development
    John Toye and Richard Toye

UN Contributions to Development Thinking and Practice
    Richard Jolly, Louis Emmerij, Dharam Ghai, and Frédéric Lapeyre

UN Voices: The Struggle for Development and Social Justice
    Thomas G. Weiss, Tatiana Carayannis, Louis Emmerij, and Richard Jolly

Women, Development, and the UN: A Sixty-Year Quest for Equality and Justice
    Devaki Jain

Human Security and the UN: A Critical History
    S. Neil MacFarlane and Yuen Foong Khong

Human Rights at the UN: The Political History of Universal Justice
    Roger Normand and Sarah Zaidi

Preventive Diplomacy at the UN
    Bertrand G. Ramcharan

The UN and Transnational Corporations

From Code of Conduct to Global Compact

Tagi Sagafi-nejad
in collaboration with
John H. Dunning

Foreword by Howard V. Perlmutter

Indiana University Press
Bloomington & Indianapolis

This book is a publication of

Indiana University Press
601 North Morton Street
Bloomington, IN 47404-3797 USA

http://iupress.indiana.edu

Telephone orders   800-842-6796
Fax orders   812-855-7931
Orders by e-mail   iuporder@indiana.edu

The paper used in this publication meets the minimum requirements
of American National Standard for Information Sciences—Permanence
of Paper for Printed Library Materials, ANSI Z39.48-1984.

Manufactured in the United States of America

Library of Congress Cataloging-in-Publication Data

Sagafi-nejad, Tagi, date-
  The UN and transnational corporations : from code of conduct to global compact /
Tagi Sagafi-nejad in collaboration with John H. Dunning.
      p.   cm. — (United Nations intellectual history project series)
  Includes bibliographical references and index.
  ISBN 978-0-253-35212-5 (cloth) — ISBN 978-0-253-22012-7 (pbk.) 1. Interna-
tional business enterprises—Social aspects. 2. Investments, Foreign—Social aspects.
3. United Nations—Developing countries—Economic assistance. I. Dunning,
John H. II. Title.
  HD2755.5.S2336 2008
  338.8'8—dc22
                                                                   2008003116

1 2 3 4 5 13 12 11 10 09 08

Contents

Boxes, Figures, and Tables

Boxes

Figures

Tables

Series Editors' Foreword

Surprisingly, no comprehensive history exists of the United Nations family of organizations. True, in the last few years, histories of the UN Development Programme (UNDP)[1] and the World Food Programme (WFP)[2] have been completed, to add to the two histories of UNICEF (UN Children's Fund) produced in the 1980s and 1990s.[3] And there is a new series of short and readable books about "global institutions" that is being edited by one of us.[4] Moreover, the UN Educational, Scientific and Cultural Organization (UNESCO), the World Health Organization (WHO), and the UN Conference on Trade and Development (UNCTAD) have been preparing internal volumes that bring together different perspectives about the evolution of these organizations.

But these are still patchy and incomplete, all the more so because more than six decades have passed since the founding of the current generation of international organizations. More serious and complete accounts of UN activities and contributions should be expected of all intergovernmental organizations, along with enhanced efforts to organize their archives so that independent researchers can document and analyze their efforts, achievements, and shortcomings. These are essential parts of compiling the record of global governance during the last half of the twentieth century and the beginning of the current millennium.

Faced with such major omissions—which have substantial implications for the academic and policy literatures—we decided to undertake the task of writing an *intellectual* history, that is, a history of the ideas launched or nurtured by the United Nations. Observers should not be put off by what may strike them as a puffed-up billing. The working assumption behind our undertaking is straightforward: ideas and concepts are a main driving force in human progress, and they arguably have been one of the most important contributions of the world organization. As the various volumes of our project have been completed, our early assumptions about the importance of ideas among the UN's various contributions have been confirmed by archival and personal records.

The United Nations Intellectual History Project (UNIHP) was launched in

1999 as an independent research effort based at the Ralph Bunche Institute for International Studies at The Graduate Center of The City University of New York. We are extremely grateful for the enthusiastic backing from the seventh Secretary-General, Kofi Annan, and other staff, as well as from scholars and analysts and governments. We are also extremely appreciative for the generosity and understanding of the governments of the Netherlands, the United Kingdom, Sweden, Canada, Norway, Switzerland, Finland, and the Republic and Canton of Geneva, as well as of the Ford, Rockefeller, and MacArthur Foundations; the Carnegie Corporation of New York; and the UN Foundation. This support ensures total intellectual and financial independence. Details of this and other aspects of the project can be found on our Web site: www.unhistory.org.

The work of the UN can be divided into two broad categories: economic and social development, on the one hand, and peace and security, on the other. The UNIHP is committed to produce fifteen volumes on major themes, mainly in the first arena, but we are also penetrating the second. These volumes are being published by Indiana University Press. Oxford University Press has published a sixteenth and related volume, *The Oxford Handbook on the United Nations*.[5]

In addition, the UNIHP has completed an oral history collection of seventy-nine lengthy interviews of persons who have played major roles in launching and nurturing UN ideas—and sometimes in hindering them! Extracts from these interviews were published in 2005 as *UN Voices: The Struggle for Development and Social Justice,* and authors of the project's various volumes, including this one, have drawn on these interviews to highlight substantive points made in the complete texts. Full transcripts of the oral histories with indices are now available on CD-ROM (essentially a searchable electronic book) to facilitate work by researchers and other interested persons worldwide.[6]

There is no single way to organize research, and certainly not for such an ambitious project as this one. We have structured this historical effort by topics—ranging from trade and finance to human rights, from transnational corporations to development assistance, from regional perspectives to sustainability. We have commissioned world-class experts for each topic, and the argument in all of the volumes is the responsibility of the authors whose names appear on the covers. All have been given freedom and responsibility to organize their own digging, analyses, and presentations. Guidance from us as the project directors as well as from peer-review groups has helped ensure accuracy and fairness in depicting where the ideas came from, how they were developed and disseminated within the UN system, and what happened with them. We are hoping that future analyses will build upon our series, and indeed go well beyond. Our intellectual history project is the first, not last, installment in depicting the history of the UN's contributions to ideas. We trust that these publications will be of help to the eighth Secretary-General, Ban Ki-moon, and his successors.

The present volume, the eleventh in our series, is about transnational corporations (TNCs) and the United Nations. The author, Tagi Sagafi-nejad, is currently the Radcliffe Killam Distinguished Professor of International Business and director of the Ph.D. program at Texas A&M International University. He has spent a lifetime studying the ups and downs of these entities as both a scholar and a consultant. He was privileged to obtain the close collaboration of one of the world's leading experts in this field and a player in many of the dramatic roles in the book, namely John Dunning, Emeritus Professor of International Business at the University of Reading, whose name also appears on the cover of this book. And what a story it is! Within the UN proper, it is mainly focused on the United Nations Commission on Transnational Corporations and on the United Nations Centre on Transnational Corporations (UNCTC), both created in 1974 upon the recommendation of the United Nations Group of Eminent Persons (GEP). This institutional configuration is called here "the enterprise." But the rest of the UN galaxy is also drawn into the analysis because the work of UN agencies impinges on TNCs.

The story is mainly one of cycles—from harmonious relationships between TNCs and society to antagonistic ones—with the UN trying to keep a cool head and mostly (but not always) succeeding. The title of this book is particularly apt in reflecting the situation during the 1970s when the reputation of TNCs came under serious attack, notably because of the ITT affair in Chile that led to the toppling and death of President Salvador Allende and the bribing scandals around the world revealed by U.S. congressional committees that almost led to a crisis in the royal family in the Netherlands, among other things. Given the attitude of the United States subsequently, it is important to underline that the UN's role was to a large extent inspired by the outcome of these American congressional committees.

The authors give a vivid account of the discussions in the UN Group of Eminent Persons in 1972 and 1973, in which legendary business executives such as G. A. Wagner of Royal Dutch Petroleum Company and Gianni Agnelli of Fiat crossed swords with trade union leaders and representatives of developing countries. The academic members of the group, at times bewildered, made every effort to move disputes back into calmer waters. The UN accepted the main recommendations of the GEP, and in 1974 the UNCTC was created, getting its directions from the UN Commission on TNCs.

Although the terms of reference of the centre were broad—covering knowledge creation, capacity-building, and policy recommendations—the main focus during the early years was to elaborate a code of conduct that would temper the revealed abuses of TNCs. That attempt was unsuccessful, and the authors make clear that this failure could have been predicted from the discussions in the GEP.

An important contribution of the commission and the centre was the creation in 1985 of a Panel of Eminent Persons to study transnational corporations in South Africa and Namibia. It came up with specific recommendations on how to limit the role of TNCs in perpetuating the apartheid regime.

Over the 1980s the climate surrounding TNCs in general and foreign direct investment (FDI) in particular started to change. Developing countries now received the investments and the vehicles carrying them with open arms. This almost led to a "race to the bottom," with countries outbidding one other to offer ever more favorable terms to TNCs. The UNCTC, which was never as extreme as some of its member states, tried with considerable success to keep the ship on an even keel. It was therefore somewhat of a surprise that the United States continued its very critical stand with respect to the work of the enterprise. This led, in 1992, to UN Secretary-General Boutros Boutros-Ghali's dismissal of Peter Hansen, the third executive director of the centre and the transfer of the work on FDI and TNCs from New York to UNCTAD in Geneva. This sad story is told in vivid detail in the pages that follow.

In the meantime, other parts of the UN system continued their activities concerning TNCs. In 1977, for instance, the International Labour Organization (ILO) adopted a Tripartite Declaration of Principles concerning Multinational Enterprises and Social Policy. It passed because it was not binding and was couched in more conciliatory terms than successive drafts of the Code of Conduct. The World Health Organization accomplished remarkable work on tobacco use, baby food, and abuses by the pharmaceutical industry. All this, and much more, comes out clearly and succinctly in the chapter examining the work of the UN system.

The Geneva years, from 1993, were more quiet and subdued. A whole chapter is devoted to the *World Investment Report* series that started in 1991 and continues to this day. Although it is attacked by some observers as too friendly to TNCs and by others as too critical of FDI, the statistical data and other information gathered over the years for these reports constitutes a remarkable source of data and is deserving of the special treatment in this volume.

The UNIHP is about future-looking history. In the last chapter, therefore, the authors attempt to identify the UN's intellectual challenges today in the area of TNCs and FDI. The focus in particular, though far from exclusively, is on the need for closer collaboration between the different stars in the UN galaxy. That may seem obvious, but is not so. Even nomenclature remains a problem, with the ILO talking about "multinational enterprises" and the UN about "transnational corporations." Both have advanced good reasons to stick to their labels. Fortunately, the authors make clear that TNCs by any other name smell the same! The volume concludes by identifying the most important challenges the UN must confront in the years ahead.

We are convinced that the UN story in general deserves to be better documented if it is to be better understood and appreciated. As Secretary-General Kofi Annan wrote in the foreword to the first publication in this book series, *Ahead of the Curve? UN Ideas and Global Challenges:* "With the publication of this first volume in the United Nations Intellectual History Project, a significant lacuna in twentieth-century scholarship and international relations begins to be filled."[7] The present volume is another important step in closing this gap in the historical record.

We hope that readers will feel engaged, confronted, and perhaps provoked by this account, at once a journey through time and ideas. As always, we welcome comments from our readers.

Louis Emmerij
Richard Jolly
Thomas G. Weiss
New York
June 2007

Foreword

The history of the relationship between transnational corporations (TNCs) and nation-states during the past half century and more may be characterized as a "tortuous evolution." As organizations that control, utilize, and distribute goods and services and create jobs, wealth, and knowledge on an increasingly global scale, TNCs have an increasingly profound impact on the world we inhabit and therefore deserve serious attention. This multifaceted relationship has been examined by scholars for many years. Among many scholars, the late Raymond Vernon, John Dunning, and I have devoted much of our professional lives to analyzing TNCs and their influence on the global economy. Since its inception, the United Nations and its various agencies have been at the forefront of understanding and studying the role of these corporations in development and international relations and on the well-being of the nation-states in which they operate.

I became increasingly interested in these entities and established the Multinational Enterprise Unit and the Worldwide Institutions Research Group at the Wharton School of the University of Pennsylvania in the mid-1960s. A few years later, when the UN established a formal entity to study TNCs, I was asked to advise them on the subject, and I was privileged to do so. I also recommended some of our best and brightest graduates at U Penn to work at the UN. Tagi Sagafi-nejad was one of these.

Sagafi-nejad, whose contribution to the field is well known, has taken up the challenge of analyzing the evolving interface between TNCs and the United Nations, which he has been studying for over four decades. In this volume, he carefully takes the reader through the many phases that have characterized this occasionally troubled relationship, from a period of relative tranquility to the stormy 1970s, when many radical Third World advocates called for a New International Economic Order that had as its centerpiece tighter control over TNCs, to the more nuanced, complicated, and accommodating phase that characterizes the relationship in early twenty-first century, when TNCs have achieved higher levels of global corporate citizenship. Sagafi-nejad chronicles this and subsequent phases in great detail, and in so doing, he makes extensive use of a wide variety of sources, including original UN documents and interviews with key players with direct involvement at various junctures. Through meticulous research, he provides, for the first time, a comprehensive and engaging story of how the United Nations became a forum for a deeper understanding of the complex web of relationships that evolved between TNCs and the members of the UN galaxy.

The book concludes with a view to the future. It rightly points out that engaging TNCs rather than confronting them is likely to yield a more sustainable future. It also argues that the constellations that form the United Nations family can be utilized effectively in harnessing this enormous power toward a collaborative and cooperative future in what I have called an "emerging global civilization." This book ends on a note of optimism, namely, that if there is cooperation and collaboration, a fertile future scenario involving TNCs will become likely.

The valued advice and active collaboration of John Dunning, a member of the original UN-appointed Group of Eminent Persons to study the impact of TNCs on development and international relations, and who continues to provide advice to the UN on a regular basis, adds first-hand knowledge and insight to this valuable and uniquely useful work.

I warmly commend Professor Sagafi-nejad and his collaborator Professor Dunning for having produced this important and notable book; and it is my sincere belief that scholars, policymakers, and executives will read it and benefit greatly from it.

Howard V. Perlmutter
The Wharton School, University of Pennsylvania and
Vice Chair, Global Interdependence Center, Philadelphia, PA
January 2008

Preface and Acknowledgments

Many ideas concerning foreign direct investment (FDI) and transnational corporations (TNCs) can be traced, in origin or maturation, to research or discourse within the United Nations. This book examines the impact of these ideas on policy, knowledge creation, and capacity-building in developing countries.

The evolution of scholarly writings on FDI and related subjects and the role of the various actors within the international community are traced from the creation of the League of Nations to the early twenty-first century. The book centers on the 1975 establishment of the Group of Eminent Persons (GEP) and its subsequent influence on the creation of the UN Commission and Centre on Transnational Corporations (UNCTC), its work in New York, and its continuation under UNCTAD in Geneva after 1993. The institutional configuration responsible for the bulk of UN activities is called "the enterprise."

The UN was instrumental in bringing attention to the need for a multilateral and multifaceted approach to harness the activities of TNCs for the benefit of all stakeholders. The centerpiece of this policy initiative, the projected Code of Conduct, did not materialize. However, many of its ideas on competition, resource allocation, labor relations, the environment, and corruption survived. They resurfaced in other places and in other forms. The world organization continued to mirror the changes related to TNCs, FDI, and nation-states from the antagonistic and confrontational era of the 1970s—exemplified by the contentious debate over the code—to the more cooperative and conciliatory one of the mid-1980s to the present. The change in tenor within the UN is exemplified by the 1999 Global Compact.

The terms "code" and "compact," captured in the subtitle of the book, form its two margins. The book also examines a number of other policy initiatives in which the UN had a pivotal role. Other specialized agencies within the UN system are part of the story, focusing on TNC and FDI-related work that has emanated from them. The world body has provided a debating forum and a mirror through which the world can see itself while gravitating close to the center as member states have swung to extremes. Through it all, the UN has remained the spawning ground for ideas that have the potential to make FDI and TNCs more beneficial to humankind.

The book has had a long gestation period, having its genesis in earlier work that has preoccupied me, namely the relationship between TNCs, developing countries, and the development process. The project began when I took a sabbatical from Loyola College in Maryland, which led to field research at UNCTAD in 2000 and to an association with UNIHP. Following retirement from Loyola, I held the Keating-Crawford Chair for the academic year 2002–2003 at Seton Hall University's Stillman School of Business. My research continued to benefit from the generous assistance of the library staff at both Loyola and Seton Hall. After I agreed to lead Texas A&M International University's efforts to establish its first doctoral program—in International Business Administration—Laredo became the site for continued work on the manuscript.

Many have further contributed to the book by providing information through interviews and discussion. I am especially grateful to Louis Emmerij, Richard Jolly, and Thomas G. Weiss—the UNIHP leadership team—as well as to Yves Berthelot, for their financial and intellectual support. I also owe special thanks to the Dag Hammarskjöld Foundation at Uppsala for two review seminars where my initial ideas were discussed and critiqued. The manuscript benefited from the insights and criticisms of three readers to whom I am immensely grateful: Padma Mallampally, Peter Utting, and Louis Wells.

From Baltimore to London, Geneva, Gaza, New York, South Orange, and Laredo, I owe much to one individual whose immeasurable contribution to this book can hardly be overstated. My collaborator, John Dunning, has combined his giant intellect and warm heart to serve as a guiding light. He has stood by me, generously shared his wisdom, and read several drafts of each chapter. His name on the title page is but a faint reflection of his contribution. Nancy, my wife, has masterfully blended her keen editorial and intellectual skills with love and grace and patience. I thank John and Nancy. I consider myself lucky, having journeyed on the wings of these two.

Debts have accumulated as I have journeyed in the course of writing this book. In addition to the sponsorship and support from the UNIHP, I am very grateful to its competent staff, including Nancy Okada, Tatiana Carayannis, Danielle Zach Kalbacher, and Zeynep Turan. I would also like to thank Kate Babbitt for her meticulous copy editing.

The following individuals, listed alphabetically, granted me interviews, and I am thankful to them all: Abebe Abate (ILO); Victoria Aranda (UNCTC/ UNCTAD); Francis Blanchard (ILO); Jean Boddewyn (Baruch College,

CUNY); Gustave Feissel (UNCTC); John Gara (UNCTAD); David Gould (UNCTC); Robert Grosse (Thunderbird School of Global Management); Donald Guertin (Exxon); Khalil Hamdani (UNCTC/UNCTAD); Aleya Hammad (WHO); Peter Hansen (UNCTC); Guriqbal Jaiya (WIPO); Kalman Kalotay (UNCTAD); Georg Kell (UNCTC/UN Global Compact); Mithat Kulur (UNIDO); Sanjaya Lall (Oxford University); Francois LeGuay (UNIDO); Anne Miroux (UNCTC/UNCTAD); Fiorina Mugioni (UNCTC/UNCTAD); Teritomo Ozawa (Colorado State University); Stephen Persey (ILO); Pedro Roffe (UNCTAD); Klaus Sahlgren (UNCTC); Jorge Simon (UNCTAD); John Stopford (London Business School); Thomas W. Walde (UNCTC); N.T. Wang (UNCTC); Jorge Weber (UNCTAD); James X. Zhan (UNCTAD); Zbigniew Zimny (UNCTC/UNCTAD).

The following scholars have provided valuable insight and support in this endeavor: Persephone Economou (UNCTAD; World Bank); Richard Franke (Loyola College in Maryland); Robert G. Hawkins (Georgia Institute of Technology); Andrew Hilton (Center for the Study of Financial Innovation, London); Howard V. Perlmutter (Wharton School, University of Pennsylvania); Alan Rugman (Indiana University); Masood Samii (Southern New Hampshire University); and John Williams (ESCAP).

I am grateful to one and all. The remaining errors and opinions are mine alone.

As the role of TNCs and the United Nations remain contested, it is my hope that this volume will help explain the past and provide insight for future action.

T. S.
Laredo, Texas
June 2007

Abbreviations

ANC	African National Congress
DESA	Department of Economic and Social Affairs
DITE	Division of Investment, Technology and Enterprise Development
ECA	Economic Commission for Africa
ECE	Economic Commission for Europe
ECLAC	Economic Commission for Latin America and the Caribbean
ECOSOC	Economic and Social Council
ESCAP	Economic and Social Commission for Asia and the Pacific
ESCWA	Economic and Social Commission for Western Asia
FAO	Food and Agriculture Organization
FCPA	Foreign Corrupt Practices Act
FCTC	Framework Convention on Tobacco Control
FDI	foreign direct investment
FIAS	Foreign Investment Advisory Services
G-77	Group of 77
GATT	General Agreement on Tariffs and Trade
GEP	Group of Eminent Persons
GDP	gross domestic product
ICC	International Chamber of Commerce
ICFTU	International Confederation of Free Trade Unions
ICSID	International Convention on the Settlement of Investment Disputes

IDB	Inter-American Development Bank
IFC	International Finance Corporation
ILO	International Labour Organization
IMF	International Monetary Fund
IPR	investment policy review
ISAR	International Standards of Accounting and Reporting
ITO	International Trade Organization
ITT	International Telegraph and Telephone Corporation
MDG	Millennium Development Goal
MNC	multinational corporation
MNE	multinational enterprise
NAM	Non-Aligned Movement
NGO	nongovernmental organization
NIEO	New International Economic Order
NIIO	New International Information Order
OPEC	Organization of the Petroleum Exporting Countries
OPIC	Overseas Private Investment Agency
SEC	Securities and Exchange Commission
SIDA	International Development Cooperation Agency
TNC	transnational corporation
TNI	index of transnationality of firms
UNCTAD	UN Conference on Trade and Development
UNCTC	UN Centre on Transnational Corporations
UNDP	UN Development Programme
UNESCO	UN Educational, Scientific and Cultural Organization
UNICEF	UN Children's Fund
UNIDO	UN Industrial Development Organization
UNIHP	UN Intellectual History Project

UNRISD   UN Research Institute for Social Development

WHO   World Health Organization

WIPO   World Intellectual Property Organization

WIR   World Investment Report

WTO   World Trade Organization

The UN and Transnational Corporations

Introduction

While the Covenant of the League of Nations referred to an open and non-discriminatory international economic environment for investment, scholarship prior to World War II dealt primarily with trade. Foreign direct investment (FDI) was rarely studied, and the paucity of formulation of FDI theory in the early twentieth century may have been proportionate to its perceived relative significance in the real world.

Since the birth of the United Nations more than sixty years ago, the twin subjects of transnational corporations (TNCs)[1] and foreign direct investment[2] have been, and remain, major issues of interest. Many UN agencies have recognized the role and impact of TNCs on international relations and on the economic development and social well-being of the people of the world. The United Nations and transnational corporations have been two of the most salient and powerful players in the post–World War II global political economy. Major global corporations have had a significant impact on their countries of origin (their "home countries") and on countries that host them ("host countries"). The UN has been the premier international institution that has developed ideas, programs, and initiatives to study and understand these corporations. The organization has worked with them and, at times, has suggested means of regulating their activities, either though government policies in host countries or as a fulfillment of corporate missions. The Preamble to the United Nations Charter stated that one goal of the organization was "to employ international machinery for the promotion of the economic and social advancement of all peoples." This study examines how the UN has influenced TNCs in terms of policy ideas.

Over the years in Geneva, New York, Paris, Vienna, and other cities, many UN agencies have devoted attention to one or another aspect of this issue. These include the United Nations Conference on Trade and Development (UNCTAD) and its Division of Technology, Investment and Enterprise Development (DITE). This was formerly the UN Centre on TNCs (UNCTC), headquartered in New York from its creation in 1974 until 1993, when it became

Box 0.1. A Note on Terminology:
Multinational Corporations by Any Other Name

Many terms have been used in the literature to identify companies that do business beyond their home-country borders. To describe these entities, the terms "global," "international," "multinational," "supranational," "transnational," and "world" are combined with "firms," "companies," "corporations," and "enterprises."

In 1934, Alfred Plummer spoke of "international trusts," as the term trust was used at the turn of the twentieth century. He referred to Rockefeller's Standard Oil Company: "While one international trust may bring together under unified control a number of existing undertakings, another may begin as a single national undertaking and spread itself and its activities out into other countries. This type of international business does not have to achieve unified control for control is unified from the beginning, but it has to create its foreign undertakings before it can control them."[1]

The term "multinational corporations" was first used by David Lilienthal (of Tennessee Valley Authority fame) when he was chief executive of Development Resources Corporation of New York in an address at the Carnegie Institute of Technology.[2]

In its preparatory work in 1972–1973 that preceded the establishment of the Group of Eminent Persons, the UN Secretariat used the term "multinational corporation," the most widely used term at the time.

Two pioneering institutions that focused on these firms beginning in the 1960s both used "multinational enterprise": one at Harvard University under Raymond Vernon called the Multinational Enterprise Project, the other at the Wharton School of the University of Pennsylvania under Howard V. Perlmutter called the Multinational Enterprise Unit. Perlmutter also developed the classic typology, classifying multinational enterprises into ethnocentric (home-country oriented), polycentric (host-country oriented), and geocentric (globally oriented).

In early UN work, multinational corporations were understood as enterprises that own or control productions or service facilities outside the country in which they were based. Such enterprises were not always incorporated or private; they could also be cooperatives or state-owned entities. The Group of Eminent Persons agreed that "enterprise" should be substituted for corporation and that "transnational" would better convey the notion that such firms operate from their home bases across national borders.

In *Multinational Corporations in World Development,* the term "enterprise" is sometimes preferred because it clearly implies a network of corporate and noncorporate entities in different countries joined together by ownership ties. The word "corporation" is used not in the legal sense but in accordance with common usage as seen in ECOSOC resolution

1721 (LIII) of July 1972. The term "multinational" signifies that the activities of the corporation or enterprise involve more than one nation. Some authors prefer the term "international" or "transnational" when corporations are basically home-country oriented but also operate abroad.

The term "multinational corporation" accords with the broad sense of the ECOSOC resolution; it covers all enterprises that control assets—such as factories, mines, or sales offices—in two or more countries. The implication of this definition is that multinational corporations are responsible for most foreign direct investment. The study of multinational corporations can include the topics of transfer of technology and goods and provision of managerial services and entrepreneurship and related business practices, including cooperative arrangements, marketing restrictions, and transfer pricing.

The distinction between "corporation" and "enterprise" has been the subject of debate. The Soviets preferred the former because it would exclude their state-owned enterprises. Scholars such as Perlmutter and Vernon preferred "enterprise" because it was more inclusive, connoting the existence of a variety of relationships between firms; "corporation" implied a private legal entity incorporated in a given jurisdiction.

The United Nations eventually settled on "transnational corporations" in the course of its 1973–1974 deliberations. Nevertheless, different specialized agencies continue to exercise their autonomy in the use of these terms.

Sources: UN, *Multinational Corporations in World Development* (New York: UN Department of Economic and Social Affairs, 1973); UN Department of Economic and Social Affairs, *Summary of the Hearings Before the Group of Eminent Persons to Study the Impact of Multinational Corporations on Development and on International Relations* (New York: United Nations, 1974); United Nations, *The Impact of Multinational Corporations on Development and on International Relations* (New York: United Nations, 1974) (this source includes the report of the Group of Eminent Persons); and personal communications with Howard V. Perlmutter and the late Raymond Vernon.

1. See John Dunning, *Explaining International Production* (London: Unwin Hyman, 1988), 134–135.

2. Ibid., 136.

part of UNCTAD in Geneva. Another specialized agency of the United Nations, also in Geneva, is the International Labour Organization (ILO), which predates the creation of the UN and has long dealt with labor-management aspects of the activities of multinational enterprises (MNEs).[3]

The World Health Organization (WHO), another Geneva-based UN organization spearheaded a convention on tobacco control.[4] Other United Nations bodies—including the World Intellectual Property Organization (WIPO) in Geneva, the United Nations Educational, Scientific and Cultural Organization

(UNESCO) in Paris, the Food and Agriculture Organization (FAO) in Rome, and the United Nations Industrial Development Organization (UNIDO) in Vienna—have had an interest in the impact of TNCs in their particular areas of concern.

Recent corporate scandals, epitomized by those that engulfed Enron, Global Crossing, Tyco, WorldCom, Parmalat, Hyundai, and Siemens, have added a new sense of urgency to the need for responsible corporate behavior and for social policies that can propel corporations to act within established laws and norms.[5] In response to calls for action and a demand for greater accountability, transparency, and social responsibility within corporations, a skeleton staff at UN headquarters in New York crusades to promote a "global compact" with TNCs and to cajole them into a greater sense of corporate social responsibility. The premise of this campaign is that companies can do well by doing good.

TNCs have profoundly affected contemporary economic life by providing dynamism in the global economy and by fashioning and furthering the process of globalization. Yet TNCs are targets of criticism; some view them as symbols of all that is negative about globalization. It is in this context that the relationship between TNCs and nation-states deserves scrutiny and study.

Some see TNCs as exploitative and driven by profit at all costs; others view them as engines of growth, necessary for economic transformation. Ideas and events have both been influenced by this Janus face of TNCs. The UN has debated, studied, and recorded the various faces of TNCs. The ambivalence with which TNCs are viewed is understandable. They are large in size, flexible, and footloose in their ability to relocate quickly, thus uprooting and dislocating production. They can display monopolistic behavior in their handling of suppliers, markets, and workers. Moreover, some, like the aforementioned companies, commit corporate misdeeds. Enron, in fact, has become a kind of generic symbol of evil in the corporate world of global capitalism. From environmentalists to labor leaders, from the right to the left, and from xenophobic government officials to reasonable ones interested in preserving their nation's economic interests, the otherwise heterogeneous antiglobalization movement seems unified in opposition to certain practices of TNCs.

The ability of TNCs to upgrade industrial productivity and enhance economic development, nonetheless, is hardly in doubt. Much of the post–World War II debate on this *problematique* of TNCs has had to do with distribution of gains. While the benefits of free trade and open economies can hardly be disputed in the abstract, disagreement over how gains are distributed between trading countries and among stakeholder groups in each country can conjure the prospect of trade wars. The UN has served the world community as a useful and relevant forum, a debating society on TNC–nation-state issues, and ideas and actions that have sprung from this debate have been influential.

In the tradition of *Ahead of the Curve?*—the inaugural volume of this series[6]—this book addresses the following questions: What are the key ideas that have emanated from or passed through the United Nations system on the subject of TNCs and their relations with nation-states? What are the sources of these ideas? How did these ideas evolve? Which were implemented? What has the impact of the ideas been?

The book focuses on the knowledge creation, capacity-building, and policy work each member of the UN galaxy has done to address these questions. We examine political and economic events as well as scholarly ideas and insights and review the UN's impact by exploring the knowledge and information created within a given unit, project, or program; the policies that have been formulated as a result of this work, and the extent to which the UN has helped develop the capacity of developing countries.

The book is divided into nine chapters. Taking a chronological approach, we travel back in time to search for the earliest traces of ideas on the FDI-TNC intercept prior to World War II. Many ideas that were pursued in subsequent years had their genesis in such pioneering institutions as the League of Nations and the International Labour Organization. As early as the mid-nineteenth century, matters of intellectual property were, in fact, already on the international agenda. Chapter 1 contains a review of these prewar developments.

With the establishment of the United Nations, ideas inherited from prewar thinking as well as newly emerging ones continued to evolve. As the world economy and international relations underwent transformation, issues regarding TNCs and FDI began to attract the world body's attention. With postwar transformations came changes in the tone and tenor of the matters under debate. Chapter 2 describes pertinent postwar changes, including initiatives within the UN Secretariat and various reports and resolutions that emerged from the Economic and Social Council (ECOSOC) and other bodies. The evolving tripartite relationship between TNCs, nation-states, and the UN is examined in this context.

As FDI and TNCs accelerated in scale and scope during the first decades after World War II, so did a wave of anti-TNC writings in the literature and a parallel series of unfriendly measures by host-country governments. The relative tranquility of the 1960s was disrupted toward the decade's end. Chapter 3 describes the storm of the 1970s that included greater criticism of TNCs and their global operations, nationalizations and expropriations, and confrontational pronouncements. This tense period formed the backdrop for the UN's intensified involvement in the subject, culminating in 1973 in the establishment of the Group of Eminent Persons (GEP), from whom new ideas emerged. This group, consisting of distinguished corporate executives, government policymakers, and academics, held hearings and received testimony, which, together with its own insights, culminated in the seminal report of the Group of Eminent Persons.[7] One of the report's recommendations was that the United Nations establish a Commission on TNCs and a Centre on TNCs. The creation of these two UN entities constitutes the most notable institutional development pertaining to TNCs and FDI. Chapter 4 delves deeper into the economic and political contexts and the scholarship that preceded the establishment of the Commission and the UNCTC and the ideas that influenced the formation, direction, and subsequent output of these two UN entities.

Chapter 5 reviews the UNCTC's work during its years in New York. For two decades from the early 1970s to the early 1990s, the Commission on Transnational Corporations and the UNCTC formed the focal point within the UN on matters related to TNCs. Their three-pronged activities included a) gathering, analyzing, and disseminating information; b) analyzing policy; and c) providing advisory services. In 1993, a major reorganization resulted in the dismantling of the UNCTC; individuals and units were redeployed and absorbed into various other UN agencies. Its functions and staff were moved to Geneva and became part of UNCTAD.

This chapter focuses on a number of major themes that grew out of the UN's interest and involvement in TNCs, notably a code of conduct for TNCs and the hearings on South Africa regarding the presence and activities of TNCs there. Chapter 5 also identifies and discusses other UNCTC publications, most notably the 20-volume *United Nations Library of TNCs* and the journal *Transnational Corporations*. It also looks at how the UNCTC provided information for university curricula.

Chapter 6 reviews the post-1993 intellectual contributions of the enterprise, reincarnated as part of UNCTAD in Geneva. It includes a discussion of the background to the move, the internal negotiations that precipitated the move, the relevant work of UNCTAD prior to the move, and how that work provided a reasonable justification for the strategic realignment of TNC-related work within the UN galaxy. UNCTAD had sought for many years to broker multilateral accords on both restrictive business practices and technology transfer. A set of principles on restrictive business practices did materialize, but negotiations on a code of conduct for technology transfer failed. The chapter details many activities in knowledge-creation, capacity-building, and policy analysis and formulation during the intervening years, including the enterprise's publications on TNCs and FDI, its diagnostic case studies, its work to promote investment, and the consultation services it offered to developing countries.

Chapter 7 contains an analysis of the annual World Investment Report series since its inception in 1991. This series is considered a prime example of knowledge creation and is a comprehensive and cumulative chronicle of the work of the UN and the global scholarly community on TNCs and FDI and related matters.

Chapter 8 surveys TNC-related work undertaken by other members of the UN galaxy. This includes the ILO's significant work on labor issues, which resulted in the Tripartite Declaration of Principles concerning Multinational Enterprises and Social Policy, and its equally noteworthy studies on multinational corporations and social policy. This chapter also examines TNC-related ideas and publications that have emerged from WIPO, UNIDO, UNESCO, and others. The chapter also discusses the UN's latest initiative, the Global Compact, an initiative that seeks to build on the respective strengths and needs of TNCs and nation-states for mutual benefit.

Finally, Chapter 9 looks toward the future. It discusses whether hurricanes might reappear or whether there will be calmer winds, a return to halcyon days, due to UN efforts to establish substantive global rules of engagement and urge good corporate conduct. Will UN intellectual output concerning TNCs and their relationship with nation-states turn out to have been instrumental in producing a calmer and mutually better working relationship? Has its work led to changes in the relationship? Has the playing field been leveled? Can the United Nations make further contributions to understanding and/or influencing the role of TNCs and of national governments and supranational agencies in the globalizing economy of the twenty-first century? Can the power of TNCs be harnessed to benefit development, as envisioned by UN ideals? Can the modalities of dialogue, partnership, and engagement be used for greater good? By monitoring the global economy, the UN has served as an early warning system to signal the approach of another hurricane. By initiating policies, from devising codes of conduct to cajoling companies into joining a global compact, it has sought to mitigate the damage of approaching hurricanes.

Even before witnessing the more dramatic events of recent years, the late pioneering scholar Raymond Vernon warned that indeed another hurricane might be on its way.[8] A more recent publication by the Economist Intelligence Unit and Columbia University[9] warns of the possibility that there may be equal probabilities for boom and backlash at the end of the new millennium's first decade. Other thinkers, including Paul Kennedy, pin hopes on the eventual fulfillment of ideas engendered by the UN and its various agencies. This chapter discusses the question of whether the United Nations is ahead of or behind the curve on issues of TNCs and FDI.

A thorough understanding of the changing role of FDI and TNCs in economic development and structural change must be framed in terms of world economic events and connected to advances in scholarly work pertaining to UN activities in this area. This book chronicles events and relates these to concurrent scholarly work with the ultimate aim of identifying ideas that emerged from the United Nations.

The eye of the hurricane may be a useful metaphor that applies to both TNCs and the UN. Both have experienced several hurricanes in the twentieth century, but both have remained relatively calm in its eye. One was the economic crash of 1929 and the wave of protectionism that ensued under the UN's predecessor, the League of Nations. Another was the devastation caused by World War II that, in turn, disrupted the normal flow of economic intercourse and prompted the creation of the UN. The third came in the 1970s when scandals in government and in the corporate world precipitated clashes over corporate codes of conduct and ambitious demands from some developing countries for a New International Economic Order. A fourth hurricane may be gathering in the early years of the third millennium. TNCs were among the targets in the wave of anti-globalization protests as the twentieth century was coming to a close, while a series of corporate scandals that erupted in close temporal proximity added more wind to the sails of these protestors and other opposing forces. If another hurricane approaches, will TNCs again be in its eye or will the UN? If these institutions are resilient and open, they will adapt and withstand the next turbulence.

Box 0.2. Sources of information

The following sources have been used in the writing of the present book:

1. Interviews with individuals within the UN and its various agencies:
   a. Permanent/semi-permanent staff
   b. Academic and other consultants to the UN[1]
2. Interviews with executives of TNCs with firsthand knowledge of relevant operations or activities
3. Material prepared in connection with seminars, workshops, and conferences organized by UN agencies or attended by UN employees or consultants
4. Informal conversations and exchanges of views within the UN system and between UN employees/consultants and those outside the UN
5. The output emanating from UN bodies in the form of:
   a. Published books, reports, and papers; the 20-volume UNCTC library; the thrice-yearly publication *Transnational Corporations*; and other publications of the UNCTC in New York and, subsequently, UNCTAD in Geneva

    b. Workshop and conference proceedings
    c. Syllabi for educational institutions
    d. Unpublished papers prepared for government agencies
    e. Internal or limited-circulation documents describing results of fieldwork of UN-sponsored technical assistance and advice to national governments or their government agencies
    f. Exchanges of views and ideas that are not formally documented
    g. Documents prepared at the behest of the Commission on Transnational Corporations
    h. UN resolutions
6. Documents pertaining to the relations between the UNCTC, UNCTAD's Division of Investment, Technology and Enterprise Development; other UN agencies; and the various constituents affected by their actions, including consumer, labor, and special-interest groups; the business community, including TNCs, Business Industry Advisory Committees of the Organisation for Economic Co-operation and Development, the International Confederation of Free Trade Unions, and the International Chamber of Commerce; and other civil society organizations
7. Material from the universities, private collections, and the archives of the UN

1. Some interviews were conducted by the author and are listed in the acknowledgements section. Others were part of a larger set of interviews conducted by UNIHP colleagues; see www.unhistory.org.

1

Ideas and Institutions Relevant to Foreign Investment and TNCs Prior to World War II

- *Early Ideas*
- *Policy Implications*
- *Frontier Institutions*
- *Conclusion*

This chapter discusses the significance of foreign direct investment and the relative importance of multinational corporations before World War II. It reviews the relevant international or multilateral institutions that existed at the time and briefly describes the early scholarship and subsequent historical work that has analyzed the path, direction, and impact of American and Western European investments abroad.

Early Ideas

Foreign economic involvement has a long history. Traders of silk, slaves, and spices across the Arabian Peninsula, Asia, and Europe; the *commendas* of medieval Europe; the Hanseatic League; the East India Company; and the Medici of Florence are some of the better-known examples of early merchant capitalism. The era of "industrial capitalism"[1] arrived in the 1800s, and as the industrial revolution began, "firms from Europe and North America began to invest in foreign plantations, mines, factories, banking, sales and distribution facilities in large numbers."[2]

There is ample evidence that FDI evolved as the result of technological change and managerial innovations in the structure and strategy of firms in

Western Europe and the United States. Revolutions in production and organizational methods, aided by the advent of new forms of transportation and energy, characterized the period up until 1914. Host countries—the recipients of FDI—had location-specific advantages (primarily natural resources), while "[multinational enterprises] acted by and large as economic colonists, often aided and abetted by their mother countries."[3] During the interwar years, "few home or host countries . . . formulated specific policies towards [multinational enterprise] activity."[4] The literature of the period[5] indicates that while policymakers were aware of the merits of portfolio capital movements, "they appeared little interested or concerned about the implications of either outward or inward direct investment."[6]

During the "beggar-thy-neighbor" 1930s, when protectionism had a devastating effect on the world economy, the international community, primarily the League of Nations, recognized the importance of an open, liberal, and nondiscriminatory economic system. This is reflected in the League's Covenant. Nonetheless, most prewar scholarship dealt primarily with trade. FDI was rarely studied, despite the fact that, as Mira Wilkins has shown, many American and European companies had substantial investments abroad.[7] The bulk of foreign operations was confined to exporting back to the home market or to new markets, taking the form of trade rather than investment, and investment—in developing countries at least—sought mostly resources rather than markets.

At the outset of the World War I in 1914, some 90 percent of all cross-border capital movements took the form of portfolio (or indirect) investment. While capital flows were severely disrupted between 1929 and 1939, "direct investment came through the depression reasonably well and even increased in volume."[8] During that time, most multinational manufacturing corporations established—albeit on a small scale—foreign branches or subsidiaries. Data is scant on stocks and flows of foreign direct investment before World War II except for some estimates of the stock of accumulated FDI by recipient and host countries for 1914 and 1938. These estimates show that 100 percent of the outflow, $14,400 million in 1914 and $26,350 million in 1938, was by firms from developed countries, with firms from the United Kingdom accounting for the bulk of the outflow—45 percent and 40 percent in 1914 and 1938, respectively.[9]

The data illustrates a number of interesting trends. While the UK's share of world FDI stock declined before World War II (and in fact continued to do so after the war, to 16 percent of the total), outward investment from the United States nearly tripled, from $2,650 million in 1914 to $7,300 million in 1938. By 1960, outward FDI from the United States accounted for 4 percent of the

$66 billion. In almost all cases, these investments were limited to a handful of firms and countries. The lion's share of FDI was done by American and British companies, with French, German, and Dutch companies trailing significantly behind. The territorial destination of firms was more diverse and widespread than had been the case before. By 1914, the United States received 10 percent and the developed countries together received 37 percent of the total stock of FDI. Latin America, by contrast, had a 33 percent share. All developing countries combined accounted for no less than 63 percent of the stock of inward FDI. That ratio remained unchanged, according to John Dunning's estimates, during the prewar period; in 1938, developed countries accounted for one-third and developing countries for two-thirds. The balance changed after the war, and by 1960, the percentages had reversed, with developed countries accounting for 67 percent of inward FDI stock.

An exhaustive discussion of the motives of these firms is beyond the scope of this study. In brief, most FDI was driven by resource-seeking or market-seeking considerations. Moreover, most economists remained focused on international trade, the mainstay of internationalization up until World War II. Classical theories of Adam Smith (absolute advantage), David Ricardo (comparative advantage), and Heckscher-Ohlin (factor proportions) all dealt with trade. The paucity of theory formulation concerning FDI in the nineteenth and early twentieth centuries may be proportionate to its perceived relative significance in the real world.[10]

Policy Implications

After 1945, governments and international organizations increasingly discussed FDI as internationalization and decolonization combined to accelerate its flow. The rapid postwar expansion of U.S. foreign investment was a response to Europe's devastation and the need of several European countries to rebuild their infrastructure. Scholars and policymakers were then drawn to the subject and to the entities that were its conduit, multinational corporations.

Before World War II, national governments were not particularly active in influencing the flow of FDI or the activities of multinational enterprises (MNEs) or their subsidiaries. However, the spread of national firms beyond their home countries created some inevitable tension and conflict, as was well documented by Cleona Lewis in 1938. The history of U.S. companies in some Latin American economies in the eighteenth and nineteenth centuries (which was characterized by the Calvo Doctrine[11]) and Mexico's nationalization of the oil industry in 1938 exemplify the tension between foreign firms and their host countries. Stories of the British East India Company and the Dutch East India Company are even earlier examples of conflict between host and home countries.

Numerous instances of conflict between MNEs and nation-states can be found in history. In *Multinationals Under Fire,* Thomas Gladwin and Ingo Walters listed numerous cases of such conflicts, which they classified according to their typology of "terrorism," "human rights," "politics," "questionable payments," "marketing," "labor relations," "technology," and "economic/finance."[12] These authors report earlier cases of conflict between the Rio Tinto Company and Spanish workers, such as the 1887 incident when more than 100 demonstrators were shot dead when workers staged the first major strike against the company. Further clashes in the late 1920s caused Spanish leftists to see Rio Tinto as a symbol of exploitative foreign capitalism. Gladwin and Walters also report on the sizeable losses Roche suffered during the Bolshevik Revolution of 1917, the lengthy dispute involving Gulf Oil's acquisition of concessions in Colombia and Kuwait in the 1920s and 1930s, and the involvement of the U.S. Central Intelligence Agency in Iran to preserve the interest of oil companies after Tehran nationalized foreign oil companies in 1953.[13] Other authors discuss similar cases of conflict between firms and nations-states.[14] The history of FDI and TNCs provides ample instances of conflict as well as cooperation.

Box 1.1. Early Concerns about Foreign Direct Investment

At the turn of the twentieth century, a few British writers bemoaned the American takeover of British firms. One such author, Fred A. McKenzie, noted in *The American Invaders* that Americans in England practically dominated "every industry created in the past fifteen years." Another 1901 book by William T. Stead, *The Americanization of the World,* stressed similar themes.[1]

The League of Nations, too, took note of the monopolistic behavior of cartels.[2] Hence anti-FDI sentiment, which at times has been intertwined with nationalism (and in the early twentieth century with socialism and communism), has a long history.

1. See Mira Wilkins, *The Emergence of Multinational Enterprise: American Business Abroad from the Colonial Era to 1914* (Cambridge, Mass.: Harvard University Press, 1970); and Mira Wilkins, *The Maturing of Multinational Enterprise: American Business Abroad from 1914 to 1970* (Cambridge, Mass.: Harvard University Press, 1974), 436.

2. See also D. H. MacGregor, *International Cartels* (Geneva: League of Nations, 1930).

In a pioneering survey, Lee Nehrt, J. Frederick Truitt, and Richard W. Wright (1970) showed that only 17 percent of the postwar research in American academia on the direction and type of international business was devoted to international business and national environments.[15] With few exceptions, political economists at this time began to give more explicit recognition to the host country instead of treating it as an exogenous factor.[16]

In his seminal study of international relations during the interwar period (1919–1939), E. H. Carr made a sober and alarming observation of idealists' view of what may be accomplished under a multilateral system:

> Article 19 of the Covenant of the League of Nations remains a lonely monument to the pathetic fallacy that international grievances will be recognized as just and voluntarily remedied on the strength of "advice" unanimously tendered by a body representative of world public opinion.[17]

In an observation that has disturbing and prophetic echoes of the first decade after the fall of the Berlin Wall (1989–2001) to the second decade, beginning with September 11, 2001, Carr noted:

> The characteristic feature of the crisis of the twenty years between 1919 and 1939 was the abrupt descent from the visionary hopes of the first decade to the grim despair of the second, from a utopia which took little account of reality to a reality from which every element of utopia was rigorously excluded.[18]

Finally, Carr identified the task ahead:

> Our task is to explore the ruins of our international order to discover on what fresh foundations we may hope to rebuild it; and like other political problems, this problem must be considered from the standpoint both of power and of morality.[19]

Carr's observations can be related to TNCs today. In the early years of twenty-first century, the UN has become increasing concerned with studying and formulating policy instruments regarding corporations and the effects of globalization. It is timely to wonder whether the decline from the visionary utopia of the 1920s to the free-for-all years of the subsequent two decades is the precursor of two subsequent eras of confrontation and tension between governments and foreign enterprises, for example, the 1970s—when this tension reached a high pitch—to the post–9/11 world of heightened tension over globalization and U.S. unilateralism.

Frontier Institutions

During the interwar years, prominent institutions, including the League of Nations, the World Intellectual Property Organization and its progenitors, and the

International Labour Office started paying attention to the potentially significant role that foreign capital and technology could play in economic development. Each of their approaches emanated from the utopian and idealistic de-
sires to improve the lot of humanity, as their respective mandates specified. The
remainder of this chapter provides the historical context and institutional background for the post–World War II era. It begins with a review of discussions of
foreign investment that took place under the League of Nations, the ILO, and
other forums. How did these noble intentions fare, and what legacy did these
institutions leave to the next generation of international organization?

The League of Nations

From its inception in 1920, the League of Nations' main focus was to establish
a system of collective defense, achieve eventual disarmament, and deal with
colonial affairs.[20] Its specialized agencies were to promote cooperation in international trade, finance, transportation, communication, health, and science.
The League's Covenant begins:

> In order to promote international co-operation and to achieve international peace
> and security
>
>> by the acceptance of obligations not to resort to war,
>> by the prescription of open, just and honorable relations between nations,
>> by the firm establishment of the understandings of international law as the
>> actual rule of conduct among Governments, and
>> by the maintenance of justice and a scrupulous respect for all treaty obliga-
>> tions in the dealings of organised peoples with one another,
>
> [the high contracting parties] agree to this Covenant of the League of Na-
> tions.[21]

Article 23 makes a brief reference to trade:

> The members of the League. . . . will make provision to secure and maintain
> freedom of communications and of transit and equitable treatment for the com-
> merce of all Members of the League.[22]

Preoccupied with constructing a new world architecture after World War I,
the collapse of the Ottoman and Austro-Hungarian Empires, and the smolder-
ing problems in colonies in Africa and elsewhere, the League paid only scant
attention to the issue of FDI. To the extent that there was explicit recognition
of "private" enterprise—domestic or international—it was limited to concern
about the private manufacture of armaments. Article 8 expresses "grave objections" to the role played by private enterprise in armaments manufacture.[23]

Trade and, to a far lesser extent, investment were included in the League's discussions only insofar as matters of competition and monopoly power were concerned. At the same time, the League succeeded in improving the legal, fiscal, and administrative bases of trade by developing and adopting a number of significant multilateral agreements. While a body of principles was worked out from 1923 to 1929 on the "Treatment of Foreigners and Foreign Enterprises," "attempts to secure general adoption of these principles by international convention failed."[24]

The League of Nations Covenant and its amendments (1924) did not contain as broad and explicit a mandate to deal with economic issues and international economic cooperation as would be included later in the UN Charter. Given the circumstances of the times, the League's relative inattention to international economic issues is understandable. After all, this was a grand attempt to shape the world political order after the collapse of old empires and the emergence of new ones—the *Pax Americana* and the Soviet Union. Nevertheless, over its short life, the League was able to undertake a variety of studies on trade, competition, and the like. Its work on quantitative restrictions on trade, most-favored-nation treatment, and other aspects of commercial policy under its Economic and Financial Committees is noteworthy. Matters relating to cross-border trade, investment, and commercial policy fell into five categories: international conventions in force, those in draft or not in force, model bilateral investment treaties, reports on trade policy, and statistics.[25]

Box 1.2. Commercial Policy Concerns of the League of Nations

Between 1923 and 1941, the League produced a number of important documents related to trade and commercial policy. They dealt, inter alia, with the following areas:

1. **International conventions in force:** Customs formalities, commercial arbitration, export prohibitions and restrictions, bills of exchange, promissory notes and checks, veterinary police regulations, and commodity agreements
2. **International conventions in draft or not in force:** Import and export prohibitions and restrictions, tariffs, treatment of foreigners, and commercial propaganda
3. **Model bilateral investment treaties and international economic disputes:** Double taxation and fiscal evasions, most-favored-nation clause, procedure for settlement of international economic disputes, tariff nomenclature, unfair commercial practices, and international rules relating to

methods for the inspection of meat intended for international
trade
4. Reports and studies relating to trade policy: Transition
from war to peace, the World Economic Conference (Geneva,
1927), the International Monetary and Economic Conference
(London, 1933), agricultural protectionism, clearing agreements and customs administration, dumping, exchange control, marks of origin, most-favored-nation clauses, nutrition
and standards of living, quotas, raw materials, tariff systems,
and contractual methods
5. Trade analysis and trade statistics: International trade statistics, monthly bulletin of statistics, world economic survey,
and statistical yearbook of the League of Nations

Source: League of Nations, *Commercial Policy in the Post-War World: Report
of the Economic and Financial Committee* (Geneva: League of Nations, 1945),
118–124.

Several important features emerged from the League's activities. Most important, many of the trade issues that were to occupy postwar policymakers
were being studied and debated as early as the 1920s. Equally important, the
League crafted, or at least recognized, many of the regulatory nuts and bolts
of doing business in the post–World War I international economy. These included the harmonization of customs procedures, arbitration, and uniform laws
concerning bills of exchange and promissory notes and a host of other functionally useful and procedural mechanisms that were necessary before financial resources can flow smoothly across borders. These ideas were promulgated
at a time when the League was preoccupied with political matters—crumbling
empires at its inception and depression and protectionism in its later years.

Perhaps more relevant to an understanding of the political economy of the
territorial expansion of firms was the League's interest in international cartels and the monopolistic behavior of international firms. This interest partly
stemmed from earlier legislative measures in the United States. In 1890, the
U.S. federal government passed the Sherman Antitrust Act, forbidding monopolistic combination of capital. With the Clayton Antitrust Act of 1914, some
two decades later, trust busters in the United States dismantled the Rockefeller
oil cartel and others like it under the act's restriction against holding companies and interlocking directorates. The Federal Trade Commission (FTC), established in that same year, was empowered to investigate and to issue orders
forbidding unfair competition. Cartels and monopolies were coming under attack in Europe and Japan as well.[26]

Finally, the League succeeded in devising conventions on customs formalities, arbitration, bills of exchange, settlement of conflicts of laws on negotiable instruments, and other matters. Its work on double taxation, including model treaties drawn up in 1928 and revised in 1935 and 1944, provided "the basis for more than 100 important bilateral agreements"—all aimed at encouraging economic cooperation, including FDI, among signatory countries.[27] Despite obstacles and preoccupations, the League of Nations left behind a legacy on international economic and financial matters at its demise in 1946.

Other Frontier Institutions

The League was the foremost international institution before World War II, but it was not the only one. Other relevant organizations included the World Intellectual Property Organization and the International Labour Organization. Both of these institutions in time joined the UN family and became specialized agencies. Any work on the UN and TNCs, therefore, must include their respective work on the protection of intellectual property and proprietary technology and on labor management issues.

The oldest of these is the World Intellectual Property Organization, which had its genesis in the Paris Union of 1883 and the Berne Convention of 1886, when a regime to protect intellectual and artistic as well as technological assets was first established. Over the last century or more, the protection of all forms of intellectual property—patents, trademarks and trade names, industrial design, and copyrights—has become central to the growth of firms. In the contemporary knowledge-intensive economy, the work of WIPO is important to the activities of TNCs because the protection of these intangible but strategically important assets must be assured and their flow across national boundaries facilitated if TNCs are to remain viable. These same assets are sought by host countries and local firms in their own quest for development and growth. There must then exist a regime within which the protection of these assets is assured and their flow across national boundaries facilitated. This had been an intractable international issue since the industrial revolution, necessitating establishment of a system to protect artistic and literary work to underpin the promotion of Schumpeterian entrepreneurship.[28]

The 1883 patent system was designed to protect the intellectual rights of artists and writers. WIPO evolved into an international forum for the protection of industrial designs, inventions, trademarks, and trade names and became a specialized agency of the United Nations in 1974. Its raison d'être has remained essentially unchanged over the last 120 years. Its most significant contribution in the absence of a universal system for the protection of intellectual property may be its drafting of "model laws," now offered to its nearly 100 member countries, many of which have incorporated them into their national legislation.

This unilateral action of individual countries' adoption of WIPO model laws can have potential consequences at the multilateral level. As more countries adopt these model laws in their legislation, a global convergence on specific issues of intellectual property protection may emerge. For example, when other international rule-making bodies like the World Trade Organization (WTO) and the World Health Organization contemplate the drafting of multilateral rules in their own areas, they must remain cognizant of efforts like WIPO's that have set a certain precedent. There may be an eventual convergence between, say, the work of WIPO on intellectual property protection and that of the WTO Agreement on Trade-Related Aspects of Intellectual Property Rights.

The lack of progress on the revision of the world intellectual property regime resulted in the inclusion of that issue into the General Agreement on Tariffs and Trade (GATT) negotiations and the resultant trade-related aspects of intellectual property protection (TRIPs) agreement.[29] Consequently, the World Trade Organization has become the main forum for negotiations on intellectual property rights. Nevertheless, WIPO continues to be of critical importance to TNCs and developing countries alike, for it is in everyone's interest to have clear rules of the game. In addition to being the focal point with respect to patent registry through the Patent Cooperation Treaty, WIPO now provides technical assistance to both developing countries and TNCs.

This potential confluence will be further explored in Chapter 9 as a part of a look into the future of matters relevant to TNCs, FDI, and host countries. Protection of intellectual property has always been a major issue in the area of technology transfer. During the heated debates over the merits of a code of conduct for transfer of technology in the 1970s, TNCs insisted on receiving guarantees for their patents, trademarks, trade names, and copyrighted material before agreeing to transfer technology. This demand was made during the negotiations over a code of conduct for technology transfer. No code ever emerged from this lengthy exercise because the gap between contending parties, namely, the United States and its western allies and the Group of 77[30] developing countries on key policy issues remained unbridgeable.[31] During this process, which took place from the mid-1970s into the 1980s, WIPO was largely sidestepped, while UNCTAD took a dominant role.

These organizations, together with the International Labour Organization, form the constellation of nascent international attempts prior to World War II that influenced, directly or otherwise, FDI and the activities of TNCs. They were distinguished by several characteristics, namely, the idealism that lay at the foundation of their existence, their relatively modest achievements, and their insularity from one another. Each seemed to be pursuing a different agenda; each seemed to be doing so in relative isolation. Finally, the international community, preoccupied with political matters such as independence and colonialism, was functioning in an economic environment overshadowed by the Great Depression. The architects of the post–World War II international economic system, wary of the devastating consequences of protectionist policies, pledged to design a liberal system that would deter protectionism among member states.

Conclusion

Ideas percolating through these organizations indicate early concerns about the issues of FDI and TNCs and how each relates to the other. The key question to be addressed is how much of a common view and coordination existed between them and, more important, to what extent TNCs influenced these institutions and were in turn influenced by them in the interwar period. Some influence came in indirect form via influencing the international commercial regime in general. The depression of the 1930s affected the level and direction of FDI and the international activities of TNCs. On the one hand, it dampened the impetus of TNCs to invest abroad. On the other hand, protectionist barriers to imports encouraged TNCs to invest as a way of overcoming barriers to entry. In this context, one must also see the role played by these institutions in the interwar period. These activities, coordinated or not, set the stage for the work that was to be done under the United Nations after World War II against the backdrop of protectionism wrought by depression and devastation wrought by war.

2

The Early Post–World War II Era:
From the Golden Years of FDI to the
Incipient Rise of Economic Nationalism

- *The Five Phases in TNC–Host Country Relations*
- *The Immediate Postwar Period: The End of Colonialism,
  the Golden Age of FDI, and the Cold War*
- *The United States and Transnational Corporations*
- *Other Home Countries' Concerns, Policies, and Institutions*
- *The United Nations*
- *Conclusion*

The first two decades after World War II ushered in a period of tremendous reconstruction and development—first in devastated Europe and then in developing countries that gained independence with the collapse of colonialism. Decolonization and political independence affected not only newly independent nations throughout the Third World but also the colonial powers that had to undergo their own adjustments.[1] Along with political independence came economic interdependence throughout the developing world, facilitated by unprecedented growth in trade and FDI. One of the outstanding features of this period was the resumption in the growth of world trade, which had been severely retarded as a result of the depression and protectionism in the 1930s. This surge was brought about largely as a result of the Bretton Woods agreements of 1944, the institutions created under this regime, and the successive trade rounds that ensued.[2] The formation of the International Bank for Reconstruction and Development (IBRD, or World Bank for short), the International Monetary Fund (IMF), and, in 1947, the General Agreement on Tariffs and Trade as the three pillars of this institutional arrangement set the stage for a surge in international trade, foreign investment, and economic interdependence.[3]

The 1950s and 1960s thus constituted the golden era in postwar internationalization. Global trade increased faster than the world's collective gross product (world GDP) as barriers to trade were lowered through a series of multilateral agreements and the tempo of internationalization, including the growth
of TNC activities, continued to accelerate. Total outward flows of FDI from
all market-economy countries increased from $2.9 billion in 1960 to $8.5 billion in 1970, while inward flow into these countries amounted to $2.3 billion in
1960 and $6.9 billion a decade later.[4] Thus, FDI flows had a cumulative growth
of about 300 percent. During the same decade, the world's gross output grew
by less than one-tenth of that figure.[5] Meanwhile, the number of independent
countries rose dramatically.[6] Membership in the organization increased from
its original 51 in 1945 to 90 in 1960, 127 in 1970, 154 in 1980, 159 in 1990, and
192 in 2006.

In addition to political independence and economic growth, a third characteristic of these two decades was the gradual rise of anti-TNC economic nationalism. This started in the mid- to late 1960s, when Latin American countries
began asserting their wish for more control over their economies and scholars
from that continent began writing about *dependencia*.[7] Economic nationalism
was manifested in a number of hostile acts against foreign firms. One was the
growth of incidents of expropriation and nationalization. From 1960 to 1978,
some 1,369 instances of nationalization of foreign assets were recorded, two-
thirds of which occurred in the final six years. The other was collective action
by oil-producing developing countries to appropriate crude oil–pricing decisions away from multinational oil companies. The latter reached its height in
1973–1979, with the spectacular success of the Organization of the Petroleum
Exporting Countries (OPEC). This group's quadrupling of oil prices gave many
developing countries a new sense of pride and power. They sensed they could
take control of their economic destiny, determine the price of commodities
they exported, and even champion the design of a new international economic
order by serving as an example.

These three dynamics—the accelerated tempo of economic development,
an unprecedented increase in the number of independent countries, and a
newfound economic nationalism—all transformed the nature and intensity of
the FDI/TNC discussion at the level of scholarship as well as policy. Scholars
differ as to the motive for FDI. Without attempting to undertake an exhaustive survey of the theoretical underpinnings of foreign direct investment, it is
important to point out that the issue of control remained at the heart of the
debate.

Indeed it was "control," by definition, that differentiated "portfolio" and
"capital movements" theories from FDI theories. In contrast to foreign direct

investment, portfolio and capital movements theories stated that capital will be invested wherever it can earn a higher return. The pioneering work of Stephen Hymer, which argued that firms invested abroad to extend the oligopolistic advantage they enjoyed in the home market, illuminated one of the major differences between FDI and portfolio theory. Hymer's thesis prompted much of the vociferous disdain for FDI that was felt in the 1970s. This strand was echoed in the work of progressive scholars such as Constantine Vaitsos and others who were disturbed by the issue of who controls the activities of MNCs and the related issue of the distribution of gains between home and host countries.

While internationalization meant the growth of FDI and the foreign activities of TNCs, the gradual rise of economic nationalism proved ultimately to have negative repercussions. As will be further discussed in the next chapter, the relative tranquility and prosperity of the immediate postwar years gave way to a more confrontational and contentious period in the 1970s. Clearly the world economy was entering a new phase.

Data show dramatic shifts in patterns of FDI as well. Before World War II, developed countries as recipients of FDI had accounted for about one-third of the stock. In 1914, 37 percent, or $5 billion, was invested in developed countries, while 63 percent, or $8 billion, went to developing countries. By 1960, the positions had switched: some 67 percent of the estimated stock of accumulated FDI was in developed countries and only 32 percent in developing ones.[8] Developing countries gradually increased their share of FDI by the early twenty-first century, thanks to a handful of major host countries, notably China and India.

The Five Phases in TNC–Host Country Relations

One can divide the last century of the relationship between host countries and TNCs into distinct phases.[9] The first, prior to World War II, consisted of two periods, the decade immediately after the end of World War I and the depression of the 1930s. The second phase began after World War II, when FDI flourished and TNCs multiplied in number, type of activity, national origin, and strategy.

Phase I: Prior to World War II

For much of the twentieth century (and for some centuries prior to it), western firms had free reign in countries across the world. Host countries were either colonial dependents or were too feeble (and corrupt) to exercise much control over the activities of foreign firms. Oil companies provide a classic example. Across Africa, Asia, the Middle East, and Latin America, oil companies signed concession contracts with unelected rulers and potentates, established enclaves (at times protected by private armies and mercenaries), and controlled integrated operations from the wellhead to the pump.

Many host countries, however, also realized that they needed foreign technology and capital to develop their economies. Their location- and resource-based advantages complemented TNCs' ownership and technological advantages, making for a mutually beneficial arrangement unencumbered by the messiness of political participation and democracy. Countries provided the raw materials while companies used their proprietary assets—capital, technology, and an integrated system—to find, extract, transport, and refine petroleum and distribute the final products. Such free-reign arrangements were not limited to the oil industry; in fact they were the rule in all extractive industries well into the first half of the twentieth century. Decisions were made at the headquarters of the multinational companies in the United States or Western Europe.[10]

Given the devastating impact of protectionism in the 1930s, the postwar international economic policy debate was focused on liberalizing the international trade regime. The aborted Havana Charter, which laid the foundations for post–World War II financial architecture, actually included provisions for international investment, the first time FDI had been brought to the international agenda. And for the first time in modern history an international agency could have proposed multilateral rules for foreign investment. The International Trade Organization (ITO), part of the Bretton Woods framework, was conceived in that charter as an overarching multilateral institution charged with promulgating and implementing rules in the areas of both trade and investment. Article 12 of the Havana Charter acknowledged the importance of international investment and capital flows.

Box 2.1. The Havana Charter: International Investment

Article 12 of the Charter deals with international investment:
"1. Member countries recognize that:
   (a) international investment, both public and private, can be of great value in promoting economic development and reconstruction and consequent social progress;
   (b) the international flow of capital will be stimulated to the extent that Members afford nationals of other countries opportunities for investment and security for existing and future investments;

(c) without prejudice to existing international agreements to which Members are parties, a Member has the right:

(i) to take any appropriate safeguards necessary to ensure that foreign investment is not used as a basis for interference in its internal affairs or national policies;

(ii) to determine whether and to what extent and upon what terms it will allow future foreign investment;

(iii) to prescribe and give effect on just terms to requirements as to the ownership of existing and future investments;

(iv) to prescribe and give effect to other reasonable requirements with respect to existing and future investments;

(d) the interests of Members whose nationals are in a position to provide capital for international investment and Members whose desire to obtain the use of such capital to promote their economic development or reconstruction may be promoted if such Members enter into bilateral or multilateral agreements relating to the opportunities and security for investment which the Members are prepared to offer and any limitations which they are prepared to accept of the rights referred to in subparagraph (c)."

Source: UNCTAD, *International Investment Instruments: A Compendium*, 3 Volumes (New York and Geneva: UNCTAD, 1996), 1:4–5.

Despite its even-handed tone, the Havana Charter was doomed when the U.S. administration, knowing that the Congress would not ratify it, withdrew its submittal for ratification, thus killing an organization that, ironically, it had proposed.[11] According to Sidney Dell, in 1945 the United States circulated a document entitled "Proposals for the Expansion of World Trade and Employment" that advocated the establishment of the ITO. One of the provisions of this proposal aimed to inhibit "restrictive business practices"—practices that would restrain competition, restrict access to markets, or foster monopolistic control in international trade. These principles were deeply rooted in the American economic tradition and philosophy.

A primary reason for the failure of the ratification of the Havana Charter was rooted in the ITO's broad mandate. Fresh from victory in World War II, the United States jealously guarded its national sovereignty and was loathe to relegate responsibilities to a supranational organization. There seemed to be then, as there is now, a certain amount of ambivalence and schizophrenia running through the decision-making process in the United States—the global power expounded multilateralism yet was wary of its consequences.

On the whole, the main features of this phase include an openness to trade, the absence of administrative and legal infrastructures in host developing countries, the dominance of TNC activities in extractive industries, a gradual shift to import substitution and occasionally to export-driven manufacturing in developing countries, and a significant increase in FDI, both within the United States and Western Europe and increasingly to developing countries.

Phase II: The Laissez-Faire (Honeymoon) Era (1945–1960s)

The post–World War II era began not with an overarching institution to deal with trade and investment but with a more modest one, the GATT of 1947, which dealt only with trade. Still, the initial postwar years saw a continuation of market-opening measures, and FDI flourished. The period from 1945 to the 1960s can be called the golden era of foreign direct investment. During this phase, FDI grew dramatically both in volume and in spread. The number of foreign affiliates of U.S.-based TNCs grew from around 7,400 in 1950 to 23,000 in 1966, with an annual growth rate averaging near 10 percent. Meanwhile, outward flow of FDI from the United States increased from $1.7 billion in 1960 to $4.4 billion in 1970, while inward FDI into the United States from the rest of the world went from $140 million in 1960 to $1 billion a decade later. Worldwide, the UN recorded FDI inflows at $3 billion in 1960 and $8.5 billion in 1970. Due to some data discrepancy, inward FDI flows were somewhat different, at $2 billion and $6.9 billion, respectively.[12]

Meanwhile, the United Nations declared the 1960s the Development Decade. The UN Charter was more explicit than that of the League of Nations with respect to economic development in general and to FDI and foreign operations of TNCs in particular. The Preamble to the Charter refers to "the promotion of the economic and social advancement of all peoples," and Articles 61 to 72, Chapters IX and X, deal in detail with economic matters. The Economic and Social Council (ECOSOC) became an important body within the United Nations on matters of direct relevance to this study.

During the conclusion of its inaugural meeting in 1964, the United Nations Conference on Trade and Development (UNCTAD I) recommended that developing countries should, with the assistance of developed countries and the UN, adopt suitable means to supply all the necessary information about investment conditions, regulations, and opportunities to prospective foreign investors. It also noted that foreign private investors should base their policies on respect for the host country's sovereignty, cooperate with local initiative and capital, rely as much as possible on existing resources in developing countries, and work within the framework and objectives of the country's development plan with a view to supplying domestic markets and, in particular, expanding exports.[13]

Toward the end of the decade, incidents of nationalization and expropriation in fact increased, not only in the socialist bloc but also in Western Europe.[14] This trend accelerated into the 1970s as more newly independent countries found that status as a sovereign nation brought with it the power to control, nationalize, and expropriate. This ushered in a new phase in the international environment pertaining to FDI and TNCs.

Phase III: The "Restrictive-Unilateral Era" (Late 1960s–Mid-1980s)

In this period, antagonism and hostility toward foreign firms escalated. This occurred for at least two reasons. It was partially a reaction to the excesses of TNCs. It was also due to decolonization following World War II. Then a wave of nationalization followed. Iran's nationalist prime minister Mohammad Mosaddegh introduced a bill in 1951 to nationalize the country's oil industry, and the Anglo-Iranian Oil Company, a firm partly owned by the British government, was forced out. It later returned in partnership with American oil companies after a coup—allegedly staged by the U.S. Central Intelligence Agency—brought back the shah of Iran and ousted Mosaddegh.[15]

The 1950s also witnessed the rise of the Non-Aligned Movement (NAM). Mosaddegh's nationalization of foreign oil companies emboldened the zeal of the NAM's leaders (Prime Minister Nehru of India, President Sukarno of Indonesia, Marshal Tito of Yugoslavia, and President Nasser of Egypt) for neutrality in the East-West power struggle as well as national control of economic assets. Other nationalizations followed, elsewhere in the Middle East as well as in Latin America and North Africa. These events form a continuum that led in 1973 to the spectacular if serendipitous success of OPEC. Within a short span of time, a number of political and economic forces (the collapse of the Bretton Woods fixed-exchange-rate regime, the 1973 Arab-Israeli war, the rise in commodity prices, and associated economic uncertainties) coalesced, enabling OPEC to quadruple oil prices, which began to spike soon after the Arab-Israeli War on October 6, 1973.

Many Third World leaders hoped—some even predicted—that OPEC's success in petroleum would be replicated in other primary commodities. The U.S. Senate hearings on multinational enterprises, the Securities and Exchange Commission's investigation into corrupt practices of multinational enterprises, the Watergate affair, and the Vietnam War compounded the tumult. The combined effect of these events was an increase in solidarity among emboldened developing countries. Their demands, articulated through the Group of 77 (G-77) for a New International Economic Order (NIEO) was legitimized by a UN declaration.[16] Subsequent UN resolutions concerning sovereignty over natural resources, the Lima Declaration of 1975, and even a call by some developing countries for a New International Information Order (NIIO) followed.[17] The relative tranquility and stability that accompanied the honeymoon years immediately after World War II thus gave way to a more tumultuous phase in the relationship between nation-states and multinational corporations.

This change was reflected in a variety of UN forums, including UNCTAD III in Santiago, Chile, in 1972. One of its resolutions called for the right of developing countries to regulate FDI in order to avoid its negative effects. Resolution 56 (III) affirmed the sovereign right of developing countries to take the necessary measures to ensure that foreign capital operated in accordance with the national development needs of the host countries. It expressed concern about the disruptive effects of FDI on domestic markets. The conference stated that FDI must facilitate the mobilization of internal resources, generate inflows and avoid outflows of foreign exchange reserves, incorporate adequate technology, and enhance savings and national investment. The location and timing of UNCTAD III are both noteworthy. The Chilean government, under Salvador Allende, had initiated massive nationalization and expropriation of foreign companies' assets, and the country was poised to become a hotbed of anti-TNC activities.

This fundamental change in the international political climate was observable as countries increasingly introduced highly restrictive policies toward FDI, TNCs, and even technology transfer. With the exception of Decision 24 of the Andean Common Market, nearly all these restrictive measures were taken at the national level.[18] Efforts to develop a coordinated international front, including those under the aegis of the G-77, remained at the rhetorical level, while country after country began expropriating assets of foreign investors and establishing exchange controls, technology transfer registries, foreign investment review boards, and similar mechanisms in an effort to govern and regulate the international market for capital and technology. Some countries such as Mexico developed science and technology policies that included the screening of technology transfer agreements; approval of contracts only if they met certain stringent conditions, including the originality test (that the imported technology be new to the country); the setting of ceilings on royalty rates; and other "restrictive business practices."[19] Such restrictions on imported technology, of course, were not limited to developing countries. Among advanced-market economies, Japan and France enacted equally restrictive policies.

Phase IV: The Open Arms Era (Mid-1980s–Present)

Beginning in the early 1980s, during the Reagan-Thatcher conservative revolution, a shift occurred in attitude and policy among developing countries and even among some socialist countries, notably Hungary and the Soviet Union. In large part this was in response to tough reactions by the developed countries, which had indicated their unwillingness to concede points in the debate on NIEO in the 1970s. It also reflected a weakening of the position of developing countries as debt rose and the Bretton Woods institutions imposed adjustment policies. All this led to a move away from controls and regulations toward the gradual adoption of a more conciliatory approach toward FDI. Competitive pressures; the need to attract investment, technology, and other ownership advantages of TNCs; and an increasing recognition that markets must be given priority over regulation propelled countries to liberalize their FDI regimes and simplify entry, establishment, and exit rules for foreign capital. Barriers to entry gave way to incentives, and many countries established proactive institutions to attract FDI and promote their country as FDI-friendly.

This shift was also observable in the United Nations and its approach toward FDI and TNCs. As nation-states became more friendly toward FDI, competing over who would give more generous incentives to attract companies, the role of the UN shifted. The emphasis on a code of conduct, which had taken center stage in the early years of the life of the UN Centre on Transnational Corporations, was relegated to a secondary position and eventually oblivion, while certain UN agencies, including UNCTAD, geared up to provide data and technical assistance to help host developing countries attract FDI and maximize its benefits. This functional approach to the role of TNCs in development became the primary mission of the UN in later years.

Phase V: Toward a Multilateral/Regulatory Regime?

While the open-arms era in the global FDI climate continued into the twenty-first century, there were signs that a new era was emerging in economic transactions, one characterized by multilateralism. Rules of engagement regarding entry, establishment, and operations of TNCs were being hammered out to the mutual benefit of all stakeholders in a give-and-take process. This may seem like an overly optimistic and idealistic notion until one begins to see the contours of such a regime emerging. The failed attempts to devise codes of conduct on TNCs, the Multilateral Agreement on Investment (MAI), the earlier Havana Charter and numerous other agreements all provide reason for pessimism, as does the tendency of the sole superpower to act alone where its national interest requires. Nevertheless, there indeed exists an international regime, the broad outlines of which are already emerging. They include numerous bilateral, regional, and multilateral agreements covering the full spectrum of TNC operations and the rights and obligations of nations in these matters. These agreements range from the creation of GATT (1947), the Treaty of Rome (1957), and the Convention on Investment Disputes (1965) to the ILO's Tripartite Declaration of Principles on Multinational Enterprise and Social Policy (1977), the many WIPO agreements on intellectual property protection, UNCTAD-sponsored guidelines on restrictive business practices (1986), the Organisation for Economic Co-operation and Development's (OECD) first use of the Convention on Bribery (1998), and the 2003 Framework Convention on Tobacco Control (FCTC), negotiated under the auspices of the World Health Organization.

The evolution of the relationship between TNCs and host countries is presented in Table 2.1. It summarizes key features of each era, the national policies that characterize each era, TNC strategies in each era, and brief comments on each. We review the events since World War II within this broad chronological framework, particularly as they relate to the interaction between TNCs and national governments. This will set the groundwork for the role of the United Nations.

The Immediate Postwar Period: The End of Colonialism, the Golden Age of FDI, and the Cold War

As the war was about to end, a conference was convened in Bretton Woods, New Hampshire, to construct the postwar international architecture of the capitalist free world. The result was the establishment of a three-pillared system consisting of the World Bank, the International Monetary Fund, and later the General Agreement of Tariffs and Trade. These institutions deserve credit for supporting much of the postwar economic expansion.

TNCs, whose ranks gradually began to swell with expanding opportunities, broadened their reach. They responded to new trends in the globalizing postwar economy, population increases, advances in technology and infrastructure, advances in organizational and production techniques, and the responses of governments to these changes by engaging in new forms of entry in their known markets while seeking new markets around the world. From 1938 to 1960, the estimated stock of accumulated foreign direct investment increased from $26 billion to $66 billion, of which all but a small fraction were investments by U.S. (48 percent) and European firms. The United Kingdom, the highest

Table 2.1. Phases in TNC–Host Country Relations in the Twentieth Century

Phase	Main features	National policies and perspectives	Responses and strategies of TNCs	Comments
I. The first half of the twentieth century	An open and liberal regime for capital flows. Few government controls on inward or outward FDI, most of which is limited in scope to the developed countries or to extractive industries in colonial dependencies and other less-developed countries.	Initially open and unencumbered, FDI slows down after the depression of the 1930s. Having recovered from one war, the world economy slides into protectionism and a second war.	Contraction of FDI in conjunction with the depression and protectionism and the collapse of the world economy. Other forms of TNC activity (e.g., vertical integration and horizontal diversification) continue and flourish.	TNCs diversify and seek new resource-based activities. The market seeking FDI extends into Europe.
II. The laissez-faire era: 1945–1960s	International economic activities are dominated by trade. Investment takes place without much hindrance from host governments. Investment is dominated by American and Western European investors.	Host countries, which are either under colonial rule or lack administrative capacity, are feeble and unable or unwilling to influence the behavior of foreign firms.	TNCs are mostly related to extractive industries or are seeking markets. They dominate the scene. They can always count on home-country governments to intervene on their behalf.	FDI expands in Europe and elsewhere, shifting from extractive to manufacturing and trade-enhancing activities.
III. The restrictive-unilateral era: Late 1960s-mid-1980s	Nationalization, expropriation, and other restrictions spread across developing countries, and host-country demands for and institution of controls on entry and operation proliferate.	Nationalistic host-country policies are intended to enhance or consolidate economic and political independence and self-reliance.	Most TNCs withdraw into safer (European) markets for investment and design other modes of entry in response to equity and other restrictions.	Foreign investment and TNC activity continues, but drops to a trickle in many developing countries. UN work on TNCs begins to gain momentum.

Continued on the next page

Table 2.1. Continued

Phase	Main features	National policies and perspectives	Responses and strategies of TNCs	Comments
IV. The open arms era: Mid-1980–present	Host countries liberalize FDI and trade policies, remove controls on TNC activities, and introduce policies to attract and protect FDI.	Competitive pressures, the need to attract investment and technology, and the need to gain access to export markets force changes in the FDI regimes of many countries.	FDI surges as barriers to entry are replaced with incentives and policies to attract and protect it.	The structures and strategies of TNCs change to benefit from the global wave of liberalization, enhanced by the enlargement of the WTO.
V. The future: multilateral/regulatory era	Rules of engagement in international business transactions are devised through multilateral negotiations.	Countries agree to multilateral rules through conventions or by incorporating them into their national legal systems.	TNCs embrace transparent and uniform rules of engagement and maximize global welfare.	Global interdependent civilization (dreamland future)

ranking in 1938 with 40 percent of estimated stock of FDI, had dropped to a distant second by 1960, accounting for 16 percent. There was a difference between the distribution of FDI by origin and destination. Whereas 99 percent of the $54 billion in stock of FDI originated in western countries, about one-third constituted investment in developing countries (16 percent in Latin America). Canada accounted for 24 percent, Western Europe for 23 percent (of which the UK alone accounted for 9 percent), and the United States for 14 percent of inward investment.[20] U.S. firms retained the dominant position they had held earlier and indeed widened their lead, while their European rivals reconnoitered. Both resource-based and market-seeking activities of TNCs rose sharply as barriers to entry were lowered. At the forefront were U.S. firms, whose expansion into Canada, Europe, and an increasing number of developing countries caused certain apprehensiveness. This resulted in writings by Kari Levitt, Richard Barnett and Ronald Muller, Constantine Vaitsos, and others who can collectively be called the radical critics of the TNCs. European multinational corporations were also active, and the extent of their international operations was sometimes felt to be overwhelming and underestimated.[21]

U.S. hegemony in the arena of foreign direct investment is a microcosm of the generally dominant role it played on the world stage at this time. The architecture of the Bretton Woods system, based as it was on the U.S. dollar as the linchpin of the fixed-exchange-rate regime, exemplified the "tight bipolar" nature of the system.[22] It was natural for the U.S. government, therefore, to contemplate a coherent policy on the matter of multinational corporations.

The United States and Transnational Corporations

The U.S. need for a coherent policy on FDI and TNCs, driven by the dominance of American firms abroad, led to a heightened awareness and a more proactive posture. In February 1969, the Bureau of Intelligence and Research and the Policy Planning Council, both in the Department of State, convened an important conference. Participants included academics, businessmen, and government officials. The goal of the conference was to discuss policy issues emerging from the growing importance of the multinational corporation in the world economy. Charles Kindleberger of MIT, who chided political scientists for abandoning to the economists the task of analyzing important international relations problems arising from the operations of multinational firms, chaired the conference. Participants included Judd Polk (U.S. Council of the International Chamber of Commerce), Jack Behrman (University of North Carolina), Raymond Vernon (Harvard University), William Diebold (U.S. Council on Foreign Relations), M. E. Littlejohn (Pfizer), August Maffry (Bank of America), and J. J. Maisonrouge (IBM World Trade Corporation). Several of these participants were (or subsequently became) involved with UN efforts on the subject; Behrman later testified before the Group of Eminent Persons, as did Maisonrouge.[23]

The policy of the United States on the issue of FDI was likely shaped in large part by deliberations such as the 1969 conference. Arguments in favor of an open FDI environment were discussed at the conference, especially its beneficial effect on domestic competition, its wealth-creating power, and the importance of a free market to economic development. Also discussed was a recognition of the unequal bargaining position of some host developing countries regarding TNCs. At the conference, there was considerable support for the idea of a multilateral system similar to GATT or the OECD.

Various U.S. ambassadors to the UN adhered to this policy position in subsequent years. But statements by succeeding ambassadors to the United Nations, including Jeanne Kirkpatrick and Alan Keyes, both of whom were hostile to the UNCTC, may indicate a reversal in the policy position implied by this 1969 statement. Evidently there was a shift in policy regarding the United Nations and its deliberations on multinational corporations during the 1980s.

By this time, other U.S. entities besides the State Department were becoming more interested in the issue of TNCs. The Joint Economic Committee of the U.S. Congress held hearings on the subject, at which labor, management, and academics testified. Issues discussed included the general problems raised, the implications of technology transfer and employment, the impact on balance of payments, and the legal and political conflicts generated by TNC activities. A few years later, the U.S. Securities and Exchange Commission became involved when it uncovered instances of bribes to foreign officials. This will be more fully discussed in the next chapter.

Toward the end of the 1960s, another aspect of U.S. policy regarding outward FDI was the establishment of a federally funded investment insurance agency, the Overseas Private Investment Corporation (OPIC), in 1969. Its mission was to promote private enterprise and free market economic policies in friendly developing countries by providing risk insurance, technical assistance, and other incentives. This was meant to be an incentive to private investors, who were weary of risking their capital in developing countries strategically important to U.S. foreign policy interests. Export-Import Bank of the United States (Eximbank), a sister institution of OPIC, was created to promote U.S. exports and had a similar mission of promoting private enterprise and free market economic policies around the world.

In the 1970s, the tone in the United States became more confrontational, in part as a response to anti-U.S. and anti-TNC rhetoric, but this will be covered in the next chapter.

Other Home Countries' Concerns, Policies, and Institutions

While the United States was by far the largest source of outward FDI and a significant destination for inward flows as well, other developed countries were considering their own policies in this regard. Occasionally, these policies were influenced by such publications as *Le Defi Americain*[24] or *National Interest and the Multinational Enterprise*[25] and exemplified the conflict between TNCs and national sovereignty within the Atlantic Alliance. In Canada, too, a similar fear of TNCs was expressed.[26] However, it was Latin America that proved to be the hotbed of anti-TNC sentiments. Echoes of former times were heard—terms such as "Yankee imperialism" and "Colossus of the north" were resuscitated—and a new term, "consumptive emulation," was used to describe how the presence of American multinational corporations affected host country markets.[27]

Among the many platforms where the subject matter of multinational corporations was debated, the 1968 Round Table, organized by the Inter-American Development Bank (IDB) in Bogotá, Colombia, and held during the Ninth Meeting of the IDB Board of Governors, is noteworthy. Participants discussed ways to facilitate the process of Latin American integration. They chose "multinational investment, public and private, in the economic development and integration of Latin America" as the theme of the meeting. A wide range of participants from North as well as South America and Western Europe, government and corporate leaders, academics, and journalists participated. Two important topics were heavily discussed and debated as necessary for the encouragement of investment toward Latin American integration and development: an integrated infrastructure and the development of Latin American multinational enterprises to operate within that integrated market. This was an attempt at regionalism, fortified with a very heavy dose of state intervention. The focus was on collective self-sufficiency assisted by foreign investment and, more important, foreign technology. In fact this was the "Japanese model" of encouraging the inflow of well-screened foreign technology and enhancing local adaptive and absorptive capabilities. The conference report stated: "Latin America could reap great advantages from a detailed inquiry into the Japanese experience in regard to the acquisition and adaptation of foreign technology, and also with respect to the creation of its own technology."[28] The policy direction, which was based on prior agreements, declarations, and proclamations (including the 1966 Declaration of Bogotá among Andean countries and the 1967 hemisphere presidents' Declaration of Punta del Este), emphasized developing strength through unification—or, in the absence of that, government-led coordination. The dream of developing the region's home-grown multinational corporations was vigorously discussed. By the turn of the century, some four decades later, that dream remained largely unfulfilled, and even the dream itself had changed.

Meanwhile, some Western European countries and Japan continued to promote the free outflow of investment capital. Each followed the U.S. example by setting up institutional machinery for promoting outward FDI, guaranteeing against risk such as expropriation and currency controls and providing other forms of assistance.[29] Obviously national policy is shaped to a great extent by the confluence and the interplay of firms and government agencies. A question of relevance to the present book is the extent to which stronger governments, in concert with their stronger firms, can tip the scale in their favor in business negotiations. To what extent did the governments of home countries of TNCs succeed in getting a better bargain or in having their way in negotiations involving, say, codes of conduct? The literature on the relative bargaining positions of developing countries and advanced countries vis-à-vis TNCs is relevant and is revisited in the concluding chapter.

A few words on academic contributions are in order. Until the mid-1960s, the lion's share of the world's FDI outflow was accounted for by U.S. firms, and perhaps some 90 percent of teaching and research on this subject, too, was centered in North American universities and/or business schools. Nevertheless, European scholars, British in particular, have made notable contributions. British scholars' contributions to FDI and TNCs can be divided into three main groups. The first, and perhaps the most numerous and influential, are the writings of scholars who have been concerned mainly with the economic determinants and consequences of FDI and the activities of TNCs. The post–World War II genesis of this research dates back to the work of Hans Singer, G. C. Allen and Audrey Donnithorne, Edith Penrose, John H. Dunning, and W. B. Reddaway, J. S. Potter, and C. T. Taylor.[30]

The second strand traces its lineage to Michael Brooke, Lee Remmers, and John Stopford.[31] Their main focus has been the determinants of internal governance and decision-making properties of TNCs, viewed from an organizational, strategic management, marketing, and financial perspective. Such studies were already flourishing in the United States in the 1960s,[32] where a strong business school tradition existed. It was not until the 1960s, when the first business schools were set up in the United Kingdom.

A third group of European scholars directed their attention to the political economy of TNC activity, particularly insofar as developing countries were concerned. Here Edith Penrose (1970, 1971), Paul Streeten (1971, 1973), Sanjaya Lall (1973), Peter Ady (1971), and Louis Turner (1970, 1974) were preeminent. Each was concerned with identifying both the costs and benefits of FDI and TNC activity to recipient economies and the policy implications for host governments. Later in the decade, at the height of the *dependencia* debate, Peter Evans (1977) undertook a classic study of the interaction between the strategies of TNCs and economic development and the policies of several Latin American governments. Meanwhile, scholars in France were making their mark in the field. Among the most noteworthy contributions are the work on technology transfer by Nicholas de Jecquier and Charles-Albert Michalet at the OECD Development Centre in Paris and the edited volume by IBM's European chief Jacques Maisonrouge (1972) in the corporate world.

In the late 1980s and 1990s, European scholars began to make significant inroads into the near-monopoly of U.S. scholarship on the internal workings of the TNCs. The work of Sumantra Ghoshal (UK), Christopher Bartlett (Australia), Yves Doz (France), Danny van den Bulcke (Belgium), and Gunar Hedlund (Sweden) stands out.

The original pioneering work of Brooke and Stopford of the 1970s was not, in general, taken up further by British scholars until the late 1980s and 1990s, when the writings emanating from the younger generation of researchers at the London and Strathclyde Business Schools and the Leeds School of Business and universities of Oxford, Reading, and Cambridge—such as Julian Birkinshaw and John Child—started to make additional contributions to the international business literature.

The United Nations

The UN Economic and Social Council

As scholarship on FDI and TNCs accumulated, the United Nations became an increasingly active arena for policy debate on the subject. This was particularly true at ECOSOC. In the late 1950s, ECOSOC decided to address the issue of "restraints on trade" and "cartels." The U.S Congress had failed to ratify the Havana Charter, causing its eventual demise. However, concerned about the resurgence of cartels, which supposedly had been dismantled half a century earlier, the United States brought Chapter V of the Havana Charter, which had called for the establishment of the International Trade Organization and for adoption of measures to curb restrictive business practices by foreign cartels, before ECOSOC.[33]

When arguing for ECOSOC action on antitrust and competition issues in 1951, the U.S. representative to the UN pointed to four types of abuses characteristic of cartels and saw these abuses as justification for the United Nations to consider limiting or controlling the cartel-like behavior of firms abroad. The first was that markets were allocated to suppliers on the basis of geographical areas and export quotas, thereby not only hindering the growth of trade but also frustrating the efforts of underdeveloped countries to promote particular export industries. Second, cartels adopted "varied and ruthless" measures to limit investment in productive facilities in countries regarded as export markets and to deny access to patents and technical knowledge, credit, and the supply of raw materials. If such measures failed to achieve their purpose, cartel members had been known to acquire shares in locally owned plants "not for the purpose of developing them, but for the purpose of retarding and limiting their growth." Third, by restricting competition, cartel arrangements also restricted production and employment. Finally, cartels impaired productivity by protecting inefficient companies, preventing full-capacity operation in low-cost plants, and using restrictive agreements to delay the introduction of new technologies and more efficient methods of production.[34]

In somewhat of a role reversal, the U.S. position of 1951 of urging that limitations be placed on cartels came to be held by developing countries in the 1970s in at least three forums: the UNCTC code on TNCs, the UNCTAD set of principles on restrictive business practices, and the UNCTAD code of conduct on technology transfer. It is significant that the United States supported the set of principles of restrictive business practices but opposed the other two—and indeed, only the set of nonbinding "principles" on restrictive business practices was approved. The distinction is important and will become more clear in the discussion of the code on TNCs. The critical distinction has to do with the legal status of these instruments and whether they would be enforced by "courts and cops." Over the succeeding years, the word "code" itself became a word that drew lines of distinction between increasingly adversarial groups.

Successive issues of the UN's annual World Economic Survey refer to the role of foreign capital and technology in a neutral and even a slightly positive tone. Jacob Mozak, who was responsible for preparing the World Economic Survey, and N. T. Wang, a junior UN officer in the late 1960s, together with Philippe de Seynes, UN under-secretary-general under Secretary-General Kurt Waldheim, began referring explicitly to multinational corporations beginning with the 1971 volume, which was by this time becoming a "topic de jour."[35]

There were two types of efforts within the UN to help shape the postwar economic order. The first type was initiatives that were part of the League's unfinished agenda. Despite its significant achievements in the functional aspect of international economic affairs, the League did not survive to see many of its ideas about economic competition among firms and nations come to fruition. The UN put these uncompleted issues on its agenda upon its establishment. The second type was developing countries' quest for economic development and its domestic and international requisites. These, too, preoccupied the majority of UN members. Thus, the UN General Assembly, the ECOSOC, and specialized agencies became arenas for debate, discourse, and occasional discord. As membership increased and the balance tilted in favor of developing countries, these issues moved front and center and the UN machinery began moving in the direction of accommodating these needs.

Development Decades

When the United Nations declared the 1960s as the First Development Decade, lofty goals were articulated and many aspirations of developing countries were cast as targets to strive for.[36] Drawing attention to the problems of development and setting targets and policy measures was noble, but in retrospect, the targets for foreign aid proved too idealistic and were largely unfulfilled. The end results were disappointing, particularly for likely recipients. Potential donors were primarily interested in power aspects: who would give, who would receive, and what national policy goals would aid accomplish? The Soviet bloc expressed solidarity with developing countries at every turn. When it came to membership in committees and working groups charged with drafting resolutions, the Soviet Union even became somewhat cantankerous.[37]

Several other parts of the UN system were involved in the often discordant debate that pitted developed-market economies (primarily the United States) against a vocal group of developing countries. They viewed the FDI development nexus both as a subject of study and a policy matter concerning which policy formulation within their respective domains was deemed appropriate. These included UNCTAD, the International Labour Organization (ILO), the United Nations Industrial Development Organization, the United Nations Food and Agriculture Organization, and others.

Conclusion

The 1960s began as the golden age of FDI and ended with clouds on the horizon. Isolated episodes that might have been perceived as mere skirmishes (oil nationalizations here and there, squabbles between a few countries and TNCs over natural resources) became cumulous clouds, and vigilante logic on both sides threatened to replace vigilance and prudence. Many ideas that emerged during this period could be characterized as being consistent with the liberal economic dictum—that FDI was on the whole positive and needed to be chan-neled through government policy in the direction of promoting economic de-velopment.

Another strand, however, viewed TNCs as exploitative, alien, and purely profit driven. This perspective saw the international operations of TNCs as a mere extension of the oligopolistic advantage that they had gained in their home markets and argued that the behavior of TNCs was not wholly consis-tent with national needs and goals. Proponents of this perspective argued that control mechanisms were needed, preferably at the international level.

Cooler heads, meanwhile, continued the tedious task of dispassionate analy-sis, studying a phenomenon that was becoming both pervasive in global eco-nomic life and diverse in nature and strategy. The scholarship and policy de-velopments of the decade had a profound effect on keeping the debate that was about to be launched within the bounds of reason. It proved to be a tough task, for scope and diversity within the TNC universe as well as nation-states brought with it the greater likelihood that more would be tempted to stray from the path of mutual cooperation between the two groups, thus providing am-munition for those who were saying all along: "I told you so," implying that an unbridgeable chasm between TNCs and nations is bound to end in conflict— as it did in Venezuela under Chavez in 2005 when that government forced oil companies who had refused to renegotiate contracts out of that country.

The following chapter looks at the events as they unfolded in the 1970s, when disagreement turned to clash and debate into confrontation. A multi-lateral solution emerged from the clouds of dust kicked up by this storm, and the UN became the arena for the clash of ideas on what to do about TNCs.

3

The 1970s: Gathering Storm

- *The Church Committee Hearings*
- *The U.S. Securities and Exchange Commission Investigations*
- *Enter the United Nations*
- *The Amsterdam and Medellín Colloquia*
- *Work in the U.S. Government*
- *Conclusion*

The 1970s were turbulent, marked by a series of corporate scandals, political and economic crises, a shift in the international political agenda, and the emergence of a major North-South confrontation. Several landmark events occurred in rapid succession which, taken together, framed the tenor of international economic relations for the decade and left an indelible mark on history. In August 1971, the United States abandoned the dollar-based fixed-exchange-rate regime that had provided global economic stability since the end of World War II. Shortly thereafter, the Watergate scandal shook the U.S. political system and the confidence of the American people in their government. The dramatic findings of the U.S. Securities and Exchange Commission (SEC) revealed a number of corporate bribery scandals around the world in 1973–1974. A series of major U.S. Senate and House of Representatives hearings on the subject followed. In 1973, Arab-Israeli War precipitated an energy crisis, and in 1974, developing countries demanded a New International Economic Order.[1]

These events signaled the advent of turbulent economic times in intergovernmental relations. The UN system found itself in the eye of a storm, if not a hurricane. Ideas that emerged during this period ranged from those having to do with the exercise of national sovereignty over natural resources and the demand for a New International Economic Order to pleas for help in mitigating the financial havoc caused in energy-importing developing countries faced with quadrupled costs for imported energy.

In Chile, a political storm in the early 1970s enveloped the International

Table 3.1. Landmark Events in the Early 1970s that Helped Shape and Frame Global Economic Relations during the Turbulent 1970s

Date	Event	Impact
15 August 1971	"Nixon shock"	Bretton Woods system of fixed exchange rates breaks down, precipitating world-wide economic uncertainty
17 June 1972–9 August 1974	Watergate affair	Nixon henchmen arrested for breaking in to Democratic Party headquarters, Congress prepares for impeachment hearings, President Nixon resigns
September 1970–19 September 1973	Chilean affair	President Allende is elected in Chile, he expropriates assets of foreign (including U.S.) TNCs, U.S. stages a coup d'etat, regime changes in Chile
October 1973	October War	Prelude to the first energy crisis, rise of OPEC
1973–1974	Energy crisis	Energy crisis, host countries assert their sovereignty over natural resources, Third World countries demand a New International Economic Order
1973–1976	Hearings in U.S. Congress	United States passes anticorruption legislation, public awareness of extent of corruption grows, corporate heads are fined and indicted, and political leaders in the United States and elsewhere fall from grace
1973–1976	U.S. Securities and Exchange Commission investigations into corporate bribery abroad	United States passes Foreign Corrupt Practices Act of 1976 and other reforms and indicts corporate executives
1972	General Assembly passes Resolution 3201 (S-VI), 1 May 1974, to study MNCs	UN establishes the Group of Eminent Persons to study impact of TNCs on development and on international relations
1974	UN Declaration on a New International Economic Order (NIEO)	UN adopts the declaration unanimously without a vote, a grand design to reconfigure the whole spectrum of international economic relations under principles including "sovereignty over natural resources" and "distributive justice"

Date	Event	Impact
1974	UN Charter of Economic Rights and Duties of States	Charter affirms the right of states to exercise permanent sovereignty over all resources and economic activity related to them
1975	Lima Declaration and Plan of Action (UNIDO)	In order to fulfill the goals of the NIEO and the "main principles of industrialization," developed countries are called upon to restructure their industries; declaration states that 25 percent of world industrial output should come from developing countries by 2000 and asks developed countries to ensure that the activities of TNCs conform to the economic and social aims of developing countries in which they operate
1975–1976	Paris Conference on International Economic Cooperation	Some 35 members from rich and poor countries gather to ease the plight of developing countries, especially those most seriously affected by the increase in oil prices
1976	UNCTAD IV (Nairobi)	The G-77 reiterates its demand for a NIEO

Telegraph and Telephone Corporation (ITT), an American multinational corporation with heavy involvement in Chile's communication and service sectors. Labeled by its critics as "the sovereign state of ITT,"[2] the company was determined to protect its vast interests at any cost, including allegedly plotting with the CIA to overthrow the democratically elected socialist government of Salvador Allende.

The UN system also entered a decade quite unlike the previous one. As was discussed in Chapter 2, the first phase in the relationship between nation-states and TNCs after World War II was relatively tranquil. Some two decades later, this honeymoon period was giving way to a more confrontational one.

Contemporary scholarship was also taking a more critical view of TNCs and economic development and restrictions.[3] In 1967–1968, Servan-Schreiber's

Le Defi Americain created a minor storm on both sides of the Atlantic.[4] He warned that American-controlled firms in Europe constituted the third largest economy in the world after the United States and Europe. An even more critical strand of the literature delivered a harsher verdict. In 1974, Richard Barnett and Ronald Muller, for instance, bemoaned the global reach and power of multinational corporations, claiming that "the rise of the global corporation represents the globalization of oligopoly capitalism,"[5] while in 1970, Kari Levitt wrote of the "silent surrender" of the Canadian economy to American multinationals.[6] Other radical critics of TNCs included Stephen Hymer, whose "law of uneven development" sought to describe the consequences of "American business abroad."[7] Osvaldo Sunkel and Miguel Wionczek were critical of TNCs because their presence led to economic dependence, and Constantine Vaitsos documented the loss of revenue in developing countries through the transfer pricing strategies of TNCs.[8]

Mounting pressure from the press and the public resulted in the involvement of the U.S. Securities and Exchange Commission, which investigated illegal political contributions and bribes U.S. TNCs paid to foreign government officials in Europe, the Middle East, Japan, and elsewhere in 1973–1974. During the same period, the U.S. Senate Subcommittee on Multinational Corporations called before it top executives from the oil industry, arms manufacturers, and banks. On the day South Vietnam collapsed and American troops retreated, the subcommittee voted to investigate Northrop Corporation's payoffs to foreign officials. These hearings revealed that Northrop and other arms manufacturers, such as Lockheed, had bribed foreign government officials. Multinational banks such as Chase Manhattan Bank were also involved in illegal transactions abroad. There also appeared to be a clear link between these corporate misdeeds and the crimes and misdemeanors in the Nixon White House.[9]

Public outrage against TNCs in the United States and elsewhere may have been exacerbated by inflation, price controls, high unemployment, and events such as the Chilean affair and Watergate. Public exposure of skullduggery and mischief by some TNCs through congressional and SEC hearings provided ample justification for such outrage.

In matters concerning the conduct of TNCs, the United States was both the source of unacceptable behavior and a source of proposed remedies. It is important to review developments in the United States for several reasons. First, it was the largest economic superpower, the leader of the free world, and home to the largest number of the world's TNCs. Second, it had a sophisticated and well-developed system to regulate the economic activity of private firms, particularly regarding antitrust and competition issues. Third, actions taken by the U.S. government normally tended to resonate in other countries.

The Church Committee Hearings

Along with the Watergate scandal, the Arab-Israeli War, the energy crisis, and the fall of Salvador Allende, the first half of the 1970s was noteworthy because of another set of events that helped shape the discourse on TNCs. Primary among these was a series of hearings in 1973–1976 held by the U.S. Senate Subcommittee on Multinational Corporations, spearheaded by Senator Frank Church a relatively young liberal senator who was a kind of "moral lighting rod" in Congress.[10] Equally noteworthy were the damning Securities and Exchange Commission investigations of the bribery of foreign officials by TNCs during the same period. These revelations shook many governments from Europe to Asia and resulted in an important piece of legislation in the United States—the Foreign Corrupt Practices Act (FCPA), Public Law 95-213, which was unanimously passed by both houses of Congress in December 1977. A look at the background to the hearings and their proceedings and consequences will elucidate how these hearings may have influenced, inadvertently or otherwise, events and actions within the United Nations on international economic issues in general and on MNC matters in particular.

The Watergate scandal, which the Nixon White House tried to brush aside as a "third rate burglary," had an enormous impact on the U.S. body politic during 1973–1974. It prompted the U.S. Congress to reassert its authority and emboldened it to put a final end to American participation in the Indochina War and to an imperial presidency.

In February and March 1972, Jack Anderson, an investigative journalist, who had honed his journalistic skills with the legendary Drew Pearson, charged that the U.S. Justice Department had settled its antitrust suit against ITT in exchange for the company's $400,000 contribution to the Republican Party's National Committee. Anderson further jarred the public with subsequent revelations that ITT had "plott[ed] in 1970 with the CIA to block the election of Chile's president, Salvador Allende, a Marxist who had threatened to nationalize ITT's 60 percent interest in the Chilean telephone company." He further alleged that Harold Geneen, president of ITT, had offered the Nixon administration "up to seven figures" in political contributions to keep Allende out of power.[11]

These allegations jolted the Senate Foreign Relations Committee into action. The ITT affair and similar activities prompted it to set up a subcommittee on multinational corporations. The subcommittee held a series of hearings between March 1973 and September 1976.[12] It passed two motions, both of which were presented by its chair, Senator Church. The first was "to undertake an in-depth study of the role of multinational corporations and their relationship to foreign policy of the United States." The second was to "obtain forthwith all ITT documents concerning Chile between September 1 and November 1, 1970."[13]

The reverberations of the Senate subcommittee hearings were manifold. The Church hearings gained an attention and importance unforeseen by its initiators. Rattled by its proceedings, many TNCs marshaled forces and engaged in damage control. In a cover story in November 1972, *Newsweek* reported that "every international lawyer in Washington worth his attaché case has been hired by one or another multinational company to prepare for the barrage."[14] It was anticipated that the orgy of recrimination would be followed by a plethora of rules and regulations, even indictments.

The composition of the subcommittee is noteworthy. Senator Jacob Javits, one of its members and a ranking Republican, subsequently served as a member of the UN Group of Eminent Persons to study TNCs. LeRoy Ashby and Rod Gramer point out in their biography that Senator Church was indeed "fighting the odds" and reveal how a single individual can make a difference in a system as complex as that of the U.S. Congress.[15] Ideas concerning TNCs and corporate conduct and social responsibility that surfaced throughout the Church hearings were closely parallel to those with which the United Nations had also been grappling. Senator Church's proactive leadership made a considerable contribution to the articulation and development of these ideas.

The ITT affair in Chile provided the original momentum for these hearings. The influence of U.S. companies on foreign policy and their political contributions to foreign governments (in the Middle East and even countries such as the Netherlands and Japan[16]), together with the global role of banks, grain companies, and weapons and aviations manufacturers were scrutinized over this series of hearings lasting more than three years. The proceedings of the subcommittee hearings were published in seventeen volumes, on subjects including:

· The International Telephone and Telegraph Company and Chile, 1970–1971
· The Overseas Private Investment Corporation
· Multinational petroleum companies and foreign policy (four volumes)
· Investments by multinational companies in the communist-bloc countries
· The political and financial consequences of the OPEC price increases
· The political contributions of foreign governments

- The role of multinational corporations in the dollar devaluation crisis and the impact of direct investment abroad on the U.S. economy
- Lockheed Aircraft Corporation
- Multinational banks and U.S. foreign policy
- International grain companies
- Grumman Aerospace Corporation's Sale of F-14s to Iran

The Church subcommittee hearings prompted a number of other actions, including the Lockheed bribery hearings, initiated by Senator William Proxmire in 1975. These resulted in fewer changes in policy than the Church hearings did, but they illustrate the international political and economic atmosphere of the period, which was characterized by confrontation and mistrust between host developing countries and TNCs.

The U.S. Securities and Exchange Commission Investigations

Around the same time that the U.S. Congress was investigating and exposing corporate misdeeds by American TNCs around the world, the SEC also became interested.[17] A small enforcement division of the SEC had uncovered corrupt behavior among some of the same firms in 1972–1973. Indeed, this division discovered a mountain of evidence showing other examples of corporate bribery, "off-the-book transactions," and "slush funds."[18] Congress, relying on the SEC findings, reported in 1977:

> More than 400 corporations have admitted making questionable or illegal payments. The companies, most of them voluntarily, have reported paying out well in excess of $300 million in corporate funds to foreign government officials, politicians, and political parties. These corporations have included some of the largest and most widely held public companies in the United States; over 117 of them rank in the top Fortune 500 industries. The abuses disclosed run the gamut from bribery of high foreign officials in order to secure some type of favorable action by a foreign government to so-called facilitating payments that allegedly were made to ensure that government functionaries discharge certain ministrial [sic] or clerical duties.[19]

Unable to pursue every lead, the SEC offered companies a chance to disclose their wrongdoing and "throw themselves at [its] mercy."[20] Some 400 companies, including Exxon and Gulf Oil, subsequently submitted "voluntary disclosures" about payoffs; notable among them was the Northrop Corporation's admission that it had made payoffs to secure sales in Saudi Arabia and Iran. The State Department, however, was pressuring the SEC to curtail its investigation "lest it inflict further damage to US interests abroad."[21] The House of

Representatives, however, praised the SEC; the house had earlier issued an extensive report in May 1976 entitled "Report on Questionable and Illegal Corporate Payments and Practices."[22]

The problem was significant enough to draw the attention of other congressional committees, including the Senate Finance Committee and the House Interstate and Foreign Relations Committee's Subcommittee on Consumer Protection and Finance. The hearings in the Senate and the House of Representatives, combined with the SEC investigations, resulted in more damning revelations and increased public pressure, which culminated in the passage of the landmark Foreign Corrupt Practices Act in 1977. This act was the first of its kind, making it illegal for American individuals and corporations to bribe foreign government officials.

In the aftermath of Nixon's resignation, the atmosphere was ripe for reform in the United States. President Carter signed the Foreign Corrupt Practices Act during his first year in office. However, the act's passage provoked considerable controversy. Some critics raised the "extraterritoriality" issue (that one country—the United States—was instituting laws that involved matters beyond its sovereign jurisdiction), while others considered it a naïve attempt to export an American brand of morality. American TNCs were particularly disturbed by its unilateral approach; they argued that the law tied their hands while German, Japanese, and French corporations were left free to make similar illicit payments and receive tax deductions for them. The more progressive executives, who agreed with the need for transparency and responsible corporate behavior, nevertheless advocated self-control through voluntary corporate codes and industry-wide self-regulation. Some executives scoffed at the law's moralizing naïveté. A former chairman of Booz, Allen, and Hamilton, a U.S.-based global consulting firm, reportedly called the proponents of criminalizing bribery "a bunch of pipsqueak moralists running around trying to apply U.S. puritanical standards to other countries."[23]

Enter the United Nations

During the first half of the 1970s, storms gathered over international economic relations after the relative tranquility of the postwar period. Multinational corporations were viewed as either saints or demons in an increasingly polarized and fractured global economic policy environment. There is an eerie similarity between the 1970s and the first years of this millennium. Then, as now, corporate scandals made headlines, as did the cost of energy. Yet one can draw another parallel between the first and second decades after the end of World

War I and later periods. E. H. Carr, in his *The Twenty Years' Crisis, 1919–1939*, described the decade from 1919 to 1929 as filled with promise, marked by the relative peace, prosperity, and optimism that was epitomized by the creation of the League of Nations. In sharp contrast, the decade that followed was marked by the depression and despair that led to the 1929 stock market crash, uncertainty, and, ultimately, war. There is indeed a resemblance between the post-1929, post-1973, and post-9/11 eras;[24] each has ushered in a period of unease, tension, and even despair.

The UN's attention to TNCs as a global *problematique* must be seen in the context of the turbulent circumstances that characterized the 1970s. The issue of foreign direct investment and the spread of TNCs across the world surfaced in various UN publications and at UN meetings. The events in the United States and the rest of the world, however, provided the atmosphere and context within which the international community could tackle issues of transparency, accountability, and good governance at the global level. Without dwelling on the direction of causality between bad times, bad behavior, and bad policy, one must appreciate at least the link between events, actors, and policies. It seems as though ideas concerning TNCs and FDI, whether they came from unilateral or multilateral sources, were related to this chain of causality. Moreover, the collusion of events during the tumultuous first half of the 1970s made the TNCs a lightning rod for the gathering storm.

Having found itself in the eye of this hurricane, the United Nations was poised for action. Developed and developing countries seemed to be on two parallel tracks; on occasion, they overlapped or crisscrossed. Sometimes they tended to be on a collision course. The United Nations changed from a forum for dialogue into a prime battleground.

The Amsterdam and Medellín Colloquia

As early as 1965, the UN General Assembly had passed resolutions on TNCs. These included General Assembly resolution 2087 (XX) in 1965, UNCTAD resolutions in 1964 and 1968, and ECOSOC resolution 1286 (XLIII) in 1967. Subsequently, ECOSOC authorized the UN Secretary-General to convene a panel on FDI.[25] This panel, which met in Amsterdam, consisted of high-level government officials and executives of manufacturing and financial enterprises from Iran, Japan, the Netherlands, Chile, Kenya, and the United States. It selected UN under-secretary-general Philippe de Seynes as its chairman, and, following four days of discussion, adopted an "Agreed Statement."[26] Highlights of the statement include:

- For FDI to contribute to the development objectives of developing countries, it must find its place within the framework of the national development program and policies of each host country.
- Governments of host countries are the best judges of their own development objective and need to make opportunities for FDI more fully known to potential investors.
- Joint ventures provide a highly desirable arrangement for bringing together private capital, host governments, and local entrepreneurs.
- Transfer of technological and managerial know-how through foreign firms is frequently as important as capital.
- Steps are needed to increase the absorptive capacity of developing countries and their ability to develop new techniques for their own special needs.[27]

A second meeting on private investment was held in Medellín, Colombia, on 8–11 June 1970 under the joint auspices of the United Nations, the Organization of American States, and the Inter-American Development Bank.[28] This panel focused on Latin America and addressed both the potential benefits that can derive from FDI and possible areas of conflict. Studies presented at the meeting reached mixed conclusions, some suggesting that host countries had benefited, others pointing to adverse effects. In contrast to the Amsterdam meeting, the Medellín meeting tended to focus more on questions of potential conflict between TNCs and host developing (i.e., Latin American) countries.[29]

On the other hand, they "recognized that the improvement of the climate for foreign investment in Latin America could be enhanced by sound development policies as well as by vigorous expansion of the domestic private sector."[30] Meeting participants urged TNCs to make significant efforts to increase exports of manufactured and semi-manufactured goods from Latin America to industrially developed countries. TNCs could also contribute significantly to technological progress in Latin America, though it was necessary to adapt technologies developed in industrial countries for use in developing countries.[31]

The Amsterdam meeting had a more positive tone than the meeting in Medellín, where more Third Word rhetoric permeated the debate. Latin American participants demanded adaptation of technologies to host country conditions and used such terms as "locus of control" and "extraterritorial." Together, these two events demonstrate the pivotal role played by the United Nations. Philippe de Seynes stands out, even at this early—and still relatively positive—phase, as an activist international civil servant determined to place the topic of MNC–host country relations on the global agenda. After serving as chair of the Amsterdam panel, he was poised to take center stage in the more tumultuous phase that followed.

The tone of the latter third of the 1960s was one of promoting "dialogue," "reconciliation," and "promotion measures." By the mid-1970s, this relative harmony had metamorphosed into anger, rebellion, and revenge. Events, as described above, had turned the table.

De Seynes, the primary player in the creation of both the Commission and the Centre on Transnational Corporations saw the new architecture as "a focal point within the United Nations for transnational corporation." He envisioned a "new paradigm . . . beyond the classical treatment of imperfect competition and oligopoly" that was devoid of "asymmetrical relationships" and "unrestricted openness," a paradigm that tended to create more polarization than harmony. His new paradigm framed the establishment of institutional machinery within the United Nations on TNCs within the broader context of a New International Economic Order.[32]

By the late 1960s the UN had become a vigorous forum where some member states aired their expectations and frustrations about the international economic system. About this time, the U.S. government became interested in policy issues surrounding multinational corporations.

Meanwhile, scholarly research, primarily U.S. and British, was shifting from an analysis of capital movements and their impact on the home and host countries to the institution most instrumental in the FDI process—the multinational corporation as an organizational entity. At Harvard University, Raymond Vernon initiated a research project on MNEs, while Howard Perlmutter created the Multinational Enterprise Unit at the Wharton School of the University of Pennsylvania. Elsewhere in academe, in Chicago (Robert Aliber), in Pennsylvania (Franklin Root), at MIT (Charles Kindleberger), in North Carolina (Jack Behrman), and in Reading (John Dunning) and London (John Stopford), scholars devoted attention to TNCs and their impact on the world economy.[33]

One of the recurrent themes in the academic literature was the policy dimension. The vexing question for host countries was how to benefit from inbound foreign investment while minimizing its negative effects, including its perceived or actual infringement on national sovereignty, exploitative behavior, and political interference and its disregard for local culture, norms, and laws. As for MNC strategies, the primary goal was freedom to pursue business opportunities and generate profit unencumbered by unreasonable constraints. A sizeable literature of the early 1970s centered on explaining this tension.[34]

The popularity of the study of issues surrounding the growth of international (and particularly U.S.) business activity of TNCs prompted Orville Freeman—a former secretary of agriculture in the Kennedy and Johnson cabinets—to change *Business International*, a hitherto sleepy publication that began in 1954, into a must-read weekly bulletin for executives in the 1970s and 1980s. Major TNCs subscribed. *Business International* monitored the international business environment and provided useful intelligence and analysis.[35]

Interest in TNCs, therefore, was by no means limited to scholarly literature. The UN's annual *World Economic Survey*[36] first explicitly referred to the importance of FDI and multinational corporations in 1971. This idea crept into the language of ECOSOC resolution 1721 of 1972, the document that catapulted the United Nations into serious study of TNCs. The resolution asserted:

> While these corporations are frequently effective agents for the transfer of technology as well as capital to developing countries, their role is sometimes viewed with awe, since their size and power surpass the host country's entire economy. *The international community has yet to formulate a positive policy and establish effective machinery for dealing with the issues raised by the activities of these corporations.*[37]

This was a pivotal resolution. It set the field in motion by laying the groundwork for policy formulation and the institutional machinery to deal with issues arising from the activities of TNCs. Under the resolution, ECOSOC formally requested the Secretary-General to appoint "a group of eminent persons" and set its terms of reference:

> to study the role of multinational corporations and their impact on the process of development, especially that of the developing countries, and also their implications for international relations, to formulate conclusions which may possibly be used by Governments in making their sovereign decisions regarding national policy in this respect, and to submit recommendations for appropriate international action.[38]

This resolution was the genesis of the Group of Eminent Persons, the establishment of the UNCTC, and all that followed.

Work in the U.S. Government

In the United States, debate between various domestic stakeholder groups, notably labor and management, was also becoming more intense. In 1969 the State Department convened a conference[39] to discuss policy issues emerging from the growing importance of TNCs in the world economy. It was attended by U.S. scholars such as Jack Behrman, John Fayerweather, Richard Robinson, and Raymond Vernon, all of whom were pioneers in the analysis of FDI and the tensions between host countries and TNCs. Some of these tensions were international; others were domestic. On the international side, critical views of TNCs were gaining currency. Even in the home countries, TNCs were becoming controversial. A pamphlet published by the National Association of Manufacturers countered "organized labor's offensive against the MNC," arguing that the key assumptions of those who criticized TNCs were erroneous. According to the pamphlet, it was not true that TNCs caused U.S. unemployment and contributed to a balance-of-payments deficit when they exported capital, it was not true that TNCs undermined the U.S. lead when they transferred technology, and it was not true that TNCs manipulated transfer pricing to take advantage of tax and tariff loopholes.[40]

The 1969 State Department conference was precipitated by undercurrents that resulted in the Burke-Hartke bill,[41] which would have become the Foreign Trade and Investment Act of 1972 if enacted. U.S. organized labor supported this proposed legislation, which intended to prevent the export of jobs via FDI by TNCs. Although the bill did not pass, it epitomized a segment of the domestic policy debate in which TNCs had become a lightening rod and target of protectionist sentiments in and out of the U.S. Congress. A similar polarization of views was evident at the United Nations when the subject of TNCs was placed on its agenda.

Conclusion

In the 1970s, the UN struggled under the cloud of the Cold War, and from the outset, its discussion of TNCs assumed political overtones. The Soviet Union saw TNCs as exploitative agents of imperialism.[42] Many developing countries also viewed them with suspicion and mistrust. The confrontational mood of the period was exacerbated by the acceleration in the activities of TNCs in host countries and the unfriendly response from some developing countries. Turbulence was compounded by the breakdown of the Bretton Woods system of fixed exchange rates, the Watergate scandal, the Chilean scandal that contributed to the overthrow of Allende, corporate bribery scandals, the hearings in the U.S. Senate, the investigation by the SEC, the first oil crisis, and the wave of expropriations and nationalizations.

At the same time, concerns about the less-desirable consequences of MNC activity must be set against a wide array of scholarly studies that detailed some of their beneficial effects, particularly with regard to their transfer of technology and other intangible assets across borders. In Europe (particularly in the United Kingdom) and in parts of Southeast Asia, host government policies toward inbound FDI continued to be generally favorable. Even countries that seemed less favorably disposed continued to court FDI. The government of India, for example, established an office in New York in the 1970s to attract FDI at the same time that its representatives at the UN were joining the chorus demanding a new international order. Southeast Asian countries were even more pro-FDI.[43] Even in Latin America, expressions of solidarity with other host countries tended to stop at the level of symbol and ceremony. It was this lack of consensus within the Third World that ultimately contributed to the demise of the NIEO agenda.[44] Chapter 4 explores these and other trends that propelled the UN system to bring the issue onto the international stage.

4

The Group of Eminent Persons:
The Eye of the Hurricane

- *The Formation of the Group of Eminent Persons*
- *The Background Report*: Multinational Corporations in World Development
- *The Testimony before the GEP*
- *The TNC: Beneficial, Neutral, or Detrimental?*
- *The Deliberations of the GEP*
- *The Report of the GEP*
- *Conclusions*

The previous chapter described the turbulence that provided the context for the launch of an ambitious effort within the UN system to study the determinants and impact of TNC activity and suggest ways and means by which these activities might best serve the interests of developing countries. We discussed the flurry of activities that followed the Senate hearings, the SEC investigations, and disclosures of numerous improprieties in which U.S. TNCs had been implicated. Around the world, particularly in Latin America, TNCs were being attacked as villains. This period in the modern history of international relations was made remarkable by volatility, discord, mistrust, and confrontation within the global economic system. It was also a time of historic transformation in TNC-state relations from confrontation toward pragmatism. Notable contributions to knowledge creation, policy formulation, and national capacity-building were made within the UN system. This chapter details the fruits of these efforts, which began in the first half of the 1970s and produced important results under the UN umbrella over the next two decades.

The Formation of the Group of Eminent Persons

Philippe de Seynes,[1] UN under-secretary-general during Secretary-General Kurt Waldheim's tenure, began the implementation of ECOSOC resolution 1721

(LIII) of 1972, of which he had been a prime architect. The resolution mandated the formation of a Group of Eminent Persons "to study the impact of multinational corporations on economic development and international relations."

The drive to place the *problematique* of TNCs before the United Nations and the call first for the establishment of the GEP and then for the formulation of related institutional and policy measures came from two distinct origins, one from inside the UN and the other from without. De Seynes drove the internal momentum, while the external impetus came from Juan Somavía[2] and others disillusioned by TNC actions. According to Somavía, he and his colleagues in the Chilean delegation to the UN also proposed the idea of establishing a group of eminent persons to spearhead a study of multinational corporations.[3] Somavía was appointed a member and, subsequently, the rapporteur of the GEP. It is significant that it was the Chileans who pioneered the initiative to lay the subject of TNCs before the United Nations, since events in Chile in 1970–1973, such as the nationalization of copper mines, telecommunications, hotels, and other foreign investments and the "ITT affair" and the attendant political events[4] had precipitated an international crisis.[5] In addition, these and subsequent events fueled the already vigorous series of Senate hearings and SEC investigations of U.S. TNCs. The Chilean crisis became an external driving force behind the Chilean delegation's proposal to ECOSOC in 1972 that the UN should initiate a study of the role TNCs in economic development. These external and internal forces converged to propel the United Nations into action.

More than any other individual, Philippe de Seynes, who was in charge of the UN Department of Economic and Social Affairs (DESA), energized the UN's work on TNCs. He elaborated on his position in the premier issue of *CTC Reporter*, the flagship publication of the UN Centre on Transnational Corporations:

> The decision of 1973 to create a focal point within the United Nations system for transnational corporations must be viewed as a landmark in the development of *institutions needed for a New International Economic Order.*[6]

Like many colleagues, de Seynes saw the UN's attitude and philosophy toward TNCs as an integral part of the broader North-South debate as it was then framed. After leaving the UN, he spoke of the inadequacy of the early post–World War II economic order. He particularly singled out the "asymmetrical relationships" between the developed countries of the West and the rest of the world, the "oligopolistic behavior" of TNCs, and the need for a new development paradigm.

De Seynes and his staff began to implement the resolution.[7] They can-

vassed universities, industry, and the UN corridors, where government delegations roamed, to locate suitable academics, politicians, and corporate executives knowledgeable about TNCs to serve as members of the GEP. The search,
undoubtedly complicated by the politicized tenor of the exercise, eventually
produced a roster from which the Secretary-General appointed twenty individuals.[8] Given the political nature of the UN system, it was imperative that
all interested stakeholders be represented, including those from a wide spectrum of countries—large and small, developed and developing, market-oriented
and socialist-oriented. The GEP was to seek input from scholarly writings and
from the accumulated capabilities and experiences of corporations and countries and conduct a series of formal hearings at which prominent persons testified on the subject.

The group included nine members from the public sector, six from academia (in the Soviet Union, Europe, Japan, and El Salvador), and five from
public and private enterprises. Since de Seynes was sensitive to the internal dynamics within the UN system and recognized that other UN departments had
already studied some aspects of TNCs and thus had a claim to the study of
the issue, he invited observers from UNCTAD, UNIDO, and the United Nations Institute for Training and Research (UNITAR) to attend the meetings of
the GEP and submit their views. Also included were representatives of other
UN specialized agencies—the ILO, the FAO, the World Bank, and the IMF.
De Seynes also appointed two consultants to the group, Raúl Prebisch, who
later became the first secretary-general of UNCTAD in 1964, and Nat Weinberg, former director of special projects and economic analysis of the United
Automobile Workers Union of the United States and Canada.[9] Their selection
is noteworthy, as both represented "left of center" perspectives on development
issues and were generally critical of the role TNCs played in economic development. Government representatives from western countries had a minimal
presence, while TNCs and developing countries were well represented, as were
academics from Europe, Japan, and developing countries.[10]

Box 4.1. The Group of Eminent Persons

Emerik Blum	General manager, Energoinvest, Yugo-slavia
Tore Browaldh	Chairman, Svenska Handelsbanken, Sweden
John J. Deutsch	Principle and vice chancellor, Queen's University and former chairman, Economic Council of Canada
Mohamed Diawara	Minister of Planning, Ivory Coast

John H. Dunning	Professor of Economics, University of Reading, United Kingdom
Antonio Estrany y Gendre	Professor of International Economic Relations, University of El Salvador, Argentina
Ahmed Ghozali	President Director-General of SONATRACH, Algeria
I.D. Ivanov	Chief of Economic Division, Institute for US Studies, USSR Academy of Sciences, USSR
Jacob Javits	U.S. Senator, United States
L. K. Jha	Governor of Jammu and Kashmir, former ambassador of India to the United States, former governor of Reserve Bank of India, India
C. George Kahama	Director-General, Capital Development Authority, United Republic of Tanzania
Ryutaro Komiya	Professor of Economics, Tokyo University
Sicco Mansholt	Former president, Commission of the European Economic Community, Netherlands
Hans Matthoefer	Federal Minister for Research and Technology, former head of the Economic Department of the Industrial Metalworkers' Trade Union, Federal Republic of Germany
J. Irwin Miller	Chairman, Cummins Engine Co., Inc., United States
Mohammad Sadli	Minister of Mining, Indonesia
Hans Schaffner	Former President of the Swiss Confederation, vice-chairman of the Board of SANDOZ, S.A., Switzerland
Juan Somavía	Former Permanent Representative to the Andean Group, former president of the Commission of the Cartagena Agreement, former chairman of the Board of the Andean Development Corporation, Chile
Mario Trindade	vice-president, National Bank of Commerce, Rio de Janeiro, Brazil
Pierre Uri	Professor of Economics, University of Paris; author and journalist, France

Secretary of the Group: Gustave Feissel, Special Assistant to the Under Secretary-General for Economic and Social Affairs

Deputy Secretary of the Group: Sotirios Mousouris, Economic Affairs Officer, Centre for Development Planning, Projections, and Policies/ESA

Source: UN Department of Economic and Social Affairs, The Impact of Multinational Corporations on Development and on International Relations (New York: United Nations, 1974), 21–22.

In 1973 and 1974, the GEP held three plenary sessions totaling over seven weeks. The first meeting took place at UN headquarters in New York on 4–14 September 1973, the second was held in Geneva on 1–16 November 1973, and the final meeting was convened in New York from 25 March to 6 April 1974.

After the first two plenary sessions, a committee of ten GEP members met in Rome on 11–21 January 1974 to discuss the structure and content of a final report. This was followed by a meeting at Kashmir House in New Delhi on 18–26 February 1974 at which Chairman L. K. Jha of India and John Dunning and three UN staff members—N. T. Wang, Sotiris Mousouris, and Gustave Feissel—prepared a final draft on the basis of the Rome deliberations. Juan Somavía, the rapporteur, who could not attend the New Delhi drafting session due to illness, added his comments and completed the draft in Geneva on 1–4 March 1974.[11] This draft, after Chairman Jha's approval, was considered by the entire group at its final plenary session in April 1974. At that meeting, members who had not been present at the Rome or New Delhi meetings provided additional material and comments. The two consultants, Prebisch and Weinberg, also participated in the process.

In addition to their own knowledge and experience and a wealth of documentation about TNCs and their impact on development, GEP members drew upon other sources. The first was a comprehensive background paper prepared at the UN Secretariat. The second was the testimonies from forty-seven experts—fifteen in New York and thirty-two in Geneva.[12] The importance of these data sources warrants further attention.

The Background Report: *Multinational Corporations in World Development*

Prepared as a background report for the GEP to consider in its deliberations by DESA in 1973, *Multinational Corporations in World Development* was a comprehensive document that helped set the tone and direction for the work of the group. Commissioned by de Seynes and prepared by his staff, it was a pioneering and original study that was rooted in ECOSOC resolution 1721 (LIII) of 1972.[13]

Around this time, the 1971 ILO General Conference[14] and UNCTAD resolution 73 (III) of May 1972[15] also recognized that the impact of TNCs was worthy of UN study and action. The DESA study drew upon data analyses from the academic community[16] as well as from the UN Centre for Development Planning, Projections and Policies, a unit within DESA at the UN Secretariat in New York. The purpose of the report was to clarify various concepts pertaining to TNCs; to provide data on their size, geographic distribution, industrial structure, and ownership patterns; and to assess their "dimensions"[17] in the world economy. It also recommended the establishment of a "multinational corporation information centre. . . . centralized in the United Nations."[18] The GEP ultimately endorsed this suggestion, which resulted in the establishment of the UN Centre on Transnational Corporations.

This seminal report looms even larger in retrospect; the GEP later endorsed many of its recommendations and incorporated them into its own. It was, perhaps, the most comprehensive review of the state of knowledge on TNCs at that time and was groundbreaking in its scope, content, and format. Its layout became a prototype for the World Investment Report and other publications. The range of policy issues it covered set the agenda for subsequent years, and the concepts it considered became springboards for later UN work.

The report first reviewed the various terminologies used for companies that engaged in value-added activities outside their home countries. These terminologies were later discussed during GEP hearings prior to agreement on the name "transnational corporations." This term was subsequently used by the UN and its various agencies; three decades later, for example, UNCTAD's annual World Investment Report depicted the extent of the foreign activities of the world's largest TNCs by a "transnationality" index.

The main body of the report consisted of analysis and recommendations in four parts. Detailed and comprehensive, the report culled the scholarly literature on both sides of the Atlantic and elsewhere to draw a detailed portrait of TNCs and FDI. Much of the pioneering scholarship was reviewed and summarized.[19] The report acknowledged the unprecedented growth of TNCs as a major phenomenon in international economic activity and the surge of interest in them among academics, mass media, and the general public. It argued that this interest, coupled with the subject's complexity, required serious analysis lest myths should prove more appealing than facts and emotion stronger than reason. It noted the distinct economic advantages arising from the activities of TNCs when put to the service of world development and reflected the diametrically opposed views of TNCs. Some saw them as saviors, "key instruments for maximizing world welfare"; others as villains, "agents of imperialism." At the outset, the report acknowledged that "the divergence of objectives between nation-states and multinational corporations, compounded by social and cultural factors, often creates tensions. Multinational corporations, through the variety of options available to them, can encroach at times upon national sovereignty by undermining the ability of nation-states to pursue their national and international objectives."[20]

The report pointed to potential contributions of TNCs to world welfare through the efficient allocation of resources but also noted the potential for conflict of interest in areas such as decision making and equitable division of benefits. It stated that TNC issues must be understood in a broader socio-political context and as part of the international economic system:

> While the conditions in the real world hardly permit an ideal system of interna-tional exchange and cooperation, a practical economic solution is required in which the political entities. . . . can co-operate to reconcile the conflicting in-terests, harmonize their policies for their mutual benefit, and achieve a greater measure of *international distributive justice.*[21]

On occasion, the report took on a proactive posture of advocacy. It noted the need for a general agreement on "some measure of accountability of multi-national corporations to the international community" and suggested that its own contribution was the start of a series of efforts for "possible lines of ac-tion."[22] The main body of the study presented a review of the literature and discussed the concept of TNCs and the dimensions of the issue—definitions as well as size, pattern (including geographic and industry spread), and trends. The broad term "multinational corporation," it stated, covered all enterprises which control assets—factories, mines, sales, and other offices—in two or more countries, with most parent companies located in the developed countries.[23] The typical TNC was a large, predominantly oligopolistic firm with sales of hundreds of millions of dollars and affiliates spread over several countries.

The presence of foreign TNCs in developing countries, it observed, was of great significance relative to total capital flows from industrial countries, reflect-ing historical ties, some of a colonial nature. Through their capacity to move capital, technology, and entrepreneurship across national borders, TNCs had become one the leading vehicles for the internationalization of production.

The report described the extractive and manufacturing activities of TNCs, how TNCs were organized and controlled, the profit and ownership strategies of TNCs, and the broader policy dimensions of those activities.[24] It reviewed both the historical evolution of TNC activities and contemporary trends. It observed that the ability and power of TNCs to shape demand patterns and values, thereby influencing people's lives and governmental policies, and their impact on the international division of labor raised concern about their role in world affairs. The report then turned to more contentious issues—the intercept between TNCs and nation-states, the challenge that TNCs posed to national sovereignty, and the "often subtle impact of TNCs on the process and patterns of development."[25] The possible divergence in objectives between nation-states and TNCs and various social and cultural factors had the potential to create tensions. These were discussed, as were the different kinds of conflicts of in-terest that might arise regarding participation in decision making and the equitable division of benefits among TNCs, host countries, and home countries. The issues raised by TNCs, the report concluded, had a direct bearing on international relations and called for immediate attention by the international community to help attain the goal of greater distributive justice. Another important issue for study, the report noted, was whether a set of institutions could be devised to guide the governance of TNCs and to ensure accountability to the world community.

The report asserted that as TNCs had expanded, flexible organizational systems had been replaced with greater centralized control. The enormous cross-border flexibility of TNCs enabled them to function well even as host governments attempted to prevent them from exerting undue influence. The TNCs, in turn, could be affected by intergovernmental relations: indeed, some governments could use them as an instrument of foreign policy. TNCs could, for example, cause jurisdictional disputes among governments and engender political confrontations if there was a conflict of interest between home and host countries. Host countries, and even some home countries, discovered that the global context in which TNCs operate could restrict the effectiveness of government policies and could affect monetary, fiscal, and trade policies.

The report acknowledged that the majority of host countries had welcomed foreign direct investment and TNC activity. However, in the view of many, TNCs could also foster a pattern of international division of labor that perpetuated political and economic dependence. It was felt that decisions taken by TNCs might sometimes threaten national sovereignty over resources, conflict with national priorities, distort consumption patterns, and unfavorably affect income distribution. The appropriateness of the technology TNCs transferred and the possibility of obtaining that technology through alternative means was also a concern of host developing countries.

Although TNC behavior could be influenced by the attitudes and actions of their home countries, the relationship between TNCs and their host countries should be defined by the latter. To that end, a coordinating body, with a nucleus of people with the capacity to understand the operations of TNCs, might aid negotiations. Adoption of the Calvo Doctrine could allay host countries' fears of foreign domination, and screening (or even auditing) the operations of TNCs could promote their accountability.

The fourth part of the report, "Towards a Programme of Action," was surprisingly proactive. It put forth a number of recommendations based on its perception of recent trends in policies in home and host countries. It cited the attempts by Western Europeans to set up rules of competition and to move toward the harmonization of tax regimes. It also noted that the "numerous Congressional investigations" in the United States[26] as well as that country's proposed legislation on TNCs were "most striking."[27] The International Confederation of Free Trade Unions[28] had approved a code of conduct in 1969, while the International Chamber of Commerce (ICC) had formulated its "Guidelines for International Investment" in 1972.

The report discussed a comprehensive program of action for policymakers at both a national and supranational level. It recommended that an international forum be established to air views and problems when tensions and conflicts arose among TNCs and host and home countries. It recommended that ECOSOC and its committees gather and publicize the relevant information and develop policies and programs for further action. Activity pertaining to technical cooperation could be supported by continuing research within the UN to help increase the bargaining capacity of host developing countries. "It has been suggested," said the report, that ECOSOC should consider making a discussion of TNCs a "more or less regular feature of its agenda" and that a "hearings procedure" on the subject might be appropriate, as would "a corresponding work programme within the Secretariat." It could include a "multinational corporation information centre" to empower developing countries by providing information on flow of goods, services, technology, and finances between TNC affiliates.[29]

The report discussed other international efforts to harmonize national policies, including taxing the profits of affiliates, transfer pricing, and restrictive business practices, as well as anti-monopoly and environmental issues. The study's preface and text referred to a topic sure to become the thorniest of all—and perhaps one that ultimately doomed the New York phase of the enterprise. It stated that various rules being proposed, such as a GATT for international investment and an International Trade Organization,[30] could be gathered and codified into an international code of conduct for TNCs.[31]

The report also suggested that a treaty or some other form of international regulation pertaining to the establishment of international corporations deserved further study because without international authority there would be no effective mechanism for resolving international disputes. This statement foreshadowed the establishment of the United Nations Centre for Transnational Corporations.

In short, the report was explicit, detailed, and prescriptive. It proposed a hearing on the topic, an international registry of multinational corporations, an international mechanism for dispute resolution, an international code of conduct, a general agreement on TNCs, and the establishment of a research information center on multinational corporations within the United Nations. In retrospect, the background study turned out to be the first of a trilogy of important documents that constituted this UN endeavor, the others being the *Sum-*

mary of the Hearings before the Group of Eminent Persons (1973–1974) and the GEP's report of 1974. Before discussing the group's deliberations and its report, it is worthwhile to examine the second set of inputs, namely, the New York and Geneva hearings and the spectrum of views aired through them.

The Testimony before the GEP

Hearings on controversial public policy issues are common in modern democracies and often provide a public venue for fact-finding and for disentangling complex problems that involve a variety of stakeholders by airing all sides of an issue. They are intended to clarify thought, eradicate misperceptions, and seek solutions and/or alternatives by tapping into collective wisdom. The Senate hearings on TNCs spearheaded by Senator Church, discussed in the previous chapter, exemplify this approach. According to one UN staff member, these hearings were the inspiration for the UN's own hearings on the subject of TNCs.[32]

Both the UN staff and GEP members made every effort to invite written statements and testimonies from experts who held a wide spectrum of views. These included leading academics, business executives, representatives from NGOs, politicians, and statesmen, each from both developed and developing countries. Particular care was taken to embrace different geographical, professional, and ideological aspects. In all, forty-seven experts testified before the GEP. The spectrum of views and recommendations expressed during these hearings revealed a great deal about the international context and the multitude of contentious issues that permeated the debate.

Participants ran the gamut from American consumer advocate Ralph Nader to OPEC secretary-general Khene, from IBM World Trade Corporation's president Jacques Maisonrouge and its chairman Gilbert Jones to Fiat's legendary Giovanni Agnelli and DuPont's equally famous Irving Shapiro. Seven academicians testified; three from the United States (Jack Behrman, Stephen Hymer, and Joseph Nye), one from the United Kingdom (Edith Penrose), and one from Canada (Detlev Vagts). Nineteen business leaders expressed their views, including those from TNCs such as IBM, Fiat, DuPont, Exxon, General Motors, Pfizer, Rio Tinto Zinc, General Tire, Unilever, Pechiney, Siemens, Massey-Ferguson, and Shell. Also testifying were two private-sector businessmen from India and Latin America, five officials from developing-country governments, and three from the socialist bloc. Public interest groups (labor, consumer groups, and other civil society organizations) and regional and international organizations also participated. Although the Senate hearings and various testimonies and investigations in the United States were among the first to investigate the activities and impact of TNCs and had served as a model on the mechanics of holding hearings, no U.S. government representative testified before the GEP. Indeed, only representatives from developing-country governments were asked to testify, since the central issue being addressed was development.[33]

The written statements of those who testified and their responses to questions asked by the GEP were published as a 455-page report in 1974.[34] The academicians who testified did their best to draw a detailed portrait of TNCs and to provide options for "taming the beast," as it was then perceived. TNCs were under attack from many quarters. Loss of sovereignty and the need for control were the hue and cry from Latin America, and some countries in Africa and Asia joined the chorus. Some academicians also considered the status quo unacceptable. Understandably, TNC executives were quick to recount the benefits of FDI and cross-border economic activity. Representatives of developing-country governments, on the other hand, tended to focus on issues of sovereignty, gains from FDI, and (what they perceived to be) unfair practices of TNCs. A question asked of an Exxon executive is illustrative: "Do you perceive yourself, typically, as a member of an oligopoly or not?" He replied: "I do not think the oil industry, which comprises innumerable companies, large and small, some integrated and some not, has any market power of the sort implicit in that remark."[35]

In sum, nine statements of those who testified can be classified as neutral vis-à-vis TNCs, fifteen in their favor, thirteen critical of their behavior and impact, and eight as mixed. The historical significance of these hearings, the issues they illuminated, and their overall importance warrant detailed examination.

The TNC: Beneficial, Neutral, or Detrimental?

Opinions of those who testified at the hearings on the impact of FDI and TNCs on the host country ran the full gamut from praise to condemnation. Executives offered evidence of how TNCs advanced economic welfare and how they could do even more if only host governments pursued more understanding and more liberal policies. Concerned that TNCs might thwart national economic and social policies and engage in unacceptable practices, representatives of socialist countries, radical critics, and some developing countries made adversarial pronouncements.

Box 4.2. On the Nature of the Beast

A sampling of views on the nature, legitimacy, and role of multinational corporations reveals the differences in perspectives:

- We have never called for the destruction or elimination of the MNCs. We have called for their regulation, the ideal form of which would be international. . . . In the absence of international regulation, we are seeking . . . the US government regulation of United-States-based MNCs. — *Nathaniel Goldfinger, AFL-CIO* (p. 52)
- MNCs should be allowed to attend to their business within the laws of countries where they operate, and they should not be politicized or their effectiveness crippled by restrictions and international control. . . . Most developing countries realize that there is a limit to the restrictions they can impose beyond which foreign capital will no longer be attracted. — *Ernest Keller, ADELA Investment* (pp. 53, 62)
- [MNCs] exist at the will of the state . . . governed by the laws, policies and customs of the countries in which they operate and by the customers they serve . . . and hence the concept of "corporate power" is neither meaningful or useful. — *Thomas A. Murphy, GM* (pp. 79, 82)
- The largest 10 "worldcorps" (by sales) are bigger than some 80 nations (by GNP), and the largest 40 firms are larger than some 65 nations. . . . The issue is one of control: who in fact controls an economy when a dominant multinational firm can pick up and leave if the local rules are changed to its displeasure? A basic way to hold [MNCs] accountable is by building controls into their birthright—the corporate charter. — *Ralph Nader* (pp. 90, 99)

Source: UN Department of Economic and Social Affairs, *Summary of the Hearings Before the Group of Eminent Persons to Study the Impact of Multinational Corporations on Development and on International Relations* (New York: United Nations, 1974).

Beneficial

Most executives of TNCs who testified before the GEP saw their companies as instruments for maximizing the interests of their stockholders and creating economic benefits to society. One of the most extensive and well articulated of those views was presented by the ICC. President Renato Lombardi reviewed the ICC's 1969 guidelines and argued against the need for new international arrangements; he suggested that the guidelines be used as a basis for review and appraisal.[36] He reiterated many points in defense of TNCs, emphasizing their contribution to the development of host countries, and said that they adhered to all national laws.

Many executives valiantly defended TNC positions, emphasizing their contributions to employment, exports, and technology creation. Giovanni Agnelli of Fiat predicted the advent of a tremendous diffusion of technological innovation and portrayed Fiat's foray into the Soviet Union and Eastern Europe as win-win situations. Gerd Tacke, former president of Siemens, asked for a more realistic understanding of the complex tasks and strategies of TNCs, a more cooperative attitude, and guarantees that the activities of TNCs would not ultimately become mired in an increasingly dense network of controls and direct intervention.[37]

Other corporate executives, including Massey-Ferguson's president Albert Thornborough, saw the crux of the matter as "a struggle for sovereignty over the multinational corporations." He credited developing countries with having skilled and well-informed negotiators who obviated the need for UN help. He disagreed with critics who believed that codes of conduct were useless unless backed by strong international authority. "The mere promulgation of a code would have a strong moral force," he argued, adding that if a general agreement on FDI could be achieved, his company would support it no less than it did the General Agreement on Tariffs and Trade. He warned, however, that "today's solution could be tomorrow's problem" if such agreements were crafted in haste.[38]

The president of Royal Dutch Petroleum Company, G. A. Wagner, reiterated that "multinational enterprises have been major contributors to the development process . . . and engines of growth" and said that they were both adaptable and amenable to change. He acknowledged concerns over loss of sovereignty but was doubtful that a general agreement on multinational enterprises was a feasible proposition.

Others besides representatives of TNCs emphasized the benefits of FDI. Sir Ronald Walker, the special advisor to the government of Australia on multinational corporations, explained how his government's position had evolved. Australia was both an exporter and importer of FDI. Besides bringing in technology and managerial expertise, FDI had accounted for one-third of domestic savings in the 1960s and had made significant contributions to the country's economic growth. Yet there was a growing recognition that foreign investment in general, and multinational corporations in particular, might be a mixed blessing. The new Labour Party government, which had come to power in December 1972, had done a reappraisal. It had a policy of "promoting Australian control of Australian resources and industries." Ronald stated that while Aus-

tralia had greatly benefited in the past from foreign capital and foreign enterprise, the Australian economy had "matured to the point at which Australians
should be in a stronger position to manage their own future industrial development."[39]

Marcus Wallenberg, patriarch of the famous Swedish banking and industrial
family, saw TNCs in the broader context of increasing the interconnectivity of
nations and the internationalization of business. He acknowledged that some
host countries might see TNCs as a threat, but observed that "when the developing countries become better equipped, many problems now attributable to
the existence of the TNCs will not make themselves felt." Wallenberg specifically and astutely recommended that TNCs accept their social responsibility
over and above what was legally required and said that they should better identify their interests with those of host countries. He agreed that there was a need
for a code of good conduct, provided it applied to both companies and governments.[40]

Sir Ernest Woodroofe and Gerrit D. A. Klijnsra, the two chairmen of Unilever,[41] presented their views in a joint statement, elaborating on themes discussed in the UN background report. They stated that Unilever preferred 100
percent ownership of subsidiaries to prevent any possible conflict of interest and
did not try to change local cultures but tried only to satisfy their needs. They
emphasized respect for national laws and warned against the danger of "throt-
tling the growth by international rules and regulations and expressed doubt
about the practicability of a supra-national body or convention on foreign investment or a UN authority to govern the relations between home and host
countries and multinationals."[42]

Box 4.3. Time for an International Mechanism to Control MNCs?

- An international agreement ratified by the parliaments of the
  world would have a tremendous educational effect. Even if final
  agreement is not reached, a thorough discussion of the question of MNCs will be very useful. — *Osvaldo Sunkel* (p. 137)
- I welcome the establishment of a UN forum aimed at the regular discussion of the problems deriving from the operations of
  MNCs. . . . In all other matters [including a code of conduct],
  thorough further consultations seem to be required. — *Gyorgy
  Adam* (pp. 141–142)
- We clearly need better rules governing the relations between
  MNCs and governments. But a binding multilateral agree-
  ment between developed and developing countries in terms

of a 'GATT for Investment' does not seem practical at the moment. — *Giovanni Angelli, Fiat* (p. 149)

· A 'General Agreement on Multinational Companies,' patterned after the General Agreement on Tariffs and Trade and laying down a number of accepted principles, is the least that the world community ought to try to offer. . . . A company should not be in a position to take advantage of its multinational power to market goods in another country to lower standards, from the consumer point of view, than those mandatory in its home market. — *Peter Goldman, International Organization of Consumers' Unions* (pp. 191, 198)

· The creation of an international forum and an information centre merit consideration, provided that these bodies do not become anti-MNC grand juries. — *Jacques Merchandise, Pechiney-Ugine-Kuhlman* (p. 307)

Source: UN Department of Economic and Social Affairs, *Summary of the Hearings Before the Group of Eminent Persons to Study the Impact of Multinational Corporations on Development and on International Relations* (New York: United Nations, 1974).

Neutral

Voices of moderation were amply represented and came from various sources, sometimes from unexpected places. The president of Delhi Cloth Mills, Bharat Ram, was a moderate voice from developing countries. He expressed concern over excessive tax concessions that some countries granted to attract TNCs and emphasized that host countries "have the ability to control the multinational corporations and [therefore] undue apprehension about [their] operations is uncalled for."[43] Jamaica's H. S. Walker also took a moderate stance by stating that his country welcomed inbound FDI provided it resulted in meaningful benefits and did not compromise Jamaica's sovereignty and its legitimate right to regulate its own affairs.

However, not all forces of moderation were in harmony, and frequently each emphasized a different angle. Altiero Spinelli of the European Community stated that without an appropriate political and social countervailing force, TNCs were more likely to engage in unacceptable business practices. Prevention could take the form of a code of conduct accompanied by sanctions or "one or two spectacular isolated measures." He did not specify what these measures might be but may have meant resort to courts and litigation.

Another appraisal came from Javed Burki, at the time a senior Pakistani official and later vice president of the World Bank for Latin America, who cautioned that the global expansion of TNC activities "may well mean that the age-old conflict between rich and poor nations will be converted into a struggle between developing countries and MNCs." He favored a set of supranational guidelines and rules of conduct for TNCs in the form of a GATT type of agreement on TNCs, but at the same time he believed that Pakistan could control the operations of multinationals through fiscal, monetary, and exchange rate policies.[44]

In the main, academic testimonies presented balanced and moderate views. Jack Behrman of the University of North Carolina believed that the fundamental issue in the relationship of TNCs and governments was one of control, not ownership. Problems existed because TNCs sought to expand their national corporate activities into the international domain. He proposed an "organization for international industrial integration" to establish better communications between governments and TNCs on issues concerning key industrial sectors and to counsel on the location and development of these sectors throughout the world. Behrman declared that the prevailing economic order was unacceptable, suggesting that industrial policies be developed at national, regional, and international levels since TNCs operated at all of these.[45]

Box 4.4. Views on Codes

· There should be a voluntary code of conduct for corporations . . . [but] we are not nearly ready to set up a body of accepted doctrine or an organization to administer and implement it. — *Emilio Collado, Exxon* (p. 42)
· Any 'guideline' or 'general agreement' on the principles to be observed by MNCs should include provisions on good citizenship and the long term social impact of MNCs. — *The Council for Social Welfare* (p. 76)
· A code of conduct for MNCs would have to be strong enough to influence their activities in countries like South Africa. . . . A GATT type of agreement regulating relations between MNCs and host countries can be usefully concluded only after major changes in the structure of economic relations between developed and developing countries are achieved. — *H. M. A. Onitiri, Nigeria* (pp. 108–109)
· A common code of behavior for multinational—and, for that matter, national—business would be a logical and constructive step so long as it was accompanied by parallel standards for the other parties to the agreements—government and labor. . . .

The concept of a GATT for investment came from an article by Michael Blumenthal [then U.S. secretary of treasury]. . . . but it will take a long time to accomplish, and there will be many hazards. — *Irving S. Shapiro, DuPont* (p. 122)

· One is not sure that much could be achieved by [a code] because some developing host countries would be so pushed that they would not be able to adhere to some of the rules because they needed the technology and capital that only MNCs can provide. — *P. O. Ahimie, Nigeria* (p. 160)

· Rio Tinto Zinc has a code of corporate behavior, the spirit of which is appropriate throughout [the mining industry] and perhaps others. Its main provisions are that one should aim for a progressive degree of local autonomy in decision-making. . . . seek to employ as high a proportion of nationals of any host country as possible. . . . . ensure that the majority of the Board of each overseas corporation are nationals of the host country . . . be sensitive to the reasonable aspirations of the host countries. . . . and ensure that the population of the host country has the opportunity to participate financially in the major enterprises of their country. — *Sir Val Duncan* (pp. 174–182)

· A common code of behaviour is an excellent idea but can only be a lowest common denominator. . . . Any registry of multi-national corporations should be the kind of list that corporations should be proud to belong to.[1] — *J. A. C. Hugill, FAO-affiliated Industry Cooperative Programme* (pp. 209–210)

· I tend to be somewhat skeptical [about codes of conduct] but they can sometimes strengthen the hands of weaker governments. . . . . Without expecting too much from codes of good behavior, I would say that they are not totally useless. — *J. S. Nye* (p. 331)

Source: UN Department of Economic and Social Affairs, *Summary of the Hearings Before the Group of Eminent Persons to Study the Impact of Multinational Corporations on development and on International Relations* (New York: United Nations, 1974).

Note: 1. In that spirit, a registry of sorts emerged about thirty years later in the form of the UN Global Compact.

The testimony of Harvard's Joseph Nye was another example of a dispassionate analysis, but it was interspersed with some warnings. He acknowledged the potential conflicts between the goals of nation-states and those of TNCs. Yet in pursuing these goals, TNCs might also stimulate the growth and restructuring of nation-states. Nye predicted that the U.S. use of force in defense of its firms would be increasingly costly and there would be more emphasis on the welfare effects of FDI than on exertion of force on behalf of TNCs, whose practice of "de-domiciling" to "remote and pleasant tropical islands" or "shopping among developing states" could increase the willingness of governments to turn to international agreements and organizations.[46]

Edith Penrose of the School of Oriental and African Studies at the University of London argued that the governments of developing countries that had refused to accept TNCs or had restricted their activities on ideological grounds had done so mainly out of fear that corporations would abuse their economic and political power. She argued that while these fears may have some basis, they were frequently exaggerated and that host countries needed to weigh the relative costs and benefits of inbound FDI.[47] Penrose stated that the UN background report's proposal to establish an organization for gathering and analyzing information about TNCs could be "the most effective type of action that an international organization could take."[48] At the same time, she felt that the adverse role of TNCs and FDI in the development process was exaggerated because in the final analysis, TNCs were subject to government regulations and control.[49]

Detlev F. Vagts of Harvard University Law School discussed the UN report and its issues within a legal framework. Vagts acknowledged that the key concern TNCs presented was the fear of "an overhang, uncurbed potential power," but he cautioned against an "understandable tendency to use the MNC as a scapegoat." He noted that the mood of the time was one of separatism, with each country "jealous of its capacity to control its own economic future." He believed that any substantive international attempt to govern the multinational enterprise, whether by chartering, regulation, or otherwise, was likely to be premature because international agencies such as GATT and the IMF had already dealt with similar issues.[50]

The president of Central El Palma, Gustavo Vollmer, also sounded a note of neutrality:

> While it is evident that the multinational corporation as it is known today is not a perfect institution, and it causes distortions in host countries, it is also true that today, and until something better comes along, it is the best instrument available to developing countries to obtain technical know-how, the expertise and the capital with which to develop their natural resources, and thus obtain the wherewithal to raise the wellbeing of their citizens to the level to which they legitimately aspire.[51]

Box 4.5 illustrates the questions uppermost in the minds of the GEP members and the responses the GEP survey received from different corners.

Box 4.5. Q&A: Barometer of the Mood?

Some of the questions raised by the Group of Eminent Persons reflected strong sentiments while some answers were equally revealing. In retrospect, it is clear that the dialogue was reflective of the mood of the times:

Q: Can developing countries hope to control the activities of MNCs?

A: *I see no problems for developing countries with an orderly administration in controlling the activities of MNCs — Investment company executive* (p. 62)

Q: Can you give an example in which GM has made a special effort to adapt technology to create more jobs than by simply transferring technology?

A: *GM's Basic Transport Vehicle (BTV), a low-cost product requiring a minimum of sheet-metal fabrication and designed with emphasis on ease of assembly and repairs, and low operating cost. [It is currently] being produced in Malaysia, Portugal, Ecuador, and the Philippines. — GM Executive* (p. 83)

Q: Would you agree that the main effect of OPEC has been an increase in the price paid by consumers rather than a reduction in the profits of multinational oil companies?

A: *Oil prices increased during 1973 in such a way that the oil-producing countries decided to increase their Government-take in an attempt to reap some of the windfall profits of the oil companies who were neither entitled to increase their prices as a consequence of this decision, nor had they the right to put the blame on the OPEC countries. — OPEC secretary-general Khene* (p. 258)

Q: Is Shell willing to bargain with its workers internationally?

A: *The world is still organized nationally or locally, with national labor laws and national unions. It is hard to see how within these constraints bargaining at an international level would be possible. — Gerrit A. Wagner, Royal Dutch Petroleum* (p. 419)

Q: What action was taken by the home Governments in response to expropriations in Algeria, Ceylon, Cuba, Egypt, Guinea, Libya, Somali, Syria and South Yemen?

A: *Action was limited to normal diplomatic representations such as expressions of concern and of expectations that adequate and effective compensation would be paid without undue delay. — Gerrit A. Wagner, Royal Dutch Petroleum* (p. 422)

Q: Has Jamaica been under external pressure to welcome foreign capital?

A: *Jamaica has always welcomed foreign capital on fair terms, and there has been no real motivation for applying external pressures either on the aid front or in the political field. — H. S. Walker, permanent representative of Jamaica to the UN in Geneva* (p. 427)

Q: Should there be a fuller disclosure of information on corporate accounting?
A: *Unilever will be happy with fuller disclosure if a reasonable basis is
   established and if competitors, including national competitors, also
   have to comply. — Sir Ernest G. Woodroofe and Gerrit D. A. Klijn-
   stra, Unilever* (p. 454)

Source: UN Department of Economic and Social Affairs, *Summary of the Hear-
ings Before the Group of Eminent Persons to Study the Impact of Multinational
Corporations on Development and on International Relations* (New York: United
Nations, 1974).

Detrimental

The socialist camp and many developing countries saw TNCs in a negative
light.

Critics saw them in the context of exploitation and the "international division of labor" and as agents of capitalism. Horst Heininger of the German
Democratic Republic said: "It is known that the implementation of the international division of labor in the non-Socialist world is, to an increasing degree,
connected with the expansion of MNCs."[52] Latin Americans had been among
the more outspoken critics, and their government representatives' statements
reflected this. Some developing and socialist countries such as Mexico, Hungary, and Poland asserted that they had the right to control their economic destiny and that TNCs were welcome only if they helped advance this goal. Jose
Campillo Sians, an undersecretary in the Mexican government, declared that
"an under-developed community is a subordinate community" but added that
"we will receive foreign investment only if it contributes to the objectives that we
have set ourselves."[53]

Attempting to further enunciate the view prevailing among Third World
countries, the Mexican representative attributed developing countries' problems to "an international order in which an unjust distribution of wealth pre-
vails." Mexico was in favor of a "code of conduct for transnational corporations,
provided that it did not in any way impair the sovereignty of the recipient countries."[54]

When asked by a panel member what effect Mexico's policies have had on
inward investment, Campillo retorted: "If we have lost any foreign investment
as a result of our policies, it has been well lost." When asked if Mexico would
accept international arbitration, as stipulated in the Calvo Doctrine, he replied
that Mexico could not agree to arbitration that would give foreigners preference

over nationals. He also noted that private investors had agreed to abide by national legislation.

Osvaldo Sunkel, a Latin American academic, cautioned against the growing economic power of many TNCs, noting that the TNC "possesses sufficient power and influence to try to set the rules of the game." Sunkel called for a study of "the nature of contemporary capitalism," adding that "mythology and ideology often preclude rational thinking."[55]

Constantine Vaitsos, a Greek-born Colombian and Harvard-educated economist—and a champion of the Pacto Andino (the Andean Pact) economic integration scheme—addressed appropriate technology and transfer pricing. He reiterated the standard arguments put forth by critics regarding the inappropriateness of much TNC technology to the basic needs of developing countries, the unfairness of the international patent system, the high prices charged, and restrictive clauses imposed by technology suppliers on recipients. In his opinion, TNCs' contribution to economic development was an open question, especially in view of their tendency to use capital-intensive technologies and the practice of transfer pricing, which he argued was a way to avoid host country taxes.[56]

Representatives from other developing countries, including Nigeria and Pakistan, echoed the views of Mexico's Campillo. However, the most vociferous critics were representatives of socialist countries. Gyorgy Adam of the Hungarian Academy of Sciences declared that the socialist bloc was introducing an alternative to TNCs that was designed to produce technologies more suited to the needs of developing countries. Adam reserved his harshest criticism for ITT, saying that it had publicly admitted to its interference in Chilean politics in U.S. Senate hearings, adding that "ITT manoeveures [sic] similar to those in Chile have taken place in Ecuador, Peru, etc." While not all TNCs indulged in practices similar to those of ITT, "in view of the historical record [Guatemala, Iran, etc.,] it can hardly be doubted that quite a few of them—particularly the biggest—do."

One of the few scholars highly critical of TNCs was Stephen Hymer, a Harvard-educated academic, socialist, and radical critic. He submitted one of the lengthiest testimonies (twenty-five pages) and provided another fifteen pages of answers to survey questions.[57] In his testimony, he called the UN background report "myopic" and "inadequate"; it did not address the dependency issue and failed to tackle the critical question of whether "a world system based on private multinational capitalism [could] ever achieve the development goals we all desire." Hymer conjectured that by century's end, the world's industrial system might be dominated by 400–500 giants and questioned whether such a system would be compatible with hopes for a peaceful and prosperous world.[58] Rather ironically, he argued in favor of national self-sufficiency, invoking a 1933 article by John Maynard Keynes, hardly a socialist. "Contrary to the belief of the 19th century free traders, the world market created in the Golden Age of Pax Brittanica [sic] did not ensure peace but ended in war and a depression."[59]

> Free traders' economic internationalization assumed the whole world was, and would be organized on the basis of private competitive capitalism. In contrast, Keynes felt that we had to go beyond capitalism if the fruits of the industrial revolution were to be realized in a humane and rational way.[60]

Hymer proposed his "law of uneven development," which, in part, states that TNCs have a Janus-like impact. On the positive side, they provide ready-made capital, technology, and organizational abilities. On the negative side, they work to maintain their advantage by centralizing control over the capacity to generate capital and technology. Furthermore, Hymer argued that as a capitalist organization, "the multinational corporate system does not seem to offer the world national independence or equality." While top executives play an influential role in the political, cultural, and social life of the host country, these countries are likely to remain as "branch plant countries" with the host country nationals occupying, at best, midlevel positions.

In answer to questions put by members of the GEP, Hymer further elaborated his views. Referring to the quasi-official "Watkins report"[61] on Canada, which he had helped write, he continued to emphasize issues of national autonomy and uneven development and the need to regulate TNCs. With respect to a research agenda, he challenged the UN to extrapolate the multinational corporate system into the future. Assuming that the flow of international capital would continue to increase at 10 percent per year (as it had done in the last fifteen years) what, he asked, would be the impact on employment and on the spread of industry to developing and underdeveloped countries? What would the international economy look like, and what types of work and income would be available to the various regions and nationalities? Hymer believed that the multinational corporate system did not offer "a promising alternative."[62] He suggested, instead, that research focus on changing the development paradigm and take aim at the "removal of misery." He argued that this goal was incompatible and inconsistent with the multinational corporate system. Why, he asked, was there no mention in the UN background report on TNCs as "agents of imperialism"?

Some speakers widened the debate to include cultural, institutional, and ideological issues. For example, Jose de la Puente of the Peruvian Foreign Affairs Ministry argued that the UN report failed to appreciate the impact of TNCs on development and on international relations "as a moral matter touching upon the innermost values of the developing countries."[63] He referred to the Andean Group's efforts to increase regional economic integration among the participating countries ("full economic union by 1980") and endorsed a standard regime for the treatment of FDI under the Cartagena Agreement, under which intraregional enterprises were nurtured. In contradistinction to traditional TNCs, these were "multinational in the true sense, to promote the harmonious and balanced development of the sub-region, with equitable distribution of the benefits of integration and reduction of disparities in the living standards" of member countries. De la Puente asserted that "a code of conduct to govern their operation is essential." Questioned why Peru would allow TNCs "when they produce such negative effects," he replied that not everything they did was negative and admitted that in any event, it was Peru's responsibility to set ground rules.[64]

The Deliberations of the GEP

The deliberations of the GEP took place within the contentious atmosphere of the time. With the background report and the testimonies before them, members began drafting their report. Coming from different geographic, ideological, professional, and educational perspectives, the members, all distinguished in their own right, found it difficult to agree on many specific ideas. This disagreement was evidenced by an appendix to the final report containing individual members' dissenting views. Those whose predilections tilted toward the benefits of TNC activity made the usual arguments about TNCs' need to make a profit and economic gains from sound business practices; they preferred to direct their criticism toward inappropriate attitudes and policy on the part of host governments. Others focused on TNCs' abuses of monopoly power and the exploitative nature of current international economic relations, of which they were an important part. Most GEP members agreed on the general need for good governance, for clear rules of engagement, and for the need to assist developing countries in their quest for economic restructuring.

According to the members of the group interviewed in the course of preparing this book, most discussions were amicable.[65] During several meetings, the group tackled the topics raised in the UN background report and the testimony of experts. Once the report of the Group of Eminent Persons was drafted, few modifications were made, and even these were nuanced and subtle. Most in the group recognized this was a more complex subject than was originally thought and that easy or straightforward answers were hard to come by. Much, it was agreed, depended on context (time, place, type of economic activity, size, and strategy of particular TNCs, etc.). Much depended, too, on the host countries' ideology, culture, development goals, and past history.

During these deliberations, many in the group were only beginning to realize that TNCs were becoming the main organizational entities for linking people, ideas, and institutions across national boundaries. TNCs were the chief harbingers of late-twentieth- and early twenty-first-century globalization. The presence of their affiliates and the transfer of intangible assets across national boundaries had turned TNCs into modern economic colonists. They embedded themselves in foreign economies, transmitted culture and alternative ways of doing things, and promoted entrepreneurship and new technologies.

During the hearings, partisan positions pitted speakers such as Nader, Sunkel, Adam, and Hymer—each critical of TNCs—against TNC executives and other proponents accused of "whitewashing" views. The group was quite forceful and far reaching in its questioning. Those who provided the most partisan testimony, either highly critical of or supportive of TNCs, came in for the most intensive criticism, mainly from those of the group who took the opposite view. According to Dunning, academics such as Behrman, Nye, and Penrose, who held dispassionate positions, probably had the greatest influence on the group's thinking, but lesser-known figures such as Peter Goldman and several representatives from developing-country governments contributed valuable insights.

The responsibility for submitting the final report to the Secretary-General fell to the chairman of the group, Ambassador L. K. Jha of India, a firm but benign chairperson.[66]

The Report of the GEP

Nine months after the hearings and after considerable deliberation, the group issued its report. A small working group, led by Chairman Jha[67] and including Gustave Feissel and John Dunning, met in Kashmere House in Delhi, India, to draft the report. This report was then circulated and discussed among GEP members and submitted to the UN Secretary-General on 22 May 1974.

The GEP report relied considerably on the background report *Multinational Corporations in World Development* as well as on the testimonies of the New York and Geneva hearings[68] and on background papers prepared by the staff of the Secretary-General. While it gave each stakeholder group something to both embrace and criticize, it focused on areas of commonality; the differences of opinion were about balancing the costs and benefits of TNC. There was general agreement regarding the facts and the recommendation that the UN establish a commission and a center on TNCs.

In its letter transmitting the report to the UN Secretary-General, the group expressly stated the key recommendations that were to form the structure and thrust of UN work on TNCs for years to come:

> We all attach particular importance to the establishment, under the Economic and Social Council, of a commission on multinational corporations. . . . As a corollary . . . we recommend the establishment, within the United Nations Secretariat or closely linked with it, of an information and research centre on multinational corporations.[69]

Significantly, both of these recommendations had been contained in the background report DESA prepared for the GEP.

Key Points and Recommendations of the Group of Eminent Persons

The body of the report the GEP sent to the Secretary-General was structured in three parts. The general and analytical section included some twenty recommendations. The second part dealt with such TNC-specific issues as ownership and control, financial flows and balance of payments, technology, employment and labor, consumer protection, competition and market structure, transfer pricing, taxation, and information disclosure and evaluation. The third part consisted of comments by nine members of the group. The analysis of each topic was followed by one or more recommendations.

The first section discussed the impact of TNCs on development. The report drew liberally from *Multinational Corporations in World Development*, especially for data on the extent of TNC involvement in particular countries and industries. In an attempt at even-handedness, the report noted:

> Most countries have recognized the potential of multinational corporations. . . . At the same time certain practices and effects of multinational corporations have given rise to widespread concern and anxiety in many quarters and a strong feeling has emerged that the present *modus vivendi* should be reviewed at the international level.[70]

The report summarized a number of concerns raised by various stakeholder groups during the course of the hearings or raised *sui sponte* in their own deliberations:

> Most *countries* are concerned about the undesirable effects that foreign investment by multinational corporations may have on domestic employment and the balance of payments, and about the capacity of such corporations to alter the normal play of competition. *Host countries* are concerned about the ownership and control of key economic sectors by foreign enterprises, the excessive cost to

the domestic economy which their operations may entail, the extent to which
they may encroach upon political sovereignty, and their possible adverse effect
on socio-cultural values. *Labor interests* are concerned about the impact of multinational corporations on employment and workers' welfare and on the bargaining strength of trade unions. *Consumer interests* are concerned about the appropriateness, quality, and price of goods produced by multinational corporations.
The *multinational corporations themselves* are concerned about the possible nationalization or expropriation of their assets without adequate compensation and
about restrictive, unclear, and often changing government policies.[71]

The report identified "fundamental new problems" that had arisen "as a direct result of the growing internationalization of production as carried out by
multinational corporations" and emphasized the need to tackle these without
delay so that "tensions are eased and the benefits which can be derived from
multinational corporations are fully realized." The use of such strong words as
"concerns," "problems," and "tensions" in the diplomatic setting of the UN is
indicative of the atmosphere at this time.

Subsequent parts of the report summarized the issues from the development
perspective, and each section contained specific recommendations. With respect to "impact on development," the report acknowledged that TNCs were
more likely to enter countries possessing large or expanding markets, higher
per capita incomes, abundant and skilled labor, stable political systems, and
auxiliary services needed by TNCs. When assessing the economic impact, the
group noted that "a wider vision and deeper probing beneath the surface" was
necessary since investment incentives to spur TNCs to predetermined activities
did not always provide a basis for sustained and sound development and "isolated foreign enclaves" had few linkages with the domestic economy.[72] In some
countries, the noneconomic impact of inward FDI was seen as perhaps even
more important because "most multinational corporations originate in countries with very different social and cultural backgrounds."[73] The report pointed
to the distribution of gains between host and home countries and policy measures at the national and international levels to which TNCs respond when developing their global strategies.

The second part contained eight recommendations concerning the impact of
TNCs on development. It began with a call for an increase in international aid,
as recommended by the United Nations International Development Strategy.[74]
Developing countries should intensify their efforts at regional cooperation and
should consider coordinating among themselves to increase their negotiating
talents and bargaining power with TNCs. The UN and its various agencies
should strengthen their capabilities to better assist developing countries in their
capacity-building efforts.

In another recommendation, again reflective of the mood of the time, the group suggested that host countries explore "the possibility of a reduction over time of the percentage of foreign ownership."[75] Without invoking the principle of "national treatment," the group advised host countries to "adopt policies towards affiliates of multinational corporations similar to those applied to indigenous companies, unless specific exceptions are made in the national interest."[76]

In the course of analyzing the impact on international relations, the report made another eight recommendations preceded by analysis and discussion. This section noted that "concern over the impact of multinational corporations on the domestic and international affairs of nation-states has been voiced at the highest government levels" and referenced the 1973 summit of nonaligned countries in Algiers and similar meetings in Ottawa, Bogotá, and Mexico City about the same time. There was general unanimity among the GEP that TNCs' interests were better served by not becoming embroiled in host countries' domestic political controversies. In fact, the group's first recommendation under the heading of impact on international relations was aimed at host countries. It urged host countries to specify as precisely as possible the conditions under which TNCs were allowed to operate, what they should achieve, and how they should fit into the overall priorities of the recipient countries. With the unacceptable actions of the International Telephone and Telegraph in Chile clearly in mind, the group:

> *unequivocally condemns* subversive political intervention on the part of multinational corporations directed towards the overthrow or substitution of a host country's Government or the fostering of internal or international situations that stimulate conditions for such action, and *recommends* that, in such an eventuality, host countries should impose strict sanctions in accordance with due process of law of the host country concerned.[77]

The group also urged host countries "not to use multinational corporations and their affiliates as instruments for the attainment of foreign policy goals."[78]

A discussion of how TNCs might find themselves in the midst of disputes between home and host countries and the need for fair treatment in cases of nationalization was followed by a recommendation concerning arbitration. The report stated that where there is nationalization, compensation should be "fair and adequate and determined according to due process of law of the country concerned, *or in accordance with any arbitration arrangements existing between the parties.*"[79] The group then proposed what was to become controversial to the United States and others—the establishment of a commission and a center on TNCs.

A fresh reading of the GEP report a quarter-century later can still provoke mixed reactions. Through a twenty-first century lens, some recommendations may appear anachronistic; others are right on target.

General Issues: Impact on Development
and on International Relations

Dealing with overarching issues of concern that had precipitated the hearings—namely, the impact of TNCs on development and international relations—the report addressed the big picture and made recommendations. The first set of eight recommendations dealt with the impact on development and began by recommending an increase in international public aid consistent with the targets of the UN's International Development Strategy. Host developing countries should set precise conditions under which TNCs should operate within their countries. Some recommendations go beyond generalities and suggest, for example, that countries should establish "centralized negotiating services" and joint regional policies vis-à-vis TNCs, perform periodic review of contracts, and reduce over time "the percentage of foreign ownership." The UN should strengthen its capacity to help host countries achieve these objectives.

A further eight recommendations dealt with the impact on international relations. They began by deferring to the sovereign right of nation-states to set their own rules regarding permissible public activities and to prescribe sanctions for infringements. The group unequivocally condemned "subversive political intervention" and recommended strict sanctions for violations. In the event that assets of TNCs should be nationalized, fair and adequate compensation should be provided in accordance with the "law of the country concerned" or in accordance with arbitration agreements between parties. Home countries should also refrain from getting involved in disputes between host countries and TNCs (reference to the Calvo Doctrine) and from using international agencies to exert pressure. Home and host countries should make sure that TNCs do not violate UN sanctions against countries that suppress human rights and follow racist policies.[80]

Four resolutions described the contours of the necessary international machinery: a "commission on multinational corporations" comprised of "individuals with a profound understanding of the issues" and "an information and research centre on multinational corporations." The center would serve the commission by collecting, analyzing, and disseminating information and undertaking research.

Issue-Specific Recommendations

The report urged host countries to identify areas where they were ready to accept foreign direct investment and any conditions attached to such acceptance. It also recommended that joint ventures be considered in which foreign equity interest would be gradually reduced. The group drew a distinction between ownership and control—an important contribution given the negative attitude of some developing countries to FDI. Control could be exercised just as easily through nonequity arrangements; thus, a gradual reduction in foreign equity participation would not address the perceived fear of control.

1. Financial flows and balance of payments: The GEP did not make any specific recommendation in this area. However, it observed that the financial impact of FDI inflow was usually welcome by recipient countries and especially those countries with balance-of-payments deficits. The group saw this in a broader context, noting that foreign exchange and balance-of-payments difficulties may sometimes force developing countries to restrict financial outflows such as royalty payments, which in turn might lead TNCs to resort to transfer pricing and other evasive practices.

2. Technology: The GEP made four recommendations and noted that the role of technology was essential for production and could have a marked impact on balance of payments, industrial restructuring, exports, and jobs. It also recognized that the international market for proprietary technology was an imperfect one and was sometimes strongly influenced by TNCs. It recommended that host countries should carefully evaluate (with international assistance, if necessary) the appropriateness of imported technology and "require multinational corporations to make a reasonable contribution towards product and process innovation of the kind most suited to national or regional needs." The report drew attention to UNCTAD's work on a code of conduct for the transfer of technology[81] and called for a revision of the international patent system and "an overall regime under which the cost of technology provided by multinationals to developing countries could be reduced." Finally, it suggested the establishment of a "world patents (technology) bank" where donations would be used by developing countries to devise alternative ways of importing technology with the help of international agencies where necessary.

3. Labor: The group made ten recommendations on employment and labor issues. In doing so, it drew upon the ILO report *Multinational Enterprise and Social Policy* (1973). The first of the recommendations was directed to home countries, who were encouraged not to hamper technology transfers associated with relocation of labor-intensive and low-skill production to developing countries. In the highly competitive global economy of the early twenty-first century, which is marked by outsourcing, loss of jobs as industries relocated abroad, and slogans in home countries about the "giant sucking sound," a phrase industrialist Ross Perot popularized in his unsuccessful bids for president in the 1990s, this concern resonates quite differently.

Another recommendation urged host countries to articulate their employment objectives and communicate them clearly to TNCs. Home and host countries should permit free entry of unionists from other countries as well as "sympathy strikes and other peaceful forms of concerted action." International accounting and reporting standards should contain data that local labor representatives could use for collective bargaining. Health and safety standards applied at home should be equally applied in host countries, and home countries should prevent their companies from entering countries where workers' rights are violated.

4. Consumer protection: The GEP made two recommendations on issues related to consumer protection. One suggested that host countries require TNCs to reveal prohibitions and restrictions in effect at home or another country with respect to health and safety so they can be disclosed to host countries. The other, also addressed to home countries, recommended that products that are hazardous to health should be prohibited from export.

5. Competition and market structure: This section was influenced by UNCTAD's working group on restrictive business practices, which for several years had sought to devise rules to prevent anti-competitive behavior by TNCs. Such behavior was perceived to include territorial restrictions on market access, export restrictions, collusive tendering, tied purchase agreements, and cartel behavior.[82] Five recommendations included the suggestion that TNCs provide clear information about the restrictions they placed on their local partners concerning exports or purchasing requirements. Another urged home and host countries to cooperate in prohibiting market allocation of exports or tied purchase clauses unless they could demonstrate tangible benefits. The group urged international recognition of the principle that "restrictive clauses and market allocation by MNCs should be eliminated."[83] It also recommended that work should commence on the drafting of an international antitrust agreement under UN auspices and that in the interim, home countries should restrain from unilaterally applying their own antitrust regulations.

6. Transfer pricing and taxation: Two recommendations addressed transfer pricing. The first was that host countries should better enforce arm's-length pricing and relevant tax rules. The other urged an exchange of price information and even "an international agreement on the rules concerning transfer pricing for the purposes of taxation." Three recommendations followed on taxation issues, including one that urged that work on tax treaties be expedited and that developing countries should join in this effort.

7. Information disclosure and evaluation: Finally, the report made recommendations on information disclosure and evaluation. It suggested that an expert group on international accounting standards be convened by the commission and that the proposed Centre on Transnational Corporations be used as a

depository for information disclosed by the companies concerning agreements between themselves and their affiliates. The group noted that information per se was of little use unless governments possessed adequate resources, capabilities, and institutions to interpret and utilize it. The GEP recommended that the UN step into the capacity-building arena, thus paving the way for the center to eventually develop a capacity-building component directed to training developing country officials.

Dissenting Voices within the GEP

The GEP's report was clearly a logical extension of the UN background report and the testimony given in the hearings and its diversity accurately reflects the moods of the time. Dissent from both sides was reflected. Some members chose to separately record their views when they diverged from those of the group. Some dissenters, including Emerik Blum of Yugoslavia, Ahmed Ghozali of Algeria, and Juan Somavía of Chile, expressed additional concerns and apprehension about the possible adverse effects of TNCs, implying that the report should have made stronger recommendations for their surveillance and control.

On the other hand, members such as Senator Jacob Javits and J. Irwin Miller of the United States, Ryutaro Komiya of Japan, and Hans Schaffner of Switzerland took the opposite views. In their lengthy commentaries, each presented a view that largely concurred with those of developed market-economy countries. Senator Javits, for example, challenged many of the assumptions underlying the report, arguing that they were predicated on "a conflict between the economic power of the multinational corporations and the political power of the host Governments and sets out various concerns expressed by various groups without any attempt to assess their validity."[84] He stated that many of the GEP recommendations were "concerned with exercising greater political control" over TNCs without taking account of "economic realities."[85] While joining other members in strongly deploring "political interference by multinational corporations," Javits insisted that "the report as a whole represents a reaction to highly atypical behavior" by only a few TNCs. The group's findings, in his view, glossed over several examples of serious abuses by developing-country governments such as vindictive nationalization, arbitrary and capricious rule-making and procedures, abrogation of contracts, and other discriminatory treatment. He argued that the report would have been more balanced if it had sought to emphasize ways and means by which the interests between TNCs and host governments might be better harmonized.

Significantly, Javits did not dismiss the code of conduct. Instead, he suggested that the idea was too important to have been given "rather unsubstantial" treatment in the report. In his view, a code of conduct should be developed from "the widest possible variety of sources over a period of time . . . and not be entrusted alone to the proposed Commission on Multinational Corporations."[86]

Conclusions

The GEP submitted its report on 22 May 1974, and it was officially released on 9 June 1974. Intense activity ensued, culminating in the establishment of the UN Commission on TNCs and the UN Centre on TNCs. The establishment of the Group of Eminent Persons was the cornerstone of the UN's early intellectual contribution to our understanding of the scope of TNC activities and their impact on economic development and international relations.

While the group was composed of men of good intentions, certain ideologically charged views almost inevitably crept into their contributions to its work and to the tenor and content of its report. Terms such as "distributive justice," "sovereignty," and a need for a general agreement on "accountability of TNCs to the international community," while seemingly innocuous, tended to agitate and antagonize those who were against this particular exercise in the first place. U.S. government officials such as Secretary of State Henry Kissinger and UN ambassador Daniel Patrick Moynihan were skeptical of its value.

While sitting calmly in the eye of the storm, the GEP represented a rainbow of views. John Dunning recalls that most of the group took their responsibilities seriously, although some were more actively involved than others. Among the more vocal developing-country members were Somavía (Chile) and Sadli (Indonesia), who often offered opposing views, and Estran y Gendre (Argentina); Browaldh (Sweden), Miller (United States), Mansholt (Netherlands), Matthoefer (Federal Republic of Germany), and Schaffner (Switzerland) were among the most vocal from developed countries.[87] As can be seen from the dissenting voices contained in the report, Mansholt and Matthoefer were most critical of the conduct of TNCs and Schaffner the most critical of host governments. The academics were more balanced—Komiya the most neoclassical and Uri the least! Weinberg, one of the two consultants, was a strong advocate of labor's anti-TNCs views.

Apart perhaps from the idea of establishing the commission and the center, the main ideas contained in both the UN background report and the GEP report came from individuals and organizations outside the UN. At the same time, ECOSOC and Philippe de Seynes and his staff acted as important catalysts for both accessing and commissioning the right experts, getting them to express their ideas, and then coordinating these ideas into a very useful document.

The GEP report received widespread coverage among member countries and in the press. It was useful as an educative document, especially for developing countries. However, many developing countries were not pleased to be told by developed home country governments to put their own economic houses in order before making judgments about the costs and benefits of TNC activity. The report was also useful in elucidating the social and cultural effects and implications of TNC activities.

Finally, it should be emphasized once more that both the UN background study and the GEP report must be seen in the context of the world economic events of the early and mid-1970s. Primary among these were the OPEC-instigated energy crisis, the bribery scandals involving U.S. and other TNCs (brought to light by the Senate hearings, the SEC investigations, and investigative reporters such as Jack Anderson), the Watergate scandal, and the Chilean affair that ended in a coup d'etat and Allende's demise. These tumultuous years lasted until the early 1980s, when there was a renaissance of belief in the virtues of the market economy, spearheaded by U.S president Ronald Reagan and British prime minister Margaret Thatcher.

Gradually over the next decade, the confrontation between developing countries and TNCs diminished.[88] Perhaps more significant, there was a growing understanding of what each could offer the other and that the end result was a positive-sum game.[89] At the end of the 1980s, the eastern bloc collapsed. The institutional apparatus crafted by the Group of Eminent Persons and UN staff continued to mature and to discharge its role in helping developing countries in their interactions with TNCs as they formulated policies to attract FDI and benefit from it. The UN Commission on TNCs and Centre on TNCs did so through gathering data and information, publishing studies, training host-country officials, and influencing policy in matters relating to TNCs. These issues are further analyzed in Chapters 5 and 6.

The UN background report and the GEP's hearings and its report and recommendations were groundbreaking and pivotal. They set the pattern and agenda for the UN contribution to the debate on TNCs for many years in the future. Terse, comprehensive, and diplomatic, the DESA background report struck a delicate balance between contending views during this period. Similarly, the twenty-member GEP recommended policy measures that, while reflecting the tensions and different opinions, nevertheless sought a middle ground. The UN's work on TNCs reflected the reality that the UN was then, as it is now, a creature of its constituent parts. Its direction and action are a sum total of the push and pull factors that bear down upon it. In times of tension, actions and output will reflect these tensions, as they did during the first half of the 1970s. Subsequent eras, particularly after the fall of the Berlin Wall, reflected both a change in perceptions of the respective role of TNCs and governments in fostering economic and social development. The UN's work inevitably reflects these changes.

It is appropriate to end this chapter with a contemporary quote from one of the original members of the GEP, namely John Dunning:

> In retrospect, I believe the main contribution of the GEP was to endorse the recommendation of an earlier report on multinational corporations and economic development for the setting up of a Centre on Transnational Corporations. At the same time, I believe that over the past 30 years, events in the global economy and further scholarly research have supported those members of the GEP (including myself) who argued that focusing on the merits and demerits of MNCs [TNCs] was only part of the story of how their activities impacted on host developing countries. For at the end of the day, most of the disputes among GEP members were as much about the goals of economic development and the means of achieving such goals as they were on the role of TNCs. Yet to a large extent, the TNCs were the scapegoats of the 1970s. Today it is recognized that all stakeholders in the global economy have a positive and important role to play in ensuring that foreign direct investment and transnational business activity works to the benefit of all. I wish the report of the GEP had better recognized this.[90]

The next chapter contains an analysis of some of the initiatives that emerged from the group's report. We will describe the commission and the UNCTC and highlight key activities. Staying with the basic analytical framework adopted throughout this book, we will explore knowledge creation, policy impact, and capacity-building efforts.

5

The Commission and the Centre: New York Years, 1974–1992

- *Origin, Architecture, and Agenda: The Commission and the Centre*
- *Impact and Legacy*
- *The Demise, Interregnum, and Reincarnation*
- *Conclusion*

The establishment of the commission and the centre on TNCs in 1973–1975 constituted a watershed event in the UN's work on transnational corporations. The centre was influenced by the UN's corporate culture as well as by its own political exigencies. Nevertheless, from the beginning, it drew extensively on the expertise and advice of scholars and a rotating committee comprised of statesmen, businessmen, and government representatives who were well versed in trade and development issues. In the meantime, the storm concerning the role of TNCs in economic development and international relations was intensifying. During the rest of the 1970s, the UN found itself in the hurricane's eye as the commission and centre became the arena of debate on the subject. By the early 1980s, the hurricane had begun to subside as the political and economic pendulum swung toward the center.[1]

This chapter chronicles the establishment and subsequent functioning of the UN Commission on Transnational Corporations and the UN Centre on Transnational Corporations (UNCTC) as part of the Department of Economic and Social Affairs in New York from 1974 to 1992. During these two decades the world economy underwent a number of transformations. An era that had begun with the ascent of OPEC, the first energy crisis, and the demand by developing countries for a new economic order and a fundamental reconfiguration of international economic relations ended about the time of the fall of the Berlin Wall, the collapse of the Soviet Union, the advent of globalization and electronic commerce, and the emergence of China as a major world economic power.

That the core competencies of the UNCTC that were created and sustained during this period in New York did not fall into the dustbin of history but were instead metamorphosed under a new division within UNCTAD in Geneva is testimony to the economic and political need it met and the intellectual void it helped fill.

Origin, Architecture, and Agenda:
The Commission and the Centre

The UNCTC was set up in accordance with ECOSOC resolution 1913 (LVII) of December 1974. It had three main functions: a) to serve as the UN's focal point on issues of TNCs; b) to initiate the formulation of a code of conduct for TNCs and, if possible, a general agreement; and c) to give guidance to and instigate projects for the Centre on Transnational Corporations.

**Box 5.1. Terms of Reference of
the Commission on Multinational Corporations**

The Commission on Transnational Corporations was established by resolution 1913 (LVII) of the United Nations Economic and Social Council to serve as an advisory body to the Council and to assist it in dealing with the full range of issues relating to transnational corporations.

The Commission is composed of 48 members elected by the Council for three-year periods on a broad geographical basis: 12 from Africa, 11 from Asia, 10 from Latin America, 10 from developed market economy countries of Western Europe, North America, and Oceania, and five from the socialist countries of Eastern Europe. . . . It will be noted that terms are staggered during the initial period of the Commission's life, one-third of the countries serving for one year, another for two years and a third for three years. This distribution was determined by lot.

Resolution 1913[1] requested that each State appoint as representative to the Commission a person with expert knowledge of the issues involved; States may also appoint alternates.

The Commission meets annually, and has the following functions:

1. Serves as the central forum within the United Nations system for the comprehensive and in-depth consideration of issues relating to transnational corporations;
2. Promotes an exchange of views among Governments, inter-

---

governmental and non-governmental organizations, trade
unions, business, consumers and other relevant groups
through the arrangement, *inter alia*, of hearings and interviews;

3. Provides guidance to the Centre on Transnational Corporations on the provision of advisory services to interested Governments and the promotion of technical co-operation activities;
4. Conducts inquiries on the activities of transnational corporations, making studies, preparing reports and organizing panels
for facilitating discussion among relevant groups;
5. Undertakes work which may assist the Economic and Social
Council in evolving a set of recommendations which, taken together, would represent the basis for code of conduct dealing
with transnational corporations;
6. Undertakes work which may assist the Economic and Social Council in considered possible intergovernmental arrangements or agreements on specific aspects relating to transnational corporations "with a view to studying the feasibility
of formulating a general agreement and, on the basis of a decision of the Council, to consolidating them into a general
agreement at a future date";
7. Recommends to the Economic and Social Council the priorities and the programmes of work on transnational corporations to be carried out by the Centre.

1. ECOSOC resolution E/Res/1913/LVII, 5 December 1974.

Source: Excerpted from "The United Nations Centre on Transnational Corporations," *CTC Reporter* 1, no. 1 (December 1976): 3–4.

The commission was composed of delegates from forty-eight member nations who were elected by ECOSOC for three-year terms. Members were
drawn from Africa (twelve), Asia (eleven), Latin America (ten), developed-
market economies (ten), and socialist countries (five).[2] It provided the forum
for many spirited debates during the confrontational 1970s.

To service the commission, ECOSOC endorsed the GEP's recommendation that a Centre on Transnational Corporations be created. The task of the
centre was fourfold:

1. To provide the necessary support to the commission (and ultimately to
ECOSOC) on matters related to TNCs
2. To develop a comprehensive information system on the activities of TNCs
and disseminate this information to all governments
3. To organize and coordinate, at the request of governments, technical coop-

eration aimed at strengthening the capacity of host countries to deal effectively with TNCs

4. To conduct research on various political, legal, economic, and social aspects relating to TNCs, including work useful to the elaboration of a code
of conduct and other specific arrangements and agreements as directed by
ECOSOC.[3]

Thus, the commission and the UNCTC provided the organizational infrastructure that became the focal point within the UN system on matters dealing with TNCs. Members of the commission were government representatives,
while the UNCTC was staffed by professionals and researchers. It was patently
clear from their terms of reference that work on a code of conduct was to be
given high priority.

Within months of the passage of the 1974 resolution, in March 1975, the UN
Commission on Transnational Corporations met in New York. At that time the
"nucleus centre"[4] presented views of governments on the report of the Group of
Eminent Persons and on the work on TNCs being undertaken elsewhere in the
UN system and offered suggestions for its initial program of work. The commission's charge to the UNCTC included constructing a comprehensive information system on the activities of TNCs, establishing a series of technical cooperation programs to strengthen the capacity of host developing countries to
deal with TNCs, and conducting research and making recommendations on
a code of conduct for TNCs. The staff took its charge seriously, and in a short
period of time it prepared several background reports, including surveys of international and regional agreements, standards on codes and corruption, and
standards of accounting and reporting.

After its self-styled status as a "nucleus center," the UNCTC[5] became fully
operational in November 1975 when Secretary-General Kurt Waldheim appointed Klaus A. Sahlgren[6] as its first executive director with the rank of
assistant-secretary-general.[7] The North-South confrontation and the East-West
rivalry had cast long shadows over the choice of the director. In retrospect, the
decision to offer this important post to a professional diplomat from a small
neutral European country such as Finland was a prudent one, given the politically charged atmosphere of the time.

Sahlgren's appointment was an antidote to the political wrangling among
various countries, not only among the G-77 and between them and the West
but also between the West and the Soviet Union and its allies, who often acted
as spoilers. Sahlgren said in a 2002 interview that the Soviet Union and some
other socialist governments in the 1970s "were of the opinion that transnational
corporations were the last poisonous flowers on the dung-heap of capitalism
[and] they should be controlled and restricted as much as possible."[8] This surely

must have colored the U.S. government's perception. It could also explain, in part at least, why Juan Somavía was passed over for the position.

The new director was given a separate budget[9] and began recruiting a professional staff. Initially, many of them were drawn from the Centre for Development Planning, Projections and Policies of the UN's Department of Economic and Social Affairs. They included Gustave Feissel, Sotiris Mousouris, and N. T. Wang, all of whom had been active in the preparation of the background report and other work for the GEP. Sahlgren adopted a strategy of relying on a nucleus of internal staff, but he drew heavily on outside consulting experts, including scholars, TNC executives, and union leaders. Some of his early recruits, who included John Stopford and Charles Albert Michalet, remained active and instrumental in the centre's operations for over a decade. Perhaps the most influential, however, were economist Sidney Dell, who succeeded Sahlgren as executive director in 1982, and Samuel Asante, former attorney-general of Ghana and an expert on international and investment law.

According to its terms of reference, the UNCTC was organized along three primary functional lines: providing information, analyzing policy, and providing advisory services. Appendix 1 summarizes the organization of the UNCTC at its inception in 1974. The task of the information provision division, which was primarily engaged in knowledge creation, was to undertake a systematic collection and assessment of all information germane to TNCs. These were to include the global activities of TNCs, bibliographical data on TNCs at both an aggregate and enterprise level, and pertinent national and regional legislation and policies related to TNCs. The information provision division was to disseminate this information on a regular and continuing basis through publications and reports or by other means requested by the commission and national governments.

The task of the policy analysis division was twofold. The first was to carry out research on economic, legal, and social matters related to TNCs; the impact of TNCs on different aspects of economic development and international relations; and the relevance of TNCs to the macro and micro policies and formation of institutions in host developing countries. The second was to conduct studies relevant to the preparation of a code of conduct and international arrangements and agreements affecting the strategy and conduct of TNCs.

The purpose of the advisory services division was to assist governments in formulating, evaluating, and implementing their policies, laws, and regulations on inward foreign direct investment and the acquisition of technology. More specifically, it was intended to help governments of developing countries strengthen their institutional arrangements and procedures for screening and monitoring projects involving TNCs, select the most appropriate contractual arrangements for specific projects, review the economic and legal provisions of specific contracts being negotiated with TNCs in all sectors, and help them with their negotiations and bargaining with TNCs. This division was also charged with organizing and conducting training workshops on negotiating with and regulating TNCs, both regarding particular issues such as transfer pricing and within specific sectors. Finally, it aimed to strengthen the skills of middle- and senior-level officials of developing countries and to assist their institutions of higher learning to prepare and implement ongoing programs of training on matters related to TNCs. Its ultimate goal was to promote developing countries' efforts to ensure that inbound FDI best met their economic and social objectives and to do so in a way that was consistent with their institutional policy framework and their social and cultural mores. From the outset, the commission and the UNCTC saw this as their primary mission and saw the formulation of a code of conduct for TNCs as an integral part of this mission.

Much of the work of UNCTC was designed to meet the agenda the commission had set. However, even in the commission's report of its first session,[10] areas of disagreement or concern among its members began to emerge. These largely reflected both differences of opinion and the direction and complexity of the tasks ahead. Among the most contentious of these was over the legal status of the code of conduct for TNCs that the GEP had earlier proposed. While most developing countries insisted on an international instrument that would be binding on TNCs, developed countries were not prepared to go beyond a voluntary set of guidelines and wanted explicit assurances from host countries about their obligations to protect FDI.[11]

A year later, the commission convened its second session in Lima, Peru. At this meeting, most developing-country members stressed the desirability of a code of conduct for TNCs, while most developed countries voiced their opposition to it. Indeed, the western governments, led by the United States, tended to view the insistence of developing countries on a code as a form of confrontation. To a certain extent, this was evidence of a clash of paradigms, in particular between government-directed development and the primacy of the market mechanism. It also reflected the perception by many developing countries that they lacked bargaining power vis-à-vis TNCs. Advanced-market-economy countries believed that FDI yielded positive-sum gains in global economic relations, while most developing countries and all socialist countries viewed it as a zero-sum game.

The commission continued to meet each year for more than a decade to receive and discuss staff reports it had mandated at previous meetings and set the agenda for subsequent sessions. At the outset, these contending trends and crosscurrents set the tone of the debate and the agenda. The succeeding years witnessed both continuity and change that amounted to a sizeable legacy under successive leaders and an organizational structure that remained relatively unchanged. Appendix 2 lists the leadership of the UNCTC in New York and Geneva.

Impact and Legacy

The UN Commission on Transnational Corporations and the UNCTC were originally conceived as twin instruments to serve the cause of economic development and the role of TNCs and FDI in that development and to do so in the context of ideas, philosophies, and economic policies prevalent among developing countries. The previous section briefly described the allocation of work within the UNCTC into three divisions. The purpose of these divisions, which, in practice, mutually reinforced each other, was to provide three sets of output:

1. Creating knowledge through information-gathering, research, and publications
2. Building capacity through advice and technical assistance to governments and educational institutions
3. Providing policy recommendations and advice on topics that included a code of conduct for TNCs, accounting and reporting standards, South Africa and its apartheid policies and practices, international accounting standards, and East-West economic relations.

Contributions to Knowledge and Information about TNCs and FDI

One of the primary functions of the UNCTC was to gather information on TNCs. It had begun this task even before it was formally established, as several of the initial UNCTC staff had been involved in producing the 1973 background report for the Group of Eminent Persons. Once the UNCTC was formally and permanently established as a think tank dedicated to TNC issues, it began publishing on a regular basis.

Reviewing the literature on TNCs was a primary task of the UNCTC; in 1976 it produced two publications: *Research on Transnational Corporations*, a preliminary report of the Secretariat,[12] and a *Survey of Research on Transnational Corporations*.[13] These were updated in 1988–1990 (*Transnational Corporations: A Selected Bibliography 1988–90*)[14] and again in 1991–1992 in a three-volume survey, *University Curriculum on Transnational Corporations*. Publications in the form of industry and regional studies included *Transnational Corporations in the International Auto Industry*,[15] *Transnational Corporations in the International Semiconductor Industry*,[16] and the *World Investment Directory*, published under UNCTAD auspices.[17]

An essential part of the UNCTC's mandate, indeed, its raison d'être, was to gather, analyze, and disseminate information to remedy what many developing countries thought was a lack of adequate information on TNC strategies and operations. The 1973 background report for the Group of Eminent Persons provided a detailed study of the universe of TNCs. It had a well-designed structure that only required updating and expanding as new information became available. Pioneering work had already been done in academia by John Dunning and John Stopford and their colleagues in Europe and by Raymond Vernon and his Harvard team and others in the United States, including Howard Perlmutter and Jack Behrman. The UNCTC engaged these and similar scholars and strengthened its in-house research capabilities. This combined intellectual force created an impressive array of publications that added considerably to the general body of knowledge regarding FDI and TNCs, including the determinants and effects of FDI and the implications of FDI for national and supranational policy issues regarding them. The UNCTC's contributions to knowledge took many forms—individual studies, periodical reports, surveys on research, curricula, industry case studies, and directories. In all, no less than 278 publications for public distribution and 710 documents of more limited circulation were produced from 1973 to 1994.

These publications have been used for researchers as a baseline for further research or empirical verification of projections made earlier. One example is the UNCTC's study of TNCs in the semiconductor industry.[18] It included data on exports of semiconductors from Asian countries, showing, for example, that they accounted for 11 percent of the Philippines' merchandise exports in 1981. Similar figures for South Korea stood at 2.1 percent, Singapore at 3.2 percent, and Taiwan at 2.6 percent. Extrapolating from this data, one might reasonably predict that in time, the Philippines' semiconductor exports would exceed those of the other countries. This did not happen, as other countries, notably South Korea and Taiwan, sped ahead. This retrospective provides a framework for future research about why this trajectory did not materialize.

Equally valuable to researchers was the UNCTC's research on TNCs' transfer of technology to host countries and its subsequent linkage effects. New scholarship could test contending propositions regarding the impact of technology transfer on host countries, namely, whether it remained as an enclave within the TNC or was diffused throughout the host country through linkages.[19] Another example is research on competition among developing countries to attract FDI after an earlier era when most had been hostile and bent on control. What accounts for these shifts, and how does one test the underlying analytical propositions? Through its numerous research activities, the UNCTC was able to contribute to a better understanding of the issues and the changes over time.

The 1973 cornerstone report, *Multinational Corporations in World Development*, was ahead of the curve; it identified issues so important that they were revisited and further explored for a quarter-century thereafter. The report issued a warning about tax policies of host developing countries as an incentive to attract FDI: "The most urgent point at issue among the developing countries is that of competition among themselves for foreign investment."[20] The report already recognized that while some developing countries were intent on controlling the entry of TNCs and setting limits, others were outbidding one another to attract FDI, even in the turbulent 1970s. This report also noted that as long as host countries specified a role for TNCs, it would be beneficial to study the relationship between linkages and economic growth, employment, income distribution, and dependence. The report acknowledged that TNCs might provide the fastest, if not the only, way to develop some sectors, but it raised two questions: "First, are linkages desirable, and second, what is the actual result of planning for linkages?"[21] These early questions illuminated the direction of future work in 2001 and beyond.[22]

The commission drove the research agenda. However, the initiative and interests of key staff members—Klaus Sahlgren and the three division heads, in interplay with the educational background and skills of the senior staff— played a role in what was considered noteworthy and beneficial to developing countries, thus worth pursuing. Whereas a minority of commission members brought an agenda, the majority were content to remain as passive observers.

The Quinquennial Surveys on TNCs and FDI

One of the early decisions of the UNCTC was to produce a series of quinquennial surveys detailing state-of-the-art knowledge on FDI and TNCs. These five-year reviews cumulatively formed an impressive compilation of information. Each analyzed the contemporary state of knowledge on the extent and pattern of TNC activity, the impact of TNCs on various aspects of economic and social development, and changes that had occurred in the period between the publications. The first of these was the 1973 background report prepared for the Group of Eminent Persons. That report was followed by *Transnational Corporations in World Development: A Re-examination* (1978), which updated data and elaborated on trends on stocks and flows of FDI.[23]

While the format of the 1978 study was similar to that of its predecessor, it contained new and updated information on FDI inflows and outflows and the stock of inward and outward FDI. The statistical tables in the 1978 study were voluminous and included details of the sales of some 400 TNCs with sales of over a billion dollars each in 1976.[24]

The 1978 volume discussed the New International Economic Order. It observed that most host countries had attempted "some form of control, structuring or regulation of [TNCs] and [had] sought to improve the terms and conditions of dealing with them",[25] capturing the gist of the policy environment of the time. The study also noted that although more options and improved terms and conditions were available to developing countries, concerted national and international action was needed for TNCs to play "an effective role in the New International Economic Order."[26]

The next survey, *Transnational Corporations in World Development: The Third Survey*, was published in 1983 as the world economy was recovering from recession. Developing countries were still coping with the effects of oil crises in 1973 and 1979 that had forced them to borrow heavily on the international capital market. The global effects of this phenomenon, the collapse of the Bretton Woods system, deteriorating terms of trade, and slow growth had created a general "period of uncertainty and instability."[27] The collapse of commodity prices and the rising debt burden compounded this malaise. After noting these conditions, the survey pointed to the growth and diversification of transnational corporations, particularly from Europe and Japan, the end of enforced expropriations of the assets of TNCs by hitherto hostile host countries, the trend toward market liberalization in developing countries, and the rise of protectionism in developed countries. It brought to light emerging policy changes in China, which had recently undergone its major policy transformation under Deng Xiaoping's Open Door Policy, as well as the emergence of joint ventures between TNCs and firms in Eastern Europe and the Soviet Union. The 1983 report made no reference to the New International Economic Order. It observed that in light of the relaxation of restrictions on foreign direct investment, internationally accepted standards were needed "if the relations between Governments and TNCs are to evolve in a mutually beneficial manner."[28] These words could be read as a cautionary note and a warning against overzealous and hasty liberalization.[29]

The fourth and last in the quinquennial surveys was *Transnational Corporations in World Development: Trends and Prospects*, published in 1988. In its preface, Peter Hansen, executive director of the UNCTC, noted that while TNCs continued to be the principal forces shaping the future of technological innovation, "a more pragmatic and businesslike relationship between host governments and TNCs has emerged within the last decade." Many developing countries had liberalized their economic policies, while TNCs had displayed greater sensitivity to the needs of these countries. "The era of confrontation has receded, replaced by a practical search for a meaningful and mutually beneficial accommodation of interests."[30] This was an important statement that set the tone for the subsequent work of the UNCTC and, later, UNCTAD. This lengthy[31] report elucidated major trends in the global economy, including the increasing pluralism in the origin and destination of international investment[32] and the growing importance of services.

Deregulation and liberalization of inward and outward FDI, which had barely been noted in the previous surveys, had taken hold in many countries and was spreading to others. The survey reported China's dramatic shift in policy toward TNCs as an important example of the numerous changes that were taking place. It continued to argue for a code of conduct, emphasizing that establishing norms and standards of TNC behavior could "help minimize the negative effects of TNCs while contributing to maximizing their positive impact."[33] The report further stated:

> Whatever the ultimate fate of the entire Code of conduct may be, it is very significant that a global body, composed of representatives of a wide variety of political and economic systems, and countries at various levels of development, have agreed, albeit *ad referendum,* on the basic principles of a Code of Conduct to be observed by TNCs in international business.[34]

In a departure from the UN's usual practice of omitting names of authors or collaborators, the 1988 volume acknowledged the contributions of no less than sixty-six scholars, corporate executives, and experts from international organizations.[35] This report was longer than the previous ones and was more comprehensive and user friendly, with graphics and case studies to highlight major findings. Its tone and content reflected the shift from confrontation toward accommodation between TNCs and host countries by emphasizing complementarities between the goals and actions of TNCs and those of host developing countries. It discussed whether this more accommodating relationship was a permanent peace or a temporary truce. It concluded that the debate had become less political.

These quinquennial reports, which were prepared primarily at the request of the commission and were used in its deliberations, were generally well received and respected by academic researchers, TNC strategists, and policymakers. They also received extensive media coverage. As comprehensive and state-of-the-art publications, they were both tangible and significant evidence of an important intellectual contribution by the UN on TNCs and FDI.[36] By the 1980s, the UNCTC had become the leading repository of data and policy-oriented research on TNCs. It had assembled a sizeable "global university without walls" to which scholars, policymakers, and executives from around the world made important contributions. This cadre helped the UNCTC with workshops, studies, research, consultation, and feedback.

The *World Investment Report 1991*, the first of its kind for the UNCTC in New York, was developed after some internal discussion about whether an annual publication modeled after the World Bank's annual *World Development Report* was desirable. The rapid accumulation of knowledge about and literature on FDI and TNCs provided ample justification for an annual publication that would assemble and synthesize the issues and options in a manner that would be useful to policymakers in developing countries. After considering several titles, *World Investment Report* was decided upon.

The WIR was destined to become the first in an annual flagship series of publications that continued at UNCTAD. It continued the tradition of monitoring TNC and FDI that was begun with the 1973 background report for the GEP and subsequent quinquennial survey series. Although this report was shorter that its predecessors, it was substantive nonetheless. Demonstrating both continuity and change, it ushered in a new phase in UN efforts to monitor TNCs and publish annually updated information and analysis to readers across the world.

Industry Studies

A second way the UNCTC contributed to knowledge about TNCs and FDI was through a series of sector-focused studies. At the request of the commission,[37] the UNCTC produced detailed case studies of the contribution or potential contribution of various industries considered to be of special significance to developing countries as they began to formulate their industry and development policies.

The UNCTC's 1986 semiconductor study was one of the more extensive of these industry studies.[38] It described the structure of the global semiconductor market and production, trade in semiconductors, and the particular characteristics of the different stages of semiconductor manufacturing and their relevance to developing countries. The study provided a detailed analysis of specific TNCs, their operations and strategies concerning FDI and technology transfer, and their adaptation to changing international conditions. It assessed the impact of this industry on the employment, balance of payments, and technological capabilities of developing countries and found that a limited number of these countries—Hong Kong, Malaysia, Singapore, South Korea, and

Taiwan—had appropriated the lion's share of assembly and the more complex operations.

This study observed that global competitive forces in the international semi-conductor industry (chiefly labor costs) had driven TNCs to offshore assembly in developing countries, while "pre-existing conditions" as well as "conditions brought into existence" (or "acquired comparative advantage") by governments of certain developing countries facilitated the process of FDI. The study con-cluded that the entries of FDI and TNCs in this sector were driven by condi-tions prevailing in the country.[39] At the same time, it found that TNC activity was by no means limited to government actions but was a function of a much wider array of factors, including local demand. It identified Asian countries, notably Taiwan and South Korea, as the most successful in developing an inte-grated semiconductor industry. In the earlier stages of their development, they concentrated on relatively simple product and process technologies to meet the demand of local consumer electronics end users. They then advanced by acquiring TNC technologies through licensing agreements while purchasing capital equipment on the open international market. Having developed this lead, these countries were more likely to play host to incoming FDI. The study suggested that Mexico and Brazil were likely to become important suppliers of semiconductors in the future. Similar industry studies were conducted on new technologies, hotels, and electronics, and the banking, plastics, biotechnology, manmade fiber, textile and clothing, and construction and design engineering industries.

Issue-Specific Studies

The UNCTC authored thirty-six issue studies and reports.[40] Some of these fo-cused on countries or regions; others were designed along certain themes. The-matic studies included technology transfer, accountancy in Africa, services, mergers and acquisitions, codes of conduct, and licensing agreements. Other themes were debt crisis, debt-equity conversion, and TNCs relative to manufac-tured exports from developing countries, transborder data flow, trade, and the environment. Other studies included those on the Uruguay Round and trends and issues in FDI. Country studies dealt with such topics as TNCs in South Africa and Namibia, transborder data flows and Mexico, and data goods and services in the socialist countries of Eastern Europe.

Some of these studies were used as background material for the training and advising services the UNCTC provided to developing countries. Selection of topics was determined in large part by the needs of developing countries. The UNCTC was only too happy to lend its expertise when asked; sometimes it collaborated with local researchers, sought external funding, and conducted research on a given topic. This was quite similar to the practices of private consulting firms; the UNCTC positioned itself such that developing countries could approach it on a given topic (such as hotel or other services or transborder data flow) for analysis and advice. The UNCTC would then tap into its in-house expertise and its external network of consultants to prepare and present the results.

The UNCTC also published over twenty studies that dealt with topics such as FDI in Latin America, electronic industries in ASEAN countries, technology acquisition strategies in Thailand, legal issues germane to codes of conduct, best manufacturing practices, free economic zones, trade negotiations, FDI and debt, and TNCs and economic integration. Seven studies were produced as part of the UNCTC's advisory services, including detailed reports on natural gas clauses in petroleum arrangements (1987), debt rescheduling (1989), hotel chain management arrangements (1990), and curricula for accounting education for East-West joint ventures (1986).

Literature Surveys

As part of its attempt to educate and provide information, the UNCTC also produced surveys of the literature; its 1976 compilation of research on TNCs is a good example.[41] Later surveys included *University Curriculum on Transnational Corporations*[42] and a bibliography on TNCs.[43] The 20-volume *UN Library on Transnational Corporations*, published in 1992–1993, contained some of the most important essays on TNCs; the library was initiated and edited by John Dunning and Karl Sauvant.[44] The volumes contained contributions on all aspects of strategy and structure, the theory of TNCs, the history of TNCs, the legal environment in which TNCs operate, and the relations of TNCs to economic development. Contributors were eminent scholars, and selections from the UN's prior publications were well represented. This state-of-the-art series became an invaluable addition to university libraries and was also of considerable use to policymakers.

The UNCTC also monitored new literature as part of its efforts to develop a comprehensive information system and help equalize the bargaining position of developing countries. It initiated a global survey of research on TNCs in 1975[45] that identified more than 200 research projects on TNCs worldwide, including the basic organizational characteristics, strategies, and motivations of TNCs; the economic and socio-cultural impact of TNCs on host and home countries and the international system; and the legal implications of the impact of TNCs for policy formulation. A second survey in 1976, based on questionnaires sent to over 7,500 individuals and institutions in all stakeholder groups worldwide, summarized the research on the political, legal, economic, and social effects of TNCs. The result was a report which identified 615 research projects, 68 percent of which were based in developed countries. Western Europe's 213 projects accounted for the largest percentage (35 percent), followed by the United States at 25 percent and international organizations at 20 percent. Sixty projects (10 percent) were based in developing countries and 2 percent in socialist countries of Eastern Europe.[46]

Directories

In the 1980s, John Dunning and John Cantwell (both at the University of Reading, UK) began to assemble data on the extent and pattern of inward and outward FDI for over eighty individual countries.[47] In 1992, the UNCTC embarked upon an ambitious project to update and augment these data. The result was a series of World Investment Directories, which was continued after the UNCTC moved to UNCTAD.

The first volume in this series, subtitled *Asia and the Pacific*, was published in 1992. By 2004, eight other volumes had been published. These embraced Central and Eastern Europe, developed countries, Latin America and the Caribbean, Africa, and West Asia.[48] Like Dunning and Cantwell's original volume, these directories contained country-specific data on the geographical and industrial composition of inward and outward stocks and flows of FDI; this information was otherwise not readily available. But they also included details of government laws and regulations relating to FDI, data on inward and outward investment, and a list of major TNCs. These publications provided detailed information on a particular host country, and host-country government officials often used them to formulate policy.

Curricula and Research Surveys

Another important contribution from the UNCTC was its curricula surveys about development. These varied studies were comprehensive, forming the knowledge base needed for internal deliberations at the UN and for academics and policymakers. The surveys were intended to help developing countries build capacity, but they proved to be equally helpful in advanced countries as more universities in the United States and Western Europe sought to internationalize their curricula. Other universities around the world soon followed. These surveys covered many aspects of business and management, as well as economic development, business strategy, law, and competitions. Through these surveys, the UNCTC built an in-house information/knowledge base which enhanced its capability to discharge its task of strengthening the negotiating capacity of host countries, especially developing countries.

The survey of university curricula was also an important pedagogical tool at colleges and universities and served as a bridge between the United Nations and academia. Other publications also had many uses in courses in political science and economics and in schools of business and law. The UNCTC surveyed faculty teaching and research on TNCs and FDI and related topics around the world to ask for copies of their syllabi. The publication of these university syllabi, coupled with the information the UNCTC provided, assisted colleges and universities in their teaching about TNCs and their course offerings in the field of international business.

In the mid-1990s, groups of three to four instructors, comprised of UN staff and consultants, taught two- and three-week courses on TNCs and economic development, business strategy, and the legal implications of TNC activities that over 150 university faculty members attended. Many seminars were directed by two UNCTC consultants, Ellen Seidensticker and Tawfigue Nawaz; academics including John Dunning, Don Lecraw, Louis Wells, and Farok Contractor also participated.[49]

The UN also contributed to knowledge about TNCs through an initiative begun in 1982 to track the evolution of research on TNCs and FDI in monographs and journal articles and books. The result was a three-volume series published from 1988 to 1993. The first volume covered 1983–1987; the second covered 1988–1990.[50] The last volume contained a bibliography. Specific issues included the nature of TNCs, FDI, and other financial flows; sector- and region-specific studies; contractual agreements; and political and economic topics.

The CTC Reporter *as Chronicler*

Among the UNCTC publications we find two periodicals. The first, *The CTC Reporter*, premiered in December 1976. Published quarterly, it chronicled the activities of the UNCTC and included short articles, interviews with scholars and policymakers, and reviews of latest developments around the world—within the UN system and in academia—on FDI and TNCs.

In many respects, the content of the thirty-one issues of *The CTC Reporter* form a concise history of the UN's work on the topic. Each issue reported on the activities of the commission, upcoming events, and summaries of studies conducted under UNCTC auspices. Each issue also included short analytical essays. The last issue was published in spring 1991. An editorial statement in that issue noted that dramatic changes in the world in which transnational corporations operate and the burgeoning academic research on the topic warranted a new focus within the UNCTC.

The successor of *The CTC Reporter* was titled *Transnational Corporations: A Journal of the United Nations Centre on Transnational Corporations* and was published three times a year. The format was somewhat of a departure from that of *The CTC Reporter*, which had functioned as an upscale news bulletin about the organization's activities. The new journal shifted the focus to more substantive articles that provide insight on policy measures related to the economic, legal, social, cultural, and political impact of transnational corporations (particularly FDI) in an increasingly global economy.

The premier issue of the journal was published in February 1992 in New York and was published thereafter under UNCTAD in Geneva. Its 3,000 copies circulated to libraries and policymakers in developing countries, academia, and international agencies. Its structure resembles that of an academic journal with an editor and editorial board, and each submitted article is subject to peer review. It is the only publication of its kind that specifically deals with the interaction between the strategies and operations of TNCs and the activities of national and supranational organizations. Many well-known scholars have contributed to the journal. On the twentieth anniversary of the establishment of the UN Commission on Transnational Corporations, the editors noted in a special commemorative issue that debates in the commission had often mirrored the evolution of attitudes toward transnational corporations. And that attitude was changing toward greater openness and interdependence in a globalizing economy.

Partnerships with Regional Commissions

The United Nations has five geographically based commissions in different parts of the world as regional hubs that contribute to the UN's mission from the field: the Economic Commission for Europe (ECE), the Economic and Social Commission for Asia and the Pacific (ESCAP), the Economic Commission for Africa (ECA), the Economic and Social Commission for Western Asia (ESCWA), and the Economic Commission for Latin America and the Caribbean (ECLAC).

Shortly after the UN Commission on Transnational Corporations and the UNCTC came into existence, joint units with these regional commissions were established to help with the tasks of capacity-building, information and knowledge creation, and policy analysis, each from its particular vantage point. Over the years these outposts have hosted regional seminars and workshops and have undertaken studies on specific topics and collected data.

Not all of these joint units with the regional commissions functioned the same way. Some became independent of administrative guidance from the regional commissions, and some were effectively absorbed by the commissions through incorporation into existing divisions. Financial arrangements for funding projects undertaken by joint unit staff also varied between regional commissions. Despite these variations, the joint units accomplished several programs and projects that highlighted the role of TNCs and FDI in the regions the commissions served.

The Asian and Latin American units were the most prolific of the joint regional units. The ESCAP/UNCTAD joint unit produced several scholarly papers, monographs, and meetings about TNCs and FDI in Asia and the Pacific. After UNCTC activities moved to Geneva in 1993, topics progressively moved from those exclusively focused on TNCs to those that were more concerned with FDI.[51] Prior to the closure of all the joint units in the late 1990s, the ESCAP/UNCTAD joint unit was engaged in organizing meetings in Malaysia, the Philippines, and Thailand on the institutional development of bond markets to attract foreign investment. Such research and activities stopped when the joint unit dissolved and its staff was absorbed into regional commission line operations in 1997.

There were a number of notable reports prepared at the request of the UN Centre on Transnational Corporations. These included: *Transnational Corporations and Their Impact on Economic Development on Asia and the Pacific,*[52] *Transnational Corporations in the Copper Industry in Zaire,*[53] and *Transnational Corporations in Africa: Some Major Issues.*[54]

After the UNCTC moved to Geneva, the liaison between regional units and the enterprise continued, albeit somewhat unevenly. In the 1990s, the Latin American partnership (ECLAC in Santiago, Chile) under the directorship of Michael Mortimer seems to have been the most successful, as judged by its annual reports, publications, and workshops.[55]

Capacity-Building

The second main mission Economic and Social Council outlined for the commission and the UNCTC was strengthening the negotiating capacity of host countries in their dealings with TNCs. In a general way, nearly all of the UNCTC's output contributed, in one way or another, to capacity-building. But one discrete component of the enterprise, originally called "advisory services," was charged with helping governments formulate, evaluate, and revise their policies, laws, and regulations with respect to FDI and acquire foreign technology; participate in joint venture projects involving TNCs; and prepare for contract negotiations, drafting contracts, and disclosure of information. Its mandate was also to organize and conduct training workshops for governments

and institutions of higher learning on matters related to regulating and negotiating with transnational corporations.

From 1975 to 1990, the UNCTC conducted many technical assistance workshops and seminars with the help of consultants from academia and business.
Especially in the later years of that period, it prepared studies specifically for
the workshops that covered the issues of appropriate legislation and regulations,
evaluating contractual arrangements and negotiations, and disclosing information, among other topics. The audiences of the workshops were primarily government officials dealing with FDI and TNCs, and the faculty that conducted
the workshops were either from within the UNCTC or were drawn from the
academic or consulting communities. The goal of the workshops was to create a core competency in FDI and TNC matters within developing countries
so the UNCTC would be able to provide assistance on these matters. Occasionally, developing countries expected more than the UNCTC was able to
deliver, but on the whole, this function was satisfactorily performed and continued into the UNCTAD years. Another example of capacity-building was a
series of seminars in the mid-1980s on joint ventures in the Soviet Union and
other socialist countries.

Box 5.2. Seminar on Joint Ventures in the USSR

In the second half of the 1980s, several socialist countries, notably the
Soviet Union and Poland, were warming to the idea of joint ventures with
western firms. Gorbachev introduced policies of perestroika and glasnost in 1985, while Hungary had already pioneered a number of such
partnerships, including the Osram joint venture with GE to manufacture
light bulbs. In January 1987, the Soviet Union adopted a decree that for
the first time since the 1920s permitted foreign firms to hold as much as
49 percent equity in joint ventures with Soviet partners. Shortly thereafter
the UNCTC organized a seminar in Moscow with the USSR State Foreign Economic Commission called Joint Ventures as a Form of International Economic Cooperation. It was conducted by its staff and consultants from U.S. law firms. Over 100 officials from ministries and industrial
enterprises attended the seminar, a harbinger of both small and gargan-
tuan changes to come. Within a month of that 1988 seminar, thirty-five
joint ventures had been formed, mostly with European firms. The UNCTC
engaged the Soviet Union as an active participant in the global economy,
as it did other UN member states.

The UNCTC provided technical assistance in service and extractive industries. Countries asked the UNCTC to evaluate management contracts and review agreements in a variety of contexts. Regional organizations sought similar
services from the UNCTC.

Another aspect of capacity-building in developing countries was training country officials on accounting and reporting techniques and helping them develop more harmonized and standardized worldwide accounting and reporting systems. To that end, the UNCTC became involved in an exercise called International Standards of Accounting and Reporting (ISAR). In 1984, in collaboration with government representatives and international accounting professionals, the UNCTC formed an Intergovernmental Working Group and began a series of studies, workshops, and training programs. Under UNCTAD, these activities continued and were reported by its Trade and Development Board, the governing body within the organization. However, the accounting profession never fully embraced this initiative and took only a secondary role in global efforts to develop international accounting rules. The OECD in Paris and the International Accounting Standards Committee in London seemed to have stolen the show. Indeed, the limited success achieved under ISAR provides an excellent case study in the limits of global rule-making and harmonization, especially where nonstandardized rules and traditions clash.

There was cross-fertilization in the preparation and conducting of these workshops, as those involved in preparing reports also conducted workshops and seminar leaders collaborated on research reports.

The Policy Arena

In the early years, the role of the commission and the UNCTC was to advise the governments of developing countries on how best to deal with TNCs rather than on FDI policy per se. Very little attention was given to broader macro- and micro-management policies. In those early years, UN staff involvement was more proactive; it was fueled by the same fire that had ignited the debate on TNCs both from inside and outside the United Nations. As the decade progressed and the UNCTC matured, internal activism gave way to professionalism. Still, the enterprise remained true to its original mandate to contribute to TNC/FDI issues by influencing policy toward TNC involvement, by helping developing countries build capacity, and by advancing the creation of knowledge about TNCs and FDI.

The UNCTC exerted influence on policy in several ways; for example, by working with China and the Soviet Union on FDI policy formulation. It tackled controversial issues such as the banking scandal at the Bank of Credit and Commerce International and the debate about whether FDI by TNCs perpetuated the apartheid regime of South Africa or accelerated its demise. But almost certainly, the most significant and contentious policy issue at the UNCTC was its extensive work on a code of conduct for TNCs, and from the beginning, this task took center stage.

The Code

As early as 1970, the renowned economist Charles Kindleberger and his co-author Paul Goldberg had suggested a general agreement on FDI, patterned after GATT.[56] The issue resurfaced in the 1973 UN background report prepared for the Group of Eminent Persons that supported the concept of setting global rules on trade matters.[57]

The GEP report highlighted the need for an international code of conduct on FDI so that the behavior and activities of corporations might be made accountable to the international community.[58] Endorsing the Kindleberger and Goldberg proposal and the earlier recommendation to establish an international trade organization, the report suggested a "GATT for international investment." Acknowledging that "such far reaching proposals may not be ripe for immediate action," the report stopped short of endorsing a "code" of behavior, as the term itself was "full of ambiguity."[59] The proposed "rules" would be prepared by the commission, be approved by ECOSOC, and be administered by an international organization empowered to investigate any breaches by TNCs and make remedial recommendations. These rules would not be compulsory but would "act as an instrument of moral persuasion" to both TNCs and governments. The report recommended that ECOSOC include negotiation on such a code in its work program. When the UNCTC was established, this became one of its primary tasks.

During the GEP hearings, the concept of a code of conduct was hotly debated, and its very premise was challenged. The Group of 77, with the support of the socialist bloc, demanded a binding international instrument aimed at TNCs, while developed-market-economy countries insisted on allowing market forces to operate, unencumbered by intervention by an international body. The GEP hearings provided a preview of the polarizing effect the discussion of a code would have.

The related concept, proposed by U.S. undersecretary of state George Ball in 1967, of international chartering of supranational corporations labeled "cosmocorps" that would be governed by "an international company law" was not well received.[60] At the time of this proposal, national sovereignty was too potent an issue to accommodate such a grand scheme.

Discussion about the desirability and/or contents of a code of conduct took a similar discordant turn when the commission took up the challenge at its first meeting in New York in March 1975. The report of the commission issued afterward was replete with bracketed phrases, demonstrating a lack of consensus on key issues. Primary areas of disagreement included the legal status of such a code. Word usage was also a source of contention. The G-77 countries preferred the mandatory "shall," while the developed countries preferred the word "should"; the disagreement symbolized the dichotomy in perspectives. The commission suggested that a general agreement on multinational corporations would contain a limited set of universally accepted principles relating to the interaction between TNCs and host and home countries. At the same time, the report admitted that "even this weaker form of proposal might be considered too ambitious at this stage."[61]

Negotiations, discussions, and discordant discourse on and about the code continued for the next decade, making it one of the most divisive topics on the international agenda. They finally doomed it altogether. Not all the blame for the demise of the code can be attributed to the negotiators. One of the many ironies of this saga is that the world changed around those who had initially championed the code. Many of its erstwhile advocates took up other challenges. For those who remained, the new realities of globalization and the emergence of Third World TNCs demanded a toned-down rhetoric, a shift toward conciliation and cooperation, and a search for common ground.

In September 1986, the *Wall Street Journal* published a negative article by a writer affiliated with the Heritage Foundation, a U.S.-based conservative think tank. The writer had claimed that the UN was "unremittingly hostile" to private enterprise in the drafting of a code of conduct for TNCs.[62] The next month, UNCTC executive director Peter Hansen wrote letter to the newspaper that refuted the assertion that the code was hostile to TNCs. Hansen attempted to set the record straight by explaining and demystifying the code's content and aims. He asserted that its main purpose was "to define—in a balanced manner and with the participation of all countries—the rights and responsibilities of both TNCs and governments, especially governments of host countries." In this respect, Hansen added, the code was little different from the guidelines agreed upon by the OECD, "an organization surely not suspected of hostility to private enterprise."[63]

Many issues addressed by the code that remained unresolved were given renewed attention at the UN and other international forums over the ensuing years. These included corruption, corporate social responsibility, labor issues, consumer issues, the environment, and competition. The Global Compact that Kofi Annan established in 1999, the 2001 WHO convention on tobacco control, the 2003 UN Convention on Corruption, and the ILO's continuing quest for a Declaration on Workers' Rights are some of the topics that a comprehensive code of conduct on TNCs would have addressed. Indeed, discussions prompted by the aborted initiative to create a UN code of conduct may well have been a catalyst for some of these later agreements and may yet prove to be useful when the world community concludes that multilateral solutions are the only viable alternatives to chaos.

One of the critical reasons for the failure of the code was the insistence of proponents that it be legally binding, in contrast to other codes and guidelines set up during the 1970s and 1980s to influence attitudes and behavior of TNCs. These ranged from the OECD's fairly comprehensive set of voluntary guidelines, originally issued in 1976, to guidelines dealing with specific issues such as UNCTAD's code on restrictive business practices.

In addition, many codes were devised by individual corporations.[64] By 2006, there were hundreds of well-known corporate codes.[65] Such TNCs as IBM, DuPont, Wal-Mart, and Boeing had codes of good business practices to which their employees (and sometimes their subcontractors as well) were expected to adhere.

Meanwhile in Paris: The OECD Guidelines

The importance of FDI and TNCs and the policy issues surrounding them were not lost on the OECD. In January 1975, when the commission and the UNCTC were working on the code, the OECD established a Committee on International Investment and Multinational Enterprises, almost certainly in response to the adversarial attitude of many countries to TNC activities. At its 21 June 1976 ministerial meeting, it approved the Declaration on International Investment and Multinational Enterprise. The declaration's primary aim was to better define and further encourage the positive contributions of multinational enterprises to economic and social progress and to minimize or resolve conflicts that might arise from the activities of TNCs. This was to be accomplished through internationally agreed guidelines of corporate behavior, intergovernmental consultation, and a review mechanism. The OECD believed that this was necessary because interested parties were "somewhat without guidance" without it and needed a common approach to international direct investment. The guidelines covered a wide range of topics including information disclosure, competition, financing, employment and industrial relations, and science and technology.

How far the OECD guidelines were intended to neutralize or render irrelevant the UN initiative on the code of conduct for TNCs is not clear. Certainly they were consistent with the western approach to corporate behavior and social responsibility—self-regulation rather than mandatory rules, informal rather than formal rules, and a bias toward fewer and more flexible rules. In addition, the guidelines served as a common position vis-à-vis the Group of 77 and the socialist bloc as they debated the code. The guidelines' emphasis on host countries' adherence to "national treatment" and the fact that they were voluntary were perhaps their most distinctive features.

Occasionally the OECD guidelines have been revisited and revised, but they have always remained voluntary instruments. Their efficacy and utility, however, have yet to be established. This is in large part due to the absence of effective enforcement mechanisms. The organization may argue that they are mere guidelines and that it leaves it up to firms to decide whether to adopt them, adhere to them, or implement them. While this approach is consistent with the OECD's mandate and modus operandi, lack of specific evidence about its efficacy casts a shadow over its ultimate utility. Complicating matters even further, in the 1990s OECD membership expanded to include the erstwhile G-77 countries of South Korea and Mexico. This signifies that these countries, which used to be considered developing countries, have now been admitted into the OECD's "western club" countries and into global capitalism, thereby causing a division within the ranks of the G-77.

The UN and South Africa: Policy in Action[66]

One very specific contribution of the UNCTC in its attempts to reconcile the interests of TNCs with those of the nation-states in which they operate—and indeed those of the wider international community—concerns its involvement in South Africa's racist apartheid practices. This case is a good example of the impact of the UNCTC on policy. The story begins in the mid-1980s, when the United Nations responded to the need and desire of the international community to help end apartheid in South Africa.[67] In the mid-1970s, the UN had become concerned about the role TNCs played in the apartheid regime. From 1960 through 1984, no less than eighteen Security Council resolutions, thirty-one General Assembly resolutions, and ten ECOSOC resolutions were passed on South Africa. In addition, other resolutions, including the New International Economic Order of May 1974 and the Charter of Economic Rights and Duties of States of December 1974, contained specific provisions regarding the freedom of labor organizations, the rights of trade unions, labor standards, and working conditions, all issues that were germane to South African apartheid. All of these resolutions provided a legal basis for the involvement of the commission and the UNCTC in South Africa.

In 1974, at the request of the commission, the UNCTC took on the issue of apartheid and TNCs in South Africa in a series of reports. It also investigated the history of TNCs in South Africa and showed that since World War II, foreign direct investment had played an important role in the economic development of the country. It concluded that in the 1970s, South Africa remained dependent on transnational financial and banking institutions. At the same time, South Africa's employment and wage policies had attracted controversy because, among other things, many TNCs did not recognize black trade unions as legitimate bargainers for the rights of workers. South Africa's repressive response to the political activity of blacks had caused the UN to impose mandatory economic sanctions. Other UNCTC reports during the 1970s found that for the most part TNCs in South Africa were conforming to the legal structure of South African apartheid.

These studies formed the background against which subsequent policy action by the UN was formulated. In 1977, the General Assembly adopted a series of resolutions condemning TNC activities and the Security Council called for an end to arms sales to that country. In the same year, the European Community proposed a voluntary code of conduct for TNCs that would ensure that blacks had equal pay and working conditions and the right to unionize.

In 1982–1983, the Commission on Transnational Corporations adopted a number of resolutions pertaining to TNCs and South Africa and urged TNCs to fully comply with the relevant UN resolutions by terminating all further investments in South Africa. The UNCTC staff prepared several background studies, and in 1985 a newly commissioned Panel of Eminent Persons held its first set of hearings under the auspices of the Group of Eminent Persons on South Africa. Background studies provided detailed information on the role of FDI and TNCs in South Africa, revealing that in 1984, the United States had the most TNCs in South Africa (406), followed by the United Kingdom (364), and Germany (142). In 1983, some 80 percent of South Africa's ten million workers were black. TNCs employed about 600,000 workers, of whom 400,000 were black. The total amount of FDI at the end of 1983 was between $15.5 and $17 billion, about 8.5 percent of South Africa's capital stock. The only developing country at the time with a stock of FDI larger than South Africa was Brazil. FDI was substantial in petroleum, cars, and other transportation equipment; chemicals and pharmaceuticals; electronics; and banking and other financial services.

In 1985, UN Secretary-General Javier Pérez de Cuéllar, working with the chairman of the UN Commission on Transnational Corporations, appointed an eleven-member panel of eminent persons to study transnational corporations in South Africa and Namibia[68] and conduct public hearings. Panel members unanimously agreed that peaceful change could be effected if pressure was applied through targeted, phased, and monitored measures and that TNCs should recognize that their long-term economic interests in South Africa would be better served if apartheid was abolished. The panel found that South Africa had persisted in its policy of apartheid in violation of principles of the UN Charter, the Universal Declaration of Human Rights, the Declaration on the Granting of Independence to Colonial Countries and Peoples, and numerous resolutions of the General Assembly, the Security Council, and the Economic and Social Council. The commission unanimously adopted the panel's report and recommendations on 11 October 1985 and were presented to the Second Committee of the General Assembly on 22 November 1985. The report was endorsed by the Commission on Transnational Corporations in April 1986 and by ECOSOC in May 1986.

The panel's report was hard-hitting and detailed. It was structured around the role of the more than 1,000 TNCs active in the military and energy sectors, both of which were of general economic significance in South Africa and Namibia. Many of the report's recommendations were based on already existing subnational, national, and international measures. What was new was the panel's call for a systematic program aimed at bringing down apartheid and its proposals for what would constitute specific acts of compliance as well as its clear delineation of what would constitute effective enforcement and monitoring measures by the UN. The panel set 1 January 1987 as a deadline[69] for South Africa to rescind its Influx Control Act and its Group Areas Act,[70] two of the major pillars of the apartheid system. It also suggested that TNCs begin a program of divestment if sufficient progress was not made. However, it did not recommend wholesale divestment by TNCs in South Africa because it believed that they could play a positive role in the abolition of apartheid. The report also asserted that business enterprises, as part of their social responsibility, cannot be oblivious of universally accepted human rights and general rules of moral and social behavior. It reminded TNCs that although "the international business community representing TNCs operating in South Africa stated that apartheid was irreconcilable with the principles of free enterprise," the practical actions TNCs had made did not match their public statements.[71] In particular, the report made very specific recommendations regarding the military, the police and security, energy, and general economic issues. These are set out in Box 5.3.

Box 5.3. Recommendations to TNCs by the Panel of Eminent Persons on South Africa

· **Military, Police, and Security:** All TNCs producing for this sector should disinvest immediately and mandatory arms embargo should be expanded immediately to include dual-use items (serving both military and civilian purposes) including cars, computers, and electronics. There should be no nuclear cooperation of any kind with South Africa and Namibia. TNCs that do not comply with these recommendations should leave the country or be forced to divestment.

· **Energy:** The existing oil embargo should be made mandatory so that TNCs that export or ship petroleum or natural gas to South Africa would be prohibited from doing so; there should be no licensing of technology and no supplies of equipment and services to this sector; and governments should prohibit future purchase of South African coal and uranium ore. Any TNC that does not comply with these recommendations should be subjected to divestment action.

· **General Economic Issues:** In addition to the general economic measures already in place by certain nations, the Panel recommended several others. These included a ban on: new loans to South Africa or renewal or rollovers of existing loans, involvement of multilateral financial institutions with South Africa unless and until the apartheid was abolished. Similarly, until this was achieved, there should be no new licensing of technology, granting of franchises, and management agreements with any entity in South Africa. No export credits or guarantees or other official trade promotion should be extended to enterprises doing business with South Africa. Furthermore, existing investment guarantees or double-taxation agreements with South Africa should be revoked immediately and no new agreements be made. Finally, gold imports from South Africa should be prohibited.

· The Panel further recommended that TNCs should:
· Not supply the military, police, or security forces with computers, cars, aircraft or other material that could be used to enforce apartheid;
· Completely desegregate all work and work-related facilities, give equal pay and benefits, and abolish job reservation;
· Allow workers to live permanently with their families and ensure full, desegregated housing etc. be provided to all workers within a reasonable distance of the workplace
· Refuse to comply with the Group Areas and the Influx Control Acts;
· Recognize trade unions and allow their workers to join the union of their choice in accord with ILO conventions;
· Pay a wage substantially above that of the minimum household subsistence level, with appropriate benefits;
· Provide appropriate education, training and other opportunities for the advancement of black employees; and
· Issue an obligatory standardized semi-annual report, prepared by workers and management, describing compliance with minimum standards.

Source: UNCTC, *Transnational Corporations in South Africa and Namibia: United Nations Public Hearings*, 4 vols. (New York: United Nations, 1986–1987); and UNCTC, *Activities of TNCs in South Africa: Impact on Financial and Social Structures* (New York: UNCTC, 1983); UNCTC, *Activities of Transnational Corporations in South Africa and Namibia and the Collaboration of Such Corporations with the Racist Minority Regime in That Area: Report of the Secretary-General*, ECOSOC document E/C.10/1989/8, 1989.

For implementation, monitoring, and follow-up, the panel recommended that

· TNCs review present business policies and strategies in South Africa in light
  of the panel's recommendations
· The Secretary-General assume overall responsibility for ensuring effective
  implementation of recommended measures
· The Secretary-General monitor the situation in South Africa, prepare a
  regular report, and take additional measures when the need arose
· The report be immediately brought to the attention of the General Assembly

Finally, the panel appealed to all governments and people throughout the world to join to contribute to the elimination of apartheid and the independence of Namibia. In his foreword to the report,[72] Secretary-General Pérez de Cuéllar asserted that the elimination of apartheid and the securing of independence for Namibia were high priorities on the agenda of the United Nations and that the role of TNCs was critical in those endeavors.

Pressure had mounted in the United States and many other countries to topple apartheid. In September 1985, President Reagan, bowing to public opinion, signed Executive Order 12532, which went into effect on 11 October 1985, banning all computer exports to South Africa's military, police, prisons, national security agencies, and any other agencies involved in the enforcement of apartheid. The order also prohibited exports of nuclear goods or technology and loans to the government and imposed a ban on export assistance to any firm with twenty-five or more employees that did not adhere to comprehensive fair employment principles, which included desegregation in work facilities, equal pay for all employees, and fair labor practices.

Reagan signed the executive order instead of signing the Comprehensive Anti-Apartheid Act of 1986, which he had promised to veto. The act stated that the United States would encourage the South African government to repeal its state of emergency, respect the principle of equal justice under law for citizens of all races, and release Nelson Mandela, trade union leaders, and all other political prisoners. The Reagan administration believed that the South African people should not be punished by economic sanctions.[73]

The United Nations continued its quest to eliminate apartheid in South Africa. At the request of ECOSOC, the UN Secretary-General appointed another panel of eminent persons in 1989 to conduct a second round of public hearings on TNC activities in South Africa and Namibia with the goal of mobilizing public opinion in Europe and inducing governments and TNCs to cease all collaboration with the apartheid regime.[74] This second round of hearings took place on 4–6 September 1989 at the United Nations in Geneva. By the time of the 1990 report describing the 1989 hearings, Nelson Mandela had been released and the ban had been lifted on the African National Congress (ANC) and other antiapartheid movements. Preliminary discussions between the ANC and the government had been held, and Namibia attained independence on 21 March 1990.

These events led to a new phase in the debate on sanctions. Some commentators believed that they should be lifted while others contended that they should be maintained as long as the foundations of apartheid remained intact. In June 1990, Nelson Mandela argued for a continuation of sanctions when he addressed the UN Special Committee Against Apartheid. This committee had been given the task of reviewing all aspects of apartheid policies, promoting the international campaign against apartheid, and reporting to and advising the General Assembly and the Security Council on these matters.

In the 1989 hearings, the International Chamber of Commerce (ICC) represented the business view, as it had done in 1985. Its representative noted that its prediction in those hearings had proved true and that disinvestment by foreign firms had weakened pressure on the South African government to make further change. The ICC believed that the combined effect of disinvestment by some 550 foreign firms and economic sanctions had delayed the demise of apartheid and had hardened attitudes opposing change among the white electorate. It argued that as the assets of TNCs had been transferred to local companies, there had been a diminution of pressure for change, an increase in black unemployment, more poverty, and an overall deterioration in the conditions for blacks in the workplace. The ICC believed that disinvestment had failed to undermine apartheid whereas the presence of TNCs had done so by improving wages and employment conditions; training and developing black management; recognizing black trade unions; contributing to improvements in housing, education, and health care for blacks; and challenging apartheid outside the workplace. It also asserted that TNCs were active in working toward the abolition of the color bar for jobs and the granting of freehold tenure to blacks.

The UNCTC invited more than 800 TNCs and banks to participate in the 1989 public hearings by submitting oral or written statements regarding their activities in South Africa, but, as was the case in the 1985 hearings, none of the TNCs took the opportunity to testify before the panel. The majority of the 200 who responded to the invitation declined to participate, ten chose to submit a brief statement,[75] and twenty-five, primarily from Germany and the United Kingdom, authorized the ICC to speak on their behalf.

The TNCs gave three reasons for not participating: 1) they had already disinvested; 2) they had no further information to contribute; or 3) their subsidiaries in South Africa were relatively small and therefore had a negligible impact on political and social developments there.

Francis Blanchard, the ILO director-general and a member of the panel, asked a witness what TNCs had done to combat or discuss the anti-union legislation passed in 1988. The ILO's Committee on Apartheid had recommended in 1985 that new FDI as well as existing investment guarantees and export credits in South Africa be stopped. Employers, trade unions, and governments were cooperating with the ILO as it sought to achieve a coordinated international monitoring policy. The International Confederation of Free Trade Unions declared that its members in ninety-eight countries were unanimous in their desire to abolish apartheid.[76]

It must be asked whether these hearings had an impact on policy and on the ultimate defeat of apartheid in South Africa. It is impossible to know or to assign credit to any single initiative, be it the candlelight vigils in Washington, the UN hearings, or pressures that resulted from the Sullivan Principles or from other civil society organizations.[77] However, it is incontrovertible that the UN, through the UNCTC, was a highly visible player in the debate. While it would be a gross exaggeration to attribute the collapse of apartheid solely to the role the UN or the UN hearings played, their importance cannot be denied.

Perhaps of greater significance were the issues that surfaced during these hearings and how the South African episode served as a microcosm for the range of possibilities and the limits the UN system can offer. In its contribution to the demise of apartheid, the UN was far more than a debating society. It identified critical concerns and brought to light and condemned deviant behavior. All this happened as a direct result of the UNCTC initiative on South Africa. The hearings also illuminated several new ways of tackling apartheid, and some of these were put into effect.

After the hearings, South Africa continued to struggle with the challenges of economic development but under a new paradigm, which was both more just and more in concert with the tempo of the times. It abandoned its drive to acquire nuclear technology in favor of rejoining the fold. In December 1988, South Africa, Angola, and Cuba signed an agreement that withdrew Cuban troops in Angola, and several months later, South Africa granted independence to Namibia. When F. W. de Klerk was elected president in September 1989, he took immediate steps to introduce fundamental political reforms to end apartheid and create a democratic South Africa. Only two months after de Klerk's election, the government decided to cease production of nuclear weapons, and on 26 February 1990, de Klerk issued written instructions to terminate the nuclear weapons program and dismantle all existing weapons. The nuclear materials were to be melted down and returned to South Africa's Atomic Energy Corporation as the nation prepared to become a signatory to the 1967 Nuclear Non-Proliferation Treaty. The changed international political climate that had helped bring down apartheid also reoriented South Africa's policy away from nuclear arms and brought the country back into the fold of the international community.[78]

Over its two decades in New York, the UNCTC tackled a vast array of TNC-related issues. The code, of course, was the most wrenching, but others were significant in their own right. Some were even amusing. One anecdote concerned Klaus Sahlgren, who was summoned to Port of Spain by Prime Minister Eric Williams of Trinidad and Tobago to provide an appraisal of a jet aircraft his government had purchased; the prime minister suspected that the jet may have been overpriced. Sahlgren admitted this was beyond his mandate, but he did make a few telephone inquiries in order to get a fair price determination. As Sahlgren tells it, Williams was under the impression that a United Nations office that deals with TNCs should have a good idea of the fair price a developing country should pay for a jet. While on the face of it this story may sound trivial, it does reflect a certain image the UNCTC projected among some developing countries—that they could rely on it for information when dealing with TNCs.[79]

The Swing of the Pendulum

By the mid-1980s, many developing countries were in the throes of structural adjustment policies to cope with deficits in their balance of payments, the aftermath of recession, and the huge debts that arose from the energy crises of 1973–1974 and 1979–1980. Many were desperate for capital and technology. Trapped in underdevelopment and sluggish economic performance, they began to change their earlier radical attitudes and policies toward TNCs. In fact, they began to court FDI by exhibiting a more welcoming attitude to TNCs in their countries, and they were often pressured to do so by the conditionalities of adjustment. The UN was moving closer to the "center" in concert with these changes, but it could not completely shed the perception of earlier years that it was "leftist" and anti-West.[80] Advanced countries like the United States had never been enthusiastic about the code and were cooling to the idea altogether.

During President Reagan's second term, the U.S. administration remained lukewarm (if not directly hostile) to the code. Indeed, in 1986, after a decade of participation in the commission and in the UNCTC's deliberations and activities, the U.S. State Department declared that it intended to limit its participation in the UNCTC's activities because the commission had "never given the Centre a clear mandate to include in its work the activities of state-owned enterprises from communist countries and MNCs from developing countries— a violation of the important UN principle of universality." It also advised the

U.S. business community to "restrict its participation in the Centre's work." It clarified that this statement was aimed only at the UNCTC and did not affect U.S. participation in the activities of the commission "or the negotiations on the UN Code of Conduct."[81]

Clearly, these statements were contradictory. The United States wanted to remain engaged in the code negotiations so it would not lose control of the direction of the debate or its outcome. The U.S. government maintained that excluding "state-owned enterprises" from compliance with any potential rules would detract from the universality of any code.[82] Since the code was aimed at governments as well as TNCs, any state-owned enterprise would have been covered in any case; the argument was a red herring. Indeed, the U.S. dislike of the code continued, and conservatives who served as U.S. ambassadors to the UN during this period, including Jeanne Kirkpatrick and Alan Keyes, were determined to block its approval.

The Demise, Interregnum, and Reincarnation

As the UNCTC matured and came of age in its second decade, its impact on research and creating knowledge, building capacity, and policy analysis began to bear fruit. At the same time, the world was changing in dramatic ways, and the UNCTC changed with it. After Mao Zedong died in 1976, Deng Xiaoping ascended to power, and the People's Republic of China established normal diplomatic relations with the United States on 1 January 1979. China also opened its doors to foreign capital and technology and in the process received technical advice from the UNCTC.

As for the Soviet Union, the UNCTC had held workshops on joint ventures in the USSR in 1983–1984. Shortly thereafter, in 1985, Gorbachev introduced changes under the policies of glasnost and perestroika and allowed foreign-owned joint ventures and adopted new accounting and legal rules to fit these new enterprises.

African countries, too, sought the UNCTC's assistance with workshops and advice. The UNCTC further assisted developing countries in their assertive quest to join the global economy and reap what benefit they could from regional integration. In all of these areas, the UNCTC was a substantial player. Most of its core competencies were preserved, even as the enterprise was dismantled and relocated at UNCTAD in Geneva.

It was the UNCTC's activity on the code of conduct on TNCs that proved to be a lightning rod. Code opponents had not forgiven the UN for having initially built this effort into the enterprise, despite accommodations to the new reality under Peter Hansen. He and many of the UNCTC staff sensed some critical changes in the world economy and believed that under the pressures of globalization, accommodation between countries and TNCs should and would replace past confrontations and radicalism. A professional international civil servant and erstwhile academic, Hansen had mustered all his diplomatic skill to moderate the ideologically charged ideas that had energized the UNCTC in its early years. The UNCTC began to focus more on capacity-building and research and less on influencing policy changes. The emphasis shifted to issues more compatible with the times, such as eliminating apartheid in South Africa and helping the Soviet Union draft joint venture laws.

The UNCTC's work also involved international banking scandals such as the infamous BCCI scandal. This international bank, established by Pakistani entrepreneur Agha Hassan Abedi, was initially touted as a Third World TNC. Abedi convinced President Jimmy Carter to accompany him on globe-trotting journeys to establish credibility for this new bank. The bank became mired in an international scandal in the mid-1980s as it lost billions of dollars in deposits from millions of depositors in over eighty countries. Lucky depositors received six cents for each dollar invested; many lost everything. The BCCI episode became one of the most infamous chapters in a string of banking scandals and a disappointment to those who wished success for Third World enterprises and entrepreneurs. The UNCTC became interested in studying the issue. One result was a number of joint publications with ESCAP. Another was the direct involvement of Peter Hansen in efforts that led to the tracking and recovery of funds and involved interface with the international banking community in London and New York.

The UNCTC's research, capacity-building, and policy activities were not enough to sustain the enterprise. In 1992, Secretary-General Boutros-Ghali dismissed Peter Hansen. Hansen's efforts were not sufficient to soothe the new secretary-general or the U.S. administration that had initially supported his appointment. The issue for the U.S. administration was fairly simple: it felt that the UNCTC was hostile to TNCs and its residence in New York was not viable. Boutros-Ghali needed to hand the American government a few victories in its battle to restructure the UN, and the UNCTC became a sacrificial lamb.

For a brief interregnum, the reorganized UNCTC volleyed from pillar to post. For 1992-1993, it was reincarnated as the Transnational Corporations and Management Division in the Department of Economic and Social Development. In 1993, it was further revamped and absorbed into UNCTAD in Geneva. This was the end of an era and the start of a new one. A major chapter in the UN-TNC interface had closed. It was time for an organization stigmatized for its animus toward TNCs to show itself capable of being reformed.

Conclusion

During the New York phase of its existence, from 1975 to 1992, the commission and the UNCTC wrestled with a number of major challenges; in some it was more successful than others. The sheer volume of work during this era is astonishing. The issues it tackled were ranged widely and can be classified into three broad categories; knowledge, capacity-building, and policy analysis.

The UNCTC's endeavor to develop an international code of conduct for TNCs became politicized and polarizing and ultimately failed. By contrast, its work on capacity-building and knowledge creation was both productive and broadly successful. In the policy arena, its initiative on South Africa's apartheid succeeded in bringing this issue to the forefront of the world's attention. The UNCTC held two sets of hearings on the question of whether the presence and activities of TNCs in South Africa prolonged the apartheid regime; the second set of hearings coincided with its demise.

The UNCTC moved ahead with what it considered its primary mandate—crafting a code of conduct for TNCs. The chairman of the Commission on Transnational Corporations, Farooq Sobhan, requested that the matter be moved to the UN General Assembly, where informal consultations took place in September 1991 and again in July 1992 but reached a stalemate. This was when the final nail was driven into the code's coffin. In his report to the General Assembly, UN Secretary-General Boutros-Ghali reported no consensus was possible on the draft code as it stood. Delegations felt that the changed international economic environment and the importance attached to encouraging foreign direct investment required a fresh approach. These consultations had come to naught and had led to the restructuring of the UNCTC and its relocation in Geneva. See Box 5.4 for the Secretary-General's 1992 report.

Box 5.4: The UN General Assembly's 1992 Report on the Code of Conduct

The Economic and Social Council's 1992 report hammered the last nail in the coffin of the code of conduct negotiations:

1. Pursuant to and understanding reached during the previous informal consultations, in September 1991 (see A/46/558 and Corr. 1), the President of the forty-sixth session of the General

Assembly convened a new round of informal consultations on the code of conduct on transnational corporations from 21 to 23 July 1992. The consultations were chaired by Ambassador Farooq Sobhan, Chairman of the eighteenth session of the Commission on Transnational Corporations.

2. It was the view of delegations that no consensus was possible on the draft code at present. Delegations felt that the changed international economic environment and the importance attached to encouraging foreign investment required that a fresh approach should be examined, which could include the preparation of guidelines and/or any other international instrument on foreign investment at the next session of the Commission on Transnational Corporations. In the meanwhile, the Division of Transnational Corporations and Management of the Department of Economic and Social Development and any interested delegation may prepare suitable background papers to facilitate this task.

Source: Report by the President of the Forty-Sixth Session of the General Assembly, General Assembly document A/47/446, 15 September 1992, Annex.

The UNCTC's relocation to Geneva was generally smooth, although some key personnel chose to stay in New York. Enough institution-building had taken place during its two decades for the enterprise to keep growing despite the upheaval. The pendulum had swung in the interim, and the enterprise adapted to the changes. It always remained closer to the center than its stakeholders who occupied the extreme fringes. During its reincarnation in Geneva, it remained both a faithful chronicler of work on TNCs and FDI—especially as they pertained to developing countries—and a source of additional contributions to capacity-building, information and knowledge creation, and policy formulation in this arena.

6

From New York to Geneva: The UNCTAD Years

- UNCTAD: *Background and Early Years*
- UNCTAD, FDI, *and TNCs*
- *The UNCTC's Move to Geneva*
- *The Intellectual Contributions of the Enterprise*
- *The Quest for Relevance*

The United Nations Commission on Transnational Corporations and the UNCTC underwent a metamorphosis during the early 1990s. In 1993, a major part of the UNCTC's work was moved from New York to UNCTAD in Geneva. The work of the enterprise continued along the path established during the New York years, although its emphasis shifted further from the confrontational to the "practical." The collection and refinement of data on FDI were given a new lease of life. Publications that included the annual reports begun in New York and a wide range of issue-based case studies were produced. Training and technical assistance continued unabated.

By this time UNCTAD, whose raison d'être had been to champion the causes of developing countries since its inception, recognized the need to become more practical, focused, and positive toward the role of TNCs in economic development. Former UNCTAD secretary-general Rubens Ricupero wrote of the 1970s:[1]

> It was even believed for a short time in the 1970s that the configuration of forces had tilted in favor of the developing countries as a result of the two successive oil shocks, the American defeat in Viet Nam, followed by Nixon's resignation after Watergate and the relative disengagement of United States forces from many international conflict areas as a result of Congressional pressure.[2]

In recalling the creation of UNCTAD, he added:

> A typical creature of the 1960s, UNCTAD . . . gave impetus to a project with which it became indissolubly linked: the dynamic movement towards the crea-

tion of a New International Economic Order, in capital letters as the phrase was written then. . . . . Today, all this sounds unbelievable and absurd.[3]

Responding to the swing in the policies and orientations of nation-states, its primary constituents, the reconstructed UNCTC, which eventually became known as the Division of Investment, Technology and Enterprise Development within UNCTAD, gradually turned toward the promotion of inward FDI, policy reviews, and other more functional and less ideologically charged material. With the advent of the Internet, this material became increasingly accessible.[4] Indeed, by the early 2000s, UNCTAD had become the premier source of information about the scope, pattern, and effects of TNC activities.

The paradigm shift began in the 1980s and propelled the UNCTC in a new direction. As Peter Hansen wrote in his preface to the fourth UNCTC survey on TNCs in 1988, major changes were taking place in the structure and content of international economic activity. A more pragmatic and businesslike relationship between many, indeed most, developing host-country governments and TNCs was beginning to emerge. Burdened by external debt and economic stagnation and under the pressure of technological change and globalization, many developing-country governments were liberalizing their attitudes and policies toward TNCs, which, in turn, were displaying "greater sensitivity" to the aspirations of host countries. Hansen observed that "the era of confrontation has receded" and was being "replaced by a practical search for a meaningful and mutually beneficial accommodation of interests."[5] Demand for codes of conduct was giving way to a "race to the bottom,"[6] with many countries competing for inbound FDI. Several developing countries, notably in East Asia, were becoming significant outward foreign investors themselves. As the 1970s rolled into the early 1980s, the demand to curb the "dominant market power" and "restrictive business practices" of TNCs gradually gave way to the promotion of FDI through incentives and the Washington Consensus.[7] Jeanne Kirkpatrick and like-minded conservatives must have felt exonerated by this swing.[8]

Circumstances—some internal to the UN, others having to do with changing attitudes toward FDI and TNCs—led to a reorganization of the UNCTC, its transfer to Geneva, and its absorption into UNCTAD. This chapter explores the background of the move, including the discussions between the UN Secretariat and UNCTAD and the internal dynamics and tensions within the organization. In doing so, it places these changes in the context of the evolution in TNC–host country relations and relevant scholarly work. The chapter will show that both have been influenced by the activities of UNCTAD with respect to knowledge creation, capacity-building, and policy. We will discuss the continuation of the enterprise in Geneva, UNCTAD's evolution, and the continued contribution of the enterprise to the understanding of the role of TNCs in economic development since the 1993 reorganization and move.

UNCTAD: Background and Early Years

In contrast to GATT and the Bretton Woods institutions, UNCTAD was created as a forum for airing the interests and concerns of developing countries on issues of trade and development and to level the playing field after centuries of colonial exploitation.[9] The background document prepared for UNCTAD's 1964 founding conference, *Towards a New Trade Policy for Development*, suggested key principles that should underpin the philosophy and work of the new organization. Chief among these was Raúl Prebisch's ardent belief that "developing countries should be compensated for past and future terms-of-trade losses." Some more radical members of G-77 developing countries, in concert with the Soviet Union, were seeking an alternative structure to GATT, whose raison d'être was freer trade.[10]

On the whole, the 1964 founding conference (UNCTAD I) struck a generally positive note on FDI. For example, it recommended that developed countries avoid limiting the flow of capital to developing countries and instead actively promote such flows through investment guarantees and tax and other incentives. It encouraged developing countries to take all appropriate steps to provide favorable conditions for direct private investment, including establishing information centers in capital markets to provide information to foreign TNCs or potential TNCs about opportunities, investment conditions, and regulations in host countries. It advised foreign investors to respect the national sovereignty of host countries and work within the framework and objectives of the development plans of host countries. It also encouraged investing firms to reinvest profits in developing countries. Although these resolutions gave a conditional nod to FDI, a careful reading reveals latent concerns among some developing countries, which were still apprehensive and ambivalent about FDI. Some Asian countries were more open than Latin American countries, which remained skeptical or outright hostile for another two decades.

Although UNCTAD, a new UN forum, was born in the relatively tranquil early 1960s, the acceleration of upheaval and chaos during the latter part of the decade affected its subsequent evolvement. Signs of this tumult included military coups in Algeria, Brazil, and Greece; China's Cultural Revolution; political violence in Latin America and Africa; and the Vietnam War, which spawned bloody protests in 1968 during the U.S. National Democratic Convention in Chicago. Political events such as these influenced UNCTAD's ethos during this era.[11] Later in that decade and into the next, various tensions and polarizations crept in, particularly between the G-77 developing countries and advanced-market-economy countries. On a broader social scale, the sexual revolution, campus sit-ins,[12] drugs, rock music, and hippie communes in the West were other signs of uneasiness during these "leaden years."[13] During the 1970s, the world witnessed further tumult—terrorism at the 1972 Munich Olympics, increased assertion of independence among oil-exporting countries, and unfolding events in Chile, from nationalizations and expropriations under Allende to his overthrow on 11 September 1973.

Since the 1970s, UNCTAD has continued to hold regular sessions, usually every four years.[14] Throughout this period, it has continued its role as a forum where developing countries can discuss their interests and concerns and develop a united front in economic and political dealings with developed countries.

UNCTAD, FDI, and TNCs

When the UNCTC was established in New York in 1974, the study of FDI and TNCs that UNCTAD had pursued were concentrated at the Centre. However, issues such as terms of trade, technology transfer, restrictive business practices, shipping, and commodities continued to engage UNCTAD's attention. The organization also kept watch over the interface between FDI and these issues as they affected developing countries and its mission.

Two major projects relating to TNC activities preoccupied UNCTAD in the mid-1970s. One was a code of conduct for transfer of technology. The other was UNCTAD's Set of Multilaterally Agreed Equitable Principles and Rules for the Control of Restrictive Business Practices (known as "the set"). UNCTAD saw technology transfer as a major vehicle through which TNCs could enhance the development process in recipient countries. It established the Intergovernmental Group on Technology Transfer in the 1970s to coordinate negotiations between contending groups of countries. In 1977, it charged this group with negotiating a universal code for technology transfer. The saga of these protracted negotiations has been well documented elsewhere.[15] The dialogue was what Perlmutter and Sagafi-nejad called "a muffled quadrilogue" among four stakeholder groups: home governments, host-country governments, suppliers, and recipients of technology. Misperception and mistrust by the participating parties marred and ultimately doomed the dialogue. UNCTAD was forced into the center of the fray. Its goal was to devise new rules of engagement in international business transactions that were more favorable to developing countries. At the time, the Group of 77 was dominated by countries whose representatives were generally opposed to TNC activities in their countries. These included Brazil, Colombia, Mexico, and India, each of which was bent on imposing controls on the inflow of FDI and the conduct of TNCs or their affiliates.

UNCTAD had more success in its effort to establish rules on restrictive business practices. The story of why the set was relatively more successful while the technology code never materialized demonstrates both the strengths and limitations of UNCTAD's achievements. It is doubtful that the code or the set has had any impact on the operations or strategies of TNCs with respect to such matters as transfer of technology, technology pricing practices, or transfer pricing. However, this raises a larger question: To what extent are TNCs aware of or responsive to declarations that emanate from various UN quarters? There is little evidence in the literature that these innovations have effectively influenced TNC activity. This was the case during the UNCTC years, and so it continued to be in the Geneva years.

The UNCTC's Move to Geneva

Besides its work on restrictive practices and a code on technology transfer during the 1970s and 1980s, UNCTAD worked on behalf of developing countries by addressing issues related to trade and commodities such as a buffer stock and commodity cartels.[16] Given this history of involvement with TNC-related issues, UNCTAD's interest in absorbing UNCTC activities was understandable. For UNCTAD, the UNCTC's move to Geneva, while it involved some adjustments, meant business as usual, albeit with some changes to the dramatis personae and the agenda of work.

Meanwhile, transformations in the global economy, new technological challenges, and the shift toward liberalization coincided with the move to Geneva of work at the UN on FDI and TNCs. In the mid-1980s, the transformations experienced elsewhere in the UN were occurring within UNCTAD. The code of conduct on technology did not come to fruition. The initial zeal to curb restrictive business practices metamorphosed into a ritual of five-year reviews and a changed focus toward competition rules. However, UNCTAD continued its technical assistance to developing countries and its focus expanded to include the overlap between restrictive business practices (or competition) and trade with international investment agreements and with voluntary peer review sought by countries who wished to have their competition laws scruti-nized.[17] Meanwhile, an intergovernmental group of experts under the aegis of UNCTAD continued to articulate a "model law" on competition.[18]

Through the transition year of 1992 until the transfer of operations and key personnel to Geneva in 1993, the basic mission of the enterprise was to help member states, particularly developing countries, gain a better understanding of the contributions inward foreign direct investment and TNCs could make. Its main task continued to be fulfilling its mandate: gathering, analyzing, and disseminating information; undertaking research studies; providing technical assistance; and continuing to be a focal point within the UN for the efforts of nation-states and TNCs to work toward a mutually beneficial relationship.

Kenneth Dadzie, who was secretary-general of UNCTAD in the early 1990s, had previously been involved with the UNCTC as the first UN director-general for development in the 1980s. Change was in the air as Boutros Boutros-Ghali took the helm as UN Secretary-General. The United States was once again pushing for reform at the UN. The end of the Cold War, the collapse of the Soviet Union, and the continued push for liberalization wrought by globaliza-tion all necessitated a reappraisal of the role of some of the critical international organizations. A strong-willed man prone to making quick decisions, Boutros-Ghali had promised to institute structural change. In short order, he eliminated some forty high posts and dismissed assistant secretary-generals en masse.

About the same time, in 1990–1991, Dadzie had begun discussions with Peter Hansen about moving the UNCTC to Geneva. Both men believed that such a merger between the two organizations could be justified on several grounds. There were natural complementarities between their respective mis-sions. The two entities had already established a close working relationship, and there was some overlap in staff expertise. On the political plane, neither the UNCTC nor UNCTAD was a favored institution in the view of several devel-oped countries. The United States in particular had consistently opposed any effort to devise codes of conduct on TNCs and transfer of technology. The UNCTC's absorption into UNCTAD suited Washington policymakers, who disliked what they perceived as the Centre's distrust of the motives and work-ings of the private sector, despite the fact that it had an Advisory Committee on the private sector that had included some top executives of TNCs as par-ticipants.[19] Hansen said:

> The Americans were never too enamored of UNCTAD either. So I don't know
> if they would have bought it, but [Boutros-Ghali] would have said "okay, instead
> of having two organizations you don't like, we can put them together to be just
> one irritant."[20]

Meanwhile, UNCTAD was attempting to shed its anti-western image and to adapt to the emerging wave of liberalization, and joining with the UNCTC would soften the image. Hansen has since noted that the original idea was to create a merger of equals. He believed that "it was artificial to keep an organization that focused completely and exclusively on trade and another . . . that focused completely and exclusively on foreign direct investment when we should look at . . . the interactions between [them]." In his words, the merger that was first proposed to him would have been concluded differently from what actually happened a short time later. He recalled the 1991 conversations on a merger between the UNCTC and UNCTAD about "different conditions than the eventual swallowing up that subsequently happened":

> It [the actual merger] cut the legs out from under CTC and incorporated parts of it in UNCTAD—as a division. At the time it seemed a downgrading, and was, in my opinion, wrong. UNCTAD could have been given a stronger lease on life if there had been a proactive merger of the two organizations.[21]

Hansen and his Centre colleagues could have accepted the terms of the merger with UNCTAD as the "senior partner," although that arrangement would have necessitated a name change "that would recognize it as a new institution that incorporated two closely related aspects of international economic conditions." Hansen believed that toward the end of 1991, UNCTAD had more or less agreed to the merger. Dadzie and Hansen had worked together for decades and could have worked out such an arrangement, possibly a newly merged configuration with UNCTAD as senior partner and possibly a new name. Hansen, in particular, saw it as unique in UN history that "one agency proposed to merge with another on a conceptual programmatic policy." But what actually happened in 1992 would have been unimaginable earlier— the Centre was abolished by the UN administration and part of it was merged into UNCTAD.

> One cannot help but think that if that merger had been done as a proactive design to deal with the globalization that was then dawning—through the expansion of trade, but more significantly through the expansion of foreign investment and transnational corporations—that the Seattle and similar reactions against it might not have occurred. . . . I think that many of the issues that these blind anti-capitalist and anti-globalization movements were attacking could have been analyzed and dealt with preemptively through such an institution.[22]

Khalil Hamdani, who described himself in 2006 as "one of the last Mohicans," having worked at the UNCTC since 1988, recalled the dissolution and move:

> UNCTC was abolished in 1992. The TNC-FDI programme was leaderless and homeless for a year as the New York Secretariat underwent restructuring. In

1993, the shift to UNCTAD provided a firmer institutional base to revive the programme. But we never regained our status and independence as an autonomous agency. Our reincarnation, the second coming, is still awaited.[23]

Meanwhile, UNCTAD was attempting to reinvent itself to keep up with changing times. The absorption of the UNCTC into UNCTAD increased the latter's prestige in the eyes of its western critics but brought strong attacks from pro–Third World advocates such as the Malaysia-based publication *SUNS*, which had offices in Geneva.[24]

Two developments during the period 1989 to 1992 converged to profoundly impact the attitudes and work of the UNCTC. The first was the collapse of communism and the end of the East-West rivalry that had often led to confrontation and the formation of alliances. The Soviet Union had encouraged policies at the UN that kept "capitalist exploiters" in check. Paradoxically, during the Brezhnev and Gorbachev eras, the Soviet Union cautiously began to adopt certain western laws and institutions that helped foster greater prosperity and alleviate chronic shortages. As early as the mid-1980s, the Soviets were experimenting with joint stock companies and the concept of limited liability. In this, they were advised by Wall Street experts and, ironically, by the UN Centre on Transnational Corporations.

The second event with significant consequences was the 1992 appointment of Boutros Boutros-Ghali as UN Secretary-General. As was noted earlier, shortly after assuming office, the new Secretary-General dismissed Peter Hansen.[25] Boutros-Ghali had become Secretary-General with the expectation that he would restructure and streamline UN operations.[26] The Centre was soon ordered to dismantle, although the more diplomatic term "reorganization" was used. Staff was given the option of remaining in New York or moving to UNCTAD in Geneva.

In retrospect, it is apparent that a "merger of equals" between the UNCTC and UNCTAD—even assuming that both institutions had equal budgets and the same number of personnel, which was not the case—would have resulted in a more profound transformation within UNCTAD than that which actually occurred. Nevertheless, even though the merger did not create a partnership of equals, the move left an indelible mark. The incorporation of FDI-related topics into UNCTAD's agenda gave that agency new relevance in the age of globalization of capital, technology, and markets. At the time of the merger discussions, Hansen believed that UNCTAD was under heavy pressure from western countries to reform or die. As GATT evolved, UNCTAD's critics saw it as superfluous and outdated and questioned whether it was still viable. It was not just western countries that were skeptical; the more advanced developing countries, particularly the Asian big and small tigers, were more interested in acquiring foreign technology and capturing export markets than they were in promoting Third World solidarity.

The UNCTC, on the other hand, was beginning to gain recognition as a constructive force. It was gaining expertise on the content and form of globalization, on new modes of international expansion, on the changing organization and strategies of the world's leading TNCs, and on the geography of the most rapidly growing industrial sectors, including information technology and business services.

Let us leave the last word of this saga to Peter Hansen:

> Whereas the merger of equals was not realized, one of UNCTC's pivotal objectives, to have "a focal point within the UN Secretariat for all matters related to transnational corporations" or "all matters related to foreign direct investment and transnational corporations," as it was rephrased in later years, nevertheless, was preserved.[27]

Under UNCTAD, the enterprise has continued to make its mark on TNC-related knowledge creation and transfer and capacity-building in response to national governments, as it had during the New York years. It has contributed to the institutional development of its primary constituents, developing countries, by advising them on how to better benefit from FDI and other potential contributions of TNCs. It has generated knowledge and information useful both to developing countries and TNCs. The continuity of its established mission has also been evident in its work on industry studies, country reports, and the World Investment Report series.

In the later years, the focus and thrust of the enterprise moved from that of advocacy and confrontation to knowledge creation and capacity-building. As a result, its modus operandi changed from how governments could control TNCs to how they could best capture gains and benefit from TNCs' strengths. UNCTAD recognized that developing countries needed to enhance their capacity to absorb imported technology and capital, and it took up the challenge to meet this need. Its impact on capacity-building took several paths.

Training programs in connection with investment policy reviews have contributed to knowledge and capacity-building, as have a series of workshops in connection with international investment agreements. The strategy regarding policy impact has been more nuanced since the merger with UNCTAD. Unlike the 1970s and 1980s, when the United Nations was much more proactive and straightforward about the need for international policy formulation to ensure that the actions of TNCs conformed to national economic and social policies, in the 1990s, the pendulum began to swing. The new development paradigm increasingly called for a reappraisal of national institutions and policies to ensure that developing countries gained the most benefit from inbound, and later outbound, FDI. More emphasis was placed on the market as regulator, the government as facilitator, and private enterprise as the wealth creator. Governments were called upon to "govern the market" rather than compete with—or even substitute for—private enterprise, as had been the propensity in the 1970s. Increasingly, the impact of TNCs on policy analysis and formulation was exerted through case studies and training and collaborative regional and international work.

After the UNCTC's absorption into UNCTAD, the enterprise became the Division of Transnational Corporations and Investment and the sole focal point of issues related to FDI and TNCs. Under a succession of leaders, the mission and its implementation continued to evolve. In 1993, when the program moved to Geneva, Roger Lawrence, a career UNCTAD staffer and former director of its Globalization Division, was appointed interim director. He headed up a nucleus of personnel who had moved from New York—among them, Victoria Aranda, Persephone Economou, Khalil Hamdani, Padma Mallampalli, Masataka Fujita, Fiorina Mugione, Karl P. Sauvant, Jorg Simon, Joerg Weber, and Zbigniew Zimny. These came to form the "core competency" and institutional capacity of the new division of UNCTAD that was dedicated to doing research and providing advisory and training services on FDI and TNCs.

Lynn K. Mytelka, a Canadian scholar with extensive expertise in science, technology, investment, and economic development, was appointed head of the division in 1995. This appointment was an interesting departure from the international macroeconomics staff that had dominated the scene at the creation of the UNCTC. In 1996, shortly after becoming UNCTAD secretary-general, Rubens Ricupero initiated another internal restructuring under pressure from the UN Secretary-General and collapsed nine divisions into four, one of which was the Division of Investment, Technology and Enterprise Development (DITE), yet another name for the enterprise. The name significantly implied a stronger focus on the microeconomic and organizational aspects of TNC activity. Since then, the division has remained the focal point within the UN for matters related to FDI, technology, and enterprise development. After Mytelka left UNCTAD in 2000, Karl P. Sauvant, a longtime UNCTC staff member whose UN career began in 1973 (shortly before the Centre was formed), became the acting officer in charge and later the director of the division, a post he held until his retirement in 2005.[28] He was succeeded by Khalil Hamdani, another long-termer who had been with the enterprise since the New York years.

Although the annual World Investment Reports continued to report on developments regarding policy, the organization began to place less emphasis on advocacy and more on institution-building options. It is true that it has given less advice during visits to foreign government departments, in seminars, and with face-to-face contacts. Nevertheless, UNCTAD has organized seminars on particular policy and related issues and the enterprise reports these activities in detail to member countries and posts them on its Web site. For example, in 2001 the DITE worked with the governments of Albania and Kyrgyzstan on investment targeting, the theme of which was export competitiveness.

UNCTAD has continued to advise governments on FDI and TNC and related policy matters, but the content of that advice has changed over time. In the 1970s and 1980s, its main advice to governments regarding policies assumed a zero-sum game and focused on extracting maximum concessions from TNCs. In the 1990s, the emphasis shifted to how, in light of globalization and technological change, governments could adapt their policies to ensure that both inward and outward FDI upgraded their comparative advantage and contributed optimally to economic development. Thus, the emphasis shifted toward developing the institutional infrastructure to facilitate achievement of this goal. UNCTAD began allocating more resources to publishing case studies and manuals and conducting workshops to disseminate research results. The agency began outsourcing field research on FDI to local experts in developing countries to build their capacities and promote good practices in attracting FDI. It contracted out much of the research for investment policy reviews to academic scholars and researchers after the basic framework and preliminary research had been completed in house. The emphasis was shifting from controlling FDI to promoting and benefiting from it. The impact of the enterprise during the latter phase on capacity-building and policy has taken several forms, ranging from advice about science policy and strategies for acquiring technology to advice about developing international standards of accounting and reporting.

Recent literature suggests that policies that strike a balance between control and promotion of FDI may need to be revised in light of globalization and TNC activity.[29] Of course one must also distinguish between policies that are specifically about FDI and general macroeconomic policies that have implications for FDI. These broader contextual changes include changes in institutions, fiscal policies, industrial policies, regional policies, and trade policies. The enterprise and indeed the whole of UNCTAD has more often benefited from these changes and has recalibrated its activities in light of them instead of playing the lead in such changes. Various WIRs deal with these policies and how the changing domestic and international contexts may need to be recalibrated.

The Intellectual Contributions of the Enterprise

There is, inevitably, an overlap between the three strands—knowledge creation, capacity-building, and policy implications—of UNCTAD's contribution to our understanding of the role of TNCs in economic development. This is seen in case studies in investment policy reviews and science and technology studies, reports that monitor bilateral investment treaties, and international investment agreements. Each of these issues involves research, either directly or in consultation with local researchers (knowledge creation); interface with local policy-makers through training (capacity-building); or the creation of new policies to enhance the efficacy of FDI (policy impact). This three-pronged contribution was made in no less than six arenas, each of which originated in the New York years of the enterprise.

Three of these six arenas were concerned with rulemaking and policy issues, each illustrating how the enterprise was engaged in articulating or influencing a policy issue. The first focused on international standards of accounting and reporting (ISARs). The second focused on bilateral investment treaties; and the third was related to the Multilateral Agreement on Investments, an international accord on FDI. The agreement was spearheaded by the OECD, but UNCTAD was an active participant in the deliberations; it may have felt that the agreement accomplished some of the same objectives that the failed code for TNCs would have accomplished.

These three arenas, while they dealt primarily with policy, affected knowledge creation and capacity-building, as did the fourth arena, investment policy reviews (IPRs), in which UNCTAD undertook diagnostic reviews of countries' FDI policies and institutions and recommended actions to promote incoming investment and enhance its benefits. Similar reviews were conducted later by Foreign Investment Advisory Services (FIAS), an arm of the International Finance Corporation, a World Bank subsidiary. The FIAS initially benefited from the expertise provided by Boris Velic, who came from the UNCTC in the mid-1990s after it was dissolved and moved to UNCTAD. Unlike IPRs, which are published, FIAS studies are confidential and limited in circulation.

The fifth arena dealt with establishing and nurturing investment promotion agencies in developing countries to aid their investment promotion efforts, including through such vehicles as the World Association of Investment Promotion Agencies. Finally, the sixth arena is constituted by the web of symbiotic relationships between the enterprise and the academic community that grew through this work. Each is elaborated on below.

International Standards of Accounting and Reporting

International standards of accounting and reporting were a concern of the United Nations as early as 1974, when the Group of Eminent Persons issued its report.[30] Since that time, the growing internationalization of firms, the increasing complexity of relations between headquarters and subsidiaries, and the persistence of inconsistent and/or nontransparent accounting rules and practices have made it more difficult for external stakeholders—including governments in home and host countries—to monitor and verify company data. Both developed and developing countries have alleged that it is possible for TNCs to use increasingly complex accounting systems to hide profits, falsify cost data, and transfer funds to maximize consolidated profits.[31] These accounting systems were initially designed for internal purposes and for reporting to internal and external stakeholders. However, these practices made it difficult, if not impossible, for host countries to judge the appropriateness of the many charges TNCs required recipient firms to pay for technology and technical services. In addition to the opacity or secrecy the new accounting practices made possible, a lack of uniform reporting requirements and standards hampered the capacity of the enterprise to standardize information. Information disclosure is a precondition to good decision making by both host countries and recipient firms.

The 1974 GEP report had stated that information about asset valuation (in different currencies), inventories, expenditures for research and development, start-up expenses, transfer prices, pension and other reserves, sources and timing of income, and wages and other workers' benefits would be particularly useful to governments and other external stakeholders. The GEP recommended that an expert group on international accounting standards be convened under the Commission on TNCs, which was about to form. The group further recommended that national governments should be prepared to disclose the principal terms of agreements between them and TNCs. However, merely possessing information was not enough for developing countries, which also needed to build up their capacity to handle the complex transactions and systems involved. This is the point at which the capacity-building functions of international standards of accounting and reporting came into play.

When the enterprise relocated in Geneva, it retained this task as part of its work program. A group within UNCTAD worked on developing universally acceptable standards of accounting and reporting in collaboration with the big accounting firms and international bodies such as the International Accounting Standards Board[32] and the Financial Accounting Standards Board.[33] Organizations in the United States, including the American Institute of Certified Public Accountants, and similar groups in the United Kingdom and elsewhere also recognized the need for accounting standardization and became involved in the effort. A wave of corporate malfeasance, epitomized by the BCCI scandal in the 1990s and the Enron and WorldCom scandals in the new millennium, propelled many hitherto passive and submissive organizations and government agencies into action. The OECD also became interested when similar scandals involving firms such as Parmalat and Royal Ahold rocked governments and boardrooms in Europe.

The move toward crafting international standards of accounting and reporting was a natural extension of UNCTAD's work on TNCs and FDI. UNCTAD seminars and workshops for host developing countries occasionally included accounting and reporting topics designed to enhance capacity-building. The development of requirements for accounting procedures and reporting can be characterized as the synchronization of disparate and occasionally conflicting national practices toward an international system. Here the record has not been stellar. Despite the proliferation of private and governmental initiatives, international accounting and reporting rules have yet to emerge. Nevertheless, the impact of the ISAR guidelines is evident in the area of environmental accounting as devised by the European Commission and stock exchanges and ministries of finance. According to a 2001 report, governments and professional accounting associations used ISARs guidelines regarding regulation, self-regulation, and the professional qualifications of accountants.[34] As social responsibility assumed a more prominent role in corporate reporting, the scope of international standards for accounting expanded to potentially encompass social accounting and reporting.

Box 6.1. Some Examples of International Standards of Accounting and Reporting and Their Uses

UNCTAD's work on international accounting and reporting standards is another facet of the organization's impact on capacity-building. Improving a country's accounting and reporting standards increases foreign investors' confidence in the country because it makes the standards more compatible with international norms. The following are cases in point:

· In 2001, UNCTAD helped the Russian Federation develop and introduce national standards for accounting and reporting con-

sistent with international accounting principles and made recommendations on accounting for small and medium-sized enterprises.

· The International Chamber of Commerce found UNCTAD's
guidelines for qualifying professional accountants useful for
strengthening accounting education in developing countries
and countries in transition.

· UNCTAD guidelines on environmental accounting and professional qualifications were used by stock exchanges, governments, regulatory bodies, professional associations, and universities. Over 220 accounting practitioners, financial analysts,
and standard setters from 29 countries and 32 trainers from 17
countries were trained in five workshops.

· The guidelines and training materials were adopted and incorporated into the syllabi of ten accounting institutions in India
and Malaysia and by the Arab Society of Chartered Accountants and the Eastern, Central, and Southern African Federation
of Accountants.

· The Development Bank of Brazil incorporated environmental
ratings into its credit analysis process using UNCTAD recommendations.

· China's Ministry of Finance participated in a workshop to help
shape Chinese accounting standards.

Bilateral Investment Treaties

In the absence of a multilateral accord on investment and partially because of
prodding by UNCTAD, many countries have chosen to make bilateral arrangements. In the area of FDI, these have taken the form of bilateral investment
treaties, agreements between two countries for the reciprocal encouragement,
promotion, and protection of investments in each other's territories.

Bilateral investment treaties had their origins in nineteenth-century treaties
of amity, friendship, competence, and navigation,[35] which intended to facilitate international business activities by providing property protection to investors and traders. The 1883 Paris Convention for the Protection of Intellectual
Property and its subsequent revisions under the World Intellectual Property
Organization, together with the establishment of the ITO in 1944, might have
rendered bilateral treaties redundant by providing multilateral frameworks for
such protection. Yet bilateral investment treaties continue to proliferate, as do
regional trade agreements, in large measure because the scope of the broader
but moribund International Trade Organization was constricted in GATT with

a narrower range of responsibilities, which replaced it. By 2007, there were over 2,000 trade or investment agreements among countries, forming a spaghetti-like system. They can be viewed as a series of small steps in the process of convergence toward global multilateral rule-making. Conversely, they may forestall or postpone the realization of such an end result.

The World Trade Organization has had an ambivalent view of regional trade blocs. On one hand, it has encouraged their development as a pathway toward global convergence on trade. On the other, it has recognized their potential to forestall continued integration into the global economy and to encourage what Ohmae has called "global regionalization" instead.[36] The large number of stakeholders in regional trade blocs makes consensus unlikely, whereas bilateral and even regional accords involve a smaller (hence more manageable) group. Bilateral agreements tend to involve more similar and likeminded countries with a greater degree of interdependence and higher level of mutual trust and confidence. The World Trade Organization and other international organizations recognize that integration is a step-by-step and gradual learning process. Bilateral, regional, or issue-specific agreements can serve as stepping-stones toward global convergence. These elements combine to explain the proliferation of bilateral agreements.

Recognizing that stability and low risk are preconditions for FDI, UNCTAD became involved in gathering information about, studying, and promoting bilateral investment treaties as part of its mandate to help developing countries promote FDI that could benefit their economies. Bilateral investment treaties are presumably "symmetrical, stipulating identical rights and obligations" for both host and home countries.[37] In the mid-1980s, the enterprise focused on these treaties, recognizing a shift in the international investment climate away from control and toward promotion of FDI. It hailed them as a new and potentially useful element in international economic relations. It issued a comparative study in 1988[38] with the belief that these agreements could help developing countries participate more effectively in setting international rules for investment.

Bilateral treaties typically define investment, admission, establishment, national treatment, most-favored-nation treatment, fair and equitable treatment, compensation in the event of expropriation or damage, guarantees of free transfers of funds, and dispute settlement mechanisms, both state to state and investor to state. They include, among other elements:

· A broad and open-ended definition of FDI to accommodate tangible and intangible assets and new and existing investments
· Avoidance of illicit payments
· Clauses that protect intellectual property rights

- Labor standards
- Provisions concerning transfer of technology
- A commitment from the home country to promote investments
- Stipulations of the responsibilities of foreign investors in host countries
- Stipulations of the obligations of subnational authorities[39]

The dramatic increase in bilateral investment treaties may suggest that they have become one of the main international instruments host governments use to ensure investor confidence and encourage the inflow of FDI. There is no systematic evidence to substantiate such a claim, and only detailed empirical evidence that we do not yet have could validate it. In theory, a multilateral agreement is considered an optimal control solution, since it creates a level playing field for all. Some economists, however, would consider the "market solution," in which the role of the government is confined to eliminating market imperfections and allowing markets to regulate economic activity, to be the optimum arrangement.[40] However, firms from advanced-market economies want to reduce the risks associated with investing in developing countries, and host countries also want to lower these risks to attract FDI. In the absence of multilateral agreements, bilateral investment treaties have become mechanisms that are helpful to both. There has been greater agreement among home countries on the details of these treaties than among the more diverse host countries. Indeed, the Calvo Doctrine, which prohibits extraterritorial intervention by foreign governments in internal disputes between host countries and foreign investors, was the prevailing view across Latin America from the nineteenth century into the 1980s. This doctrine was designed to preempt any treaty that diluted or undermined national sovereignty. In the early twenty-first century, many Latin American countries were more interested in attracting FDI than they were in preserving the less tangible ideal of national sovereignty, which continued to erode with global interdependence. The more radical political and anti-TNC developments in Venezuela, Ecuador, and Bolivia may portend the end of the open-arms era when TNCs were actively courted, at least in some countries.

Many host developing countries have found it prudent, even necessary, to be party to bilateral treaties, partly because many developed countries, including the United States, have discouraged their firms from investing in countries that have not signed such treaties. The primary reason for this insistence is the strong belief among market economies in the nondiscrimination "national treatment" clause, which is routinely included in bilateral investment treaties.[41] But tensions exist between bilateral investment treaties and work that has been done at UNCTAD and elsewhere at the UN on labor standards and corporate social responsibility.

The Multilateral Agreement on Investments

The multilateral agreement on investments, spearheaded by the OECD, was yet another international attempt to develop multilateral rules concerning FDI and TNCs. Although the agreement was outside UNCTAD's realm, it overlapped with its work, and thus the enterprise was involved in the negotiations. In May 1995, after several years of preparation under the OECD's Committee on International Investment and Multinational Enterprise,[42] OECD ministers hoped to reach a multilateral agreement on investment.[43] The multilateral agreement on investments was intended to provide a broad multilateral framework for international investment, standards for liberalizing investment regimes, protection of investments, and an effective process for settling disputes. The agreement was to be a freestanding international treaty open to both OECD members and nonmembers, as were the OECD's 1976 Guidelines for Multinational Enterprises.

After four years of intense negotiations, this multilateral accord was abandoned in December 1998, despite the fact that it was a joint effort of a small number of like-minded countries. Some wanted to liberalize the investment regime more quickly than others, some sought exceptions for various reasons, and others saw potential conflicts between this instrument and existing international accords such as those under the World Intellectual Property Organization. In addition to complexities arising from technical issues such as extraterritoriality, the broader political context contributed to its failure. For those who strive for such multilateral solutions, this episode should serve as a cautionary tale.[44]

Investment Policy Reviews

Investment policy reviews, which UNCTAD began in the mid-1990s, are country-based case studies intended to help national governments improve their investment policies and familiarize the international private sector with their investment environment. Investment policy reviews are a good example of the intersection between research, knowledge creation, capacity-building, and policy formation. They study a developing country's economic conditions, inward investment strategies, institutions, and legal framework and recommend ways the country can attract FDI and benefit from it. UNCTAD begins each study by tapping into its in-house database. Then the staff, often through in-country and external consultants, draws a broad portrait of the country's macroeconomic position, institutions, and FDI situation. The team then conducts surveys of investors and holds workshops and roundtable meetings of stakeholders prior to publishing the report. A country expert (often from the country under review) or a specialist from academia or business is then contracted to undertake a background survey. Data collection may entail brief country visits by UNCTAD staff.

Once a background report has been prepared, seminars are conducted in the country to present and discuss the results. Feedback from these workshops—about new knowledge on FDI matters, policy advice, and capacity strengthening—is then incorporated into a final report and presented at UNCTAD's annual Trade and Development Board meetings in Geneva. Since more than one report is often prepared for each Trade and Development Board meeting, participating countries have an opportunity to compare notes, learn from each other's experiences, and fine-tune their FDI regimes. In the preparation of each investment policy review, new knowledge is created, the policy of the host country is critically evaluated, and the host country's capacity is strengthened through the use of local researchers in the preparation of the report and through the dissemination of results as drafts, final reports, and seminars.

The first investment policy review was conducted in 1999 for Egypt. This was followed by studies on Uzbekistan, Uganda, Peru, Mauritania, Ecuador, Tanzania, Ghana, Botswana, and others. Funding for these studies is normally provided from a combination of UN resources (UNDP, UN Development Account) and extrabudgetary contributions from Switzerland, Scandinavian countries, and a few other advanced states. Other UN institutions provide assistance as well. The report on Tanzania, for example, was conducted in collaboration with UNIDO.[45] Box 6.2 illustrates the process of one investment policy review.

Box 6.2. Investment Policy Review: Ecuador

The investment policy review on Ecuador began in 1999 with help from local researchers and UNCTAD's database. Drafts were discussed, reviewed, and revised in seminars with local government, business, and community leaders. The review concluded that the country's FDI performance was below its potential.

The investment policy review recommended these policies and actions to boost FDI inflow and to increase its benefits to the country:

· *Restoring stability and resuming growth.* Dollarization would help stabilize currency markets, and restoring political stability would bolster investor confidence.
· *Achieving social consensus.* Stakeholders should arrive at a social consensus that takes account of the poorest segment of

society and makes burden-sharing possible. The review suggested that Ecuador set up a Solidarity Fund for the poorest segment of the population.

· ***Further improving the legal framework for investment.*** While recent changes had provided a legal framework for FDI treatment and dispute resolution that compared favorably with other Latin American countries, enforcement remained problematic and the proliferation of secondary legislation often led to confusion.

· ***Implementing a viable privatization program.*** The report saw privatization as a key to the immediate realization of FDI potential in the state-owned sector, which was still quite large. The report drew special attention to infrastructure services and the banking industry, where privatization could play an important role.

· ***Improving physical infrastructure.*** Drawing further attention to the quality of infrastructure in attracting FDI, the report noted that the country needed to give priority to elements of Ecuador's infrastructure that facilitated access to international markets for exports, including air, maritime, rail, and road facilities. The report said that the public sector needed to shoulder the burden of these investments.

· ***Designing policies aimed at increasing long-term benefits from FDI.*** The report singled out four policy areas as particularly crucial in attracting FDI: human resource development, science and technology, competition, and establishing and strengthening linkages between foreign and local enterprises.

Source: UNCTAD, *Investment Policy Review: Ecuador* (Geneva, UNCTAD, 2001).

Promoting Investment: The World Association of Investment Promotion Agencies

UNCTAD's capacity-building initiatives have included strengthening investment promotion agencies in developing countries and aiding efforts in those countries to promote inbound FDI through the World Association of Investment Promotion Agencies. This association was created as a nongovernmental organization under UNCTAD's tutelage in 1995 to help countries attract foreign investment through the exchange of ideas and the use of best practices. By 2006, it had nearly 200 member agencies from some 150 countries. It had received $1 million US from the Swiss government and had moved its office from the Palais des Nations, where it was born, to downtown Geneva.[46]

UNCTAD's work on investment promotion benefited from extrabudgetary resources, voluntary donations made by many developed countries. The General Trust Fund on Transnational Corporations and a number of subject-specific funds were established by the enterprise and were tapped to support investment-related programs.[47] In addition, international bodies such as UNDP, UNIDO, the World Bank, and the European Commission provided extrabudgetary funding for specific collaborative projects. In 2006 the Swedish government's International Development Cooperation Agency (SIDA) pledged €1 million to fund the Capacity Building and Transfer of Knowledge to Investment Developing Countries project. UNCTAD will operate this project from 2006 to 2008 to support World Association of Investment Promotion Agencies activities at UNCTAD.[48]

UNCTAD's shepherding of this investment promotion umbrella organization is significant in several respects; it is symbolic of the importance both host countries and the enterprise attach to orchestrated, well-conceived, and effectively executed investment promotion. Under the umbrella of the World Association of Investment Promotion Agencies, countries can measure their investment promotion efforts against best practices. That a UN agency would spearhead and nurture such an idea at a time when attraction of FDI was being pursued by nearly all countries signals that the UN responded to the mood change and may have even been ahead of the curve.

UNCTAD Collaboration with TNCs and Academia

UNCTAD has benefited from collaboration with academia in its many activities. Its collaboration with TNCs since 1993 has been different from that of the UNCTC years in New York, when a business advisory group existed and the Centre tapped it for ideas and funding. During the Geneva years, participation by TNCs has been more ad hoc. To maintain, validate, and update its data, UNCTAD has relied on companies and academic scholars whose core business is collecting, using, and selling information on FDI, mergers and acquisitions, and licensing. Companies have been invited to participate in the enterprise's deliberations, be they on accounting and reporting, policies and practices to promote investment, or other matters. Industry associations, primarily the International Chamber of Commerce, continue to be involved. Yet there is currently no formal structure comparable to the UNCTC model, with the possible exception of the International Advisory Council, in which the ICC, as the representative of TNCs, participates on work related to the least-developed countries.

The practice of involving representatives of the private sector is consistent with the mandate of the enterprise to act as a liaison and catalyst for interface between TNCs, governments, and the international community. However, as the world changed and the influence of the private sector increased, the enterprise did not bring the private sector on board as effectively as it might have. This could be due in part to the much more activist posture of the enterprise as the UNCTC, as was demanded by the times. The relocation to Geneva may have also served as a deterrent; many TNCs are headquartered in New York. That said, there continued to be some private sector and TNC involvement, albeit in an ad hoc manner. UNCTAD has invited auditing firms such as KPMG-Peat Marwick to audit its FDI data. It has also collaborated with private firms such as Arthur Andersen to publish studies and reports.[49]

Since the relocation to Geneva, the enterprise has collaborated with academia in a sustained and more diverse way. UNCTAD made ad hoc arrangements with commercial publishers to reissue some of its publications such as WIRs or anthologies from issues of its journal, *Transnational Corporations*, in collaboration with academics. Although some university teachers and researchers have used UNCTAD's publications in classrooms, the enterprise has been underutilized as a source of information. Hundreds of academic scholars have participated in its work by writing research reports, conducting seminars on FDI around the developing world, and serving as consultants and advisors across the full spectrum of its research and advisory services. For example, there was, and is, widespread academic involvement in the preparation of the annual World Investment Reports, where the acknowledgements read like an international who's who of the academy. Other project-specific collaborations with academia include UNCTAD's partnership in 1997 with the database of the Studies and Competence Center for Organizational and Policy Research in European Business at Erasmus University in the Netherlands to document the internationalization and competition strategies of the world's largest firms.[50] Textbooks and scholarly publications that tap into UNCTAD publications may simply cite "United Nations" as their source, rendering traceability impossible. Still, a search of the scientific information database Scirus for "World Investment Report" ground to a halt after the first 1,000 hits, which is the maximum that particular database returns.[51] Google Scholar and similar Web sites generate comparable results.

The Quest for Relevance

The transition of the main body of the UN's work on TNCs from New York to Geneva was a defining moment both of the mission articulated by the GEP in 1973 to maximize the benefits of TNC activity and for UNCTAD, the champion of developing countries. The passage of time and the changed context of international economic relations transformed both the enterprise and the larger institution of which it became a part. Some work went on as before, but the UN Secretary-General ultimately found another venue, the UN Global Compact, through which the world body would reach out to TNCs. The following passage from a 2003 report provides a clear portrait of how the UN saw the world investment climate in the early twenty-first century:

> Greater openness to international market forces and competition is expected to strengthen growth prospects by improving resource allocation, by attracting foreign savings and by deepening technological capacities through greater inflows of foreign direct investment (FDI). Together with political stability, good governance, respect for property rights and public investment in human capital, these elements make up what is regarded as a generally applicable strategy for sustainable growth in a globalizing world.[52]

From the 1970s to the 1990s, from New York to Geneva, the enterprise achieved much in the areas of creating knowledge and building capacity, although it achieved less in the policy arena. The lingering effects of the mistrust and misperceptions that had characterized the previous era were still discernible throughout the 1980s. Even though several incremental events were happening that would ultimately result in the sea change of the 1990s, some scholars continued to focus on such issues as the "relative bargaining power" between host countries and TNCs and the "opportunities, constraints and dangers"[53] of the latter's involvement in development.

The enterprise has been an instrument of change even as it has been affected by megatrends beyond its control. One of these trends of the last two decades has been the growing economic and political power of certain developing countries known as emerging markets.[54] Sources of FDI have also become more dispersed from the traditional home countries (primarily the United States, the United Kingdom, and France) to other European countries, China, Hong Kong, Taiwan, and other Asian countries.

Changes in the dynamics affecting FDI and TNCs have not been limited to those in host countries. Concerns in the home countries of TNCs have ranged from a fear that TNCs will have a negative impact on investing countries' balance of payments; fear of job exports, exemplified by H. Ross Perot's use of the phrase "giant sucking sound" (warning American voters against the North American Free Trade Agreement in 1993); and more recent attacks on outsourcing to de-industrialization and loss of manufacturing competitiveness.[55] Navigating conflicting loyalties and jurisdictions between host and home countries remains a major challenge for many TNCs.

A divergence of interest among developing countries has added to the complexity of the landscape. Since the late 1990s, several developing countries have tried to redefine their relationship with TNCs. Countries rich in natural resources (such as oil exporters and mineral-rich countries, from Africa and the Middle East to India and Mexico) persisted in defining the rules of engagement, only to reverse course two decades later. In 1975, the Mexican government established a joint venture with six TNCs to gather, process, and sell barbasco, a plant native to Mexico whose roots are used to make steroidal hormones. The government held 80 percent of the stock, while the foreign partners held the remaining 20 percent. The joint venture was President Echeverria's attempt at "reformist nationalism"—not a total break with global capitalism or Mexico's own capitalist path but "a redefinition of dependency" aimed at accelerating the development process by "expanding the margin of autonomy and bargaining power" of local players.[56]

Likewise, in the 1980s, the earlier propensity to use state-owned enterprises as countervailing forces against TNCs lost much of its appeal as countries, including some in the Soviet orbit, realized the inefficiencies associated with such enterprises. In many countries the fall of the Berlin Wall may have been another nail in the coffin, but for some developing countries (Venezuela, Iran, Argentina, Ecuador, and even Mexico), the temptation to retain control was strong, as state-owned enterprises remained politically powerful and opaque and continued to be subsidized.

One of the threshold questions both TNCs and national governments are asking is whether UNCTAD's work on TNCs is indispensable, irrelevant, duplicative, or serves a special niche. Has it outlived its usefulness or has it been able to transform itself as the world has changed? Some of these concerns, of course, date back many years; and they manifest themselves in different contexts. The debate in the 1980s regarding rules against restrictive business practices is one such example. That discussion began almost the day UNCTAD was born. Some developing countries considered it important to control the activities of TNCs or their affiliates as a necessary step toward promoting the development of Third World countries. All subsequent actions followed from this basic mission.

The battle lines were first drawn between developed and developing countries in the 1980s when such contentious issues as codes of conduct for transfer of technology and restrictive business practices were debated at UNCTAD. One point of disagreement concerned whether GATT or UNCTAD should serve as the forum for discussing rules regarding restrictive business practices. Developed countries preferred GATT, whereas the G-77, itself an UNCTAD creature, wanted to retain work on restrictive business practices at UNCTAD.

As talk of restructuring fill UN corridors once again in 2007, it is an opportune time to ask whether UNCTAD will continue to reinvent itself or drift toward irrelevance. Its direction changed somewhat in the mid-1980s, when its earlier development paradigm became increasingly obsolete as the renaissance of a market-driven paradigm of global capitalism took root. National planning gave way to open-door liberalism and competitive liberalization, only to be later moderated by those who advocated a balance in "governing the market."[57]

As with other UN agencies, UNCTAD was transformed by the same forces that brought the primacy of the market to the fore. As a product of its stakeholders' positions, the UN reconfigured itself to reflect the views of its stakeholders. Note, however, that the stakeholders are both internal and external and each has its perspectives and vested interests. Such is the case at UNCTAD, where certain internal players have shown greater resilience than others in accommodating the changing times. The investment division, a relatively new addition, embraced the new paradigm somewhat more readily than the rest of the organization. The established macroeconomists at UNCTAD were mainly interested in documenting and analyzing patterns of world trade, the role of commodities and cartels, and broader economic development issues. The former UNCTC economists preferred to stress the importance of FDI and TNCs as the most important component of global exchange.

This lack of internal consensus, compounded by transitions in personnel in 2005, may be the source of what appears to be a kind of organizational schizophrenia. Shortly after Rubens Ricupero ended his term as UNCTAD secretary-general in 2005, Karl Sauvant, head of the enterprise during most of the UNCTAD years, retired. Supachai Panitchpakdi succeeded Ricupero. One of his first initiatives was to establish a Panel of Eminent Persons to advise him on how to enhance the development role and impact of UNCTAD. The panel recommended streamlining operations, focusing on the organization's comparative advantages, cooperating with other agencies, and generally serving its traditional advocacy role on behalf of developing countries.[58]

Even after Panichpakdi took over, tensions remained and seemed likely to persist; these helped keep the organization vibrant. One source of tension was internal, the other external, and they tended to pull in opposite directions, with those who remained skeptical of TNCs pitted against those who were working with a new paradigm of engaging TNCs. External tensions also remained (and, if anything, were likely to grow), as each of the organs of the UN galaxy strove for relevance. Who shall carry the mantle of serving as the focal point within the UN system as its member states seek counsel in their relations with TNCs? Will it be the UN Secretariat, UNCTAD, the ILO, UNIDO, or the WTO? Is there a healthy competition for a legitimate role in international economic challenges for each? Are there enough complementarities, or do redundancies outweigh them? Could strategic partnership among existing units be part of such a future configuration? Interest and productivity on the subject of TNCs has ebbed and flowed over time, partly due to changes in leadership and personnel and partly due to organizational reconfigurations and evolution. Ever since the WTO was created in 1995, some individuals and interest groups have viewed it as a natural home for matters concerning FDI. It was under the WTO's auspices, after all, that agreements on trade-related investment measures, trade-related intellectual property agreements, and the General Agreement on Trade in Services were hammered out and made practicable. An argument could be made that even under GATT, the enterprise's organizational framework, expertise, and conceptual overlap between trade and investment made it reasonable to suggest that it should have been given a broader mandate to include a greater focus on FDI, as the proponents of the aborted International Trade Organization had hoped.

However, since UNCTAD was created with the express purpose of helping developing countries, its proponents within the UN, primarily the G-77, could not let that happen. Whereas GATT was seen as a global institution with the mandate to facilitate trade by eliminating barriers and creating a more trade-friendly global economic environment, UNCTAD was seen as an advocate of developing countries.

Earlier we spoke of an ideological chasm within UNCTAD. It was inevitable that UNCTAD should either reinvent itself in concert with the exigencies of the time or be relegated to irrelevance or even doomed to extinction. A cursory comparison of UNCTAD's two flagship publications, namely the World Investment Reports and the Trade and Development Reports, reveals that the latter reflect a more tempered view of globalization. That is not to suggest that the World Investment Reports embrace all that is implied by globalization. Nevertheless, Trade and Development Reports tend to be more circumspect. Even the academic advisors to the investment and trade sides of the house had different world views. This also created a certain amount of internal tension that was evident in a number of other ways.[59] Peter Hansen observed such tensions inside the organization when he was negotiating the move to Geneva back in the early 1990s:

> When I was discussing the move to Geneva with Ken Dadzie . . . there was also some jealousy in UNCTAD that the Centre was on a roll, widely . . . respected as a research organization. I'm sure their economists thought that their research was better than ours.[60]

This important topic, which concerns both international organizations and other stakeholders, will be further elaborated in the concluding chapter. Given

the profound influence of the World Investment Report series—UNCTAD's
flagship publication on FDI and TNCs—in knowledge and information creation, capacity-building, and policy and institution-building, a detailed study of
that compendium is in order.

7

The World Investment Report Series: 1991–2007

- *Common Features*
- *Themes and Special Features*
- *Future Challenges*

The UNCTC and UNCTAD have contributed in many ways to a fuller and better understanding of the phenomena of foreign direct investment and transnational corporations as they relate to development. One of the more significant contributions has been the World Investment Report, begun in 1991 and published annually since.

The WIR is important for three reasons. First, it contains and examines data on the most significant trends, developments, and forms of international business activity of TNCs. Second, it analyzes key issues relating to the activities and role of FDI and TNCs in developing countries, focusing on a special topic or theme each year. Third, the series draws on work within the UN, canvassing the literature and extracting the most significant and relevant scholarly contributions on the relations between host countries and TNCs. The contribution of the series is also threefold: knowledge-creation, capacity-building, and policy analysis.

The literature on foreign direct investment and TNCs has mushroomed since the 1950s. The substance and development of this literature is inexorably intertwined with the intellectual legacy of ideas that have percolated through the United Nations system.

In 1989, Peter Hansen approved the publication of an annual report on FDI and TNCs modeled on the World Bank's World Development Report.[1] The UNCTC commissioned consultants to prepare a number of background papers on trends and issues. A team that included Karl P. Sauvant and others integrated three of these reports into a final product, the World Investment Report, which published its first issue in 1991.[2]

During the intervening years, scholars inside and outside the UN system formed an invisible college that became part of the core competency of the

Centre.[3] By assembling an impressive number of studies from experts in the field from around the world, this modestly endowed enterprise has proven to be very useful to academic, corporate, and governmental entities and individuals that engage in the study of FDI and TNCs. Indeed, one of the main contributions of the enterprise has been to act as a catalyst for scholarly research on TNCs and economic development.

This chapter examines the WIR series and its symbiotic relationship with other activities at UNCTAD. Embodying much of the large store of knowledge spawned at UNCTC and UNCTAD, the reports are interlinked with other works, which I will expand upon in Chapter 9. The interconnectedness between the World Investment Report and other UNCTAD activities is depicted in Figure 7.1, which can be found toward the end of this chapter.

Common Features

The origin of the World Investment Report is traceable to the historic 1973 report by the Group of Eminent Persons and the quinquennial reports on trends and developments in FDI and TNC activity UNCTC issued from 1978 to 1988. In 1990, directors of the enterprise decided to replace these reports with annual ones. By the time the first volume was published in 1991, knowledge about TNCs and economic development was increasing at a rapid rate. The World Investment Report attained maturity alongside the changes that were occurring in the late 1980s and early 1990s, both within the UN and in the global environment. More important, as it evolved, the series reflected the changing international mindset toward the role of TNCs, namely that they could and should be more effectively used to promote economic development through a variety of collaborative and positive-sum measures. The WIR's focus on the relationship between TNCs and FDI and economic development has always been at the heart of the series. Another common feature is that FDI is the focus, the pivot around which all else revolves. As the World Investment Report evolved in a changing global context, its authors were quick to recognize that FDI through TNCs could be an important factor in economic development. The 1992 report, *Transnational Corporations as Engines of Growth*, captured this notion early in the series.

Over time, the WIR broadened the domain of FDI-related issues to embrace other forms of corporate international economic involvement. Another common thread is the WIR's continuous monitoring of FDI policy; each report contains the latest and most important policy changes at national, regional, and international levels with respect to the overall FDI process and to policy developments directly relevant to the volume's theme. Other features common to all WIRs are:

- Collection and analysis of data and underlying themes and trends
- Explorations of global and regional trends in foreign direct investment, such as FDI stock, FDI flow in and out of major countries and regions, and key factors underlying FDI, including upswings or downturns in the world economy
- Analysis of global trends in international production
- Analysis of the significance of particular TNCs and their foreign affiliates by country of origin, industry, size, and other parameters
- Contemporary scholarly research on and review of major developments in FDI and TNCs
- Analysis of recent and emerging FDI-related policy developments at the corporate, national, and international levels
- Discussion of lessons learned and implications of trends for governments, particularly those of developing countries
- A separate *Executive Summary* begun in 1992 (renamed *Overview* in 1995) that includes charts and tables

Coverage of certain issues has become standard. These include analysis of trends in inward and outward stocks and flows of FDI, annual lists of the world's top 100 TNCs and the top fifty TNCs from developing countries, and statistics on the flow and stock of FDI and summaries of FDI policies of key countries. The underlying premise of the series has been not only that foreign direct investment is an important and growing form of international economic transactions but that it is a catalyst or complement to domestic investment in shaping economic restructuring and in development. The report consistently acknowledges that TNCs have made positive contributions to economic development but points out that maximizing their contribution and their absorptive and spillover effects, particularly to smaller and least-developed countries, remains a challenge.

Box 7.1. World Investment Reports, 1991–2007

1. *1991: The Triad in Foreign Direct Investment*
2. *1992: Transnational Corporations as Engines of Growth*
3. *1993: Transnational Corporations and Integrated International Production*
4. *1994: Transnational Corporations, Employment and the Workplace*
5. *1995: Transnational Corporations and Competitiveness*
6. *1996: Investment, Trade and International Policy Arrangements*
7. *1997: Transnational Corporations, Market Structure and Competition Policy*
8. *1998: Trends and Determinants*
9. *1999: Foreign Direct Investment and the Challenge of Development*

10. *2000: Cross-border Mergers and Acquisitions and Development*
11. *2001: Promoting Linkages*
12. *2002: Transnational Corporations and Export Competitiveness*
13. *2003: Foreign Direct Investment Policies for Development: National and International Perspectives*
14. *2004: The Shift towards Services*
15. *2005: Transnational Corporations and the Internationalization of Research and Development*
16. *2006: Foreign Direct Investment from Developing and Transition Economies: Implications for Development*
17. *2007: Transnational Corporations, Extractive Industries, and Development*
18. *2008: Transnational Corporations and the Infrastructure Challenge*

Seventeen World Investment Reports have been produced since 1991. Although the subtitle of each volume (see Box 7.1) describes the annual theme, other volumes contain information on that particular subject. For example, several volumes address competitiveness, social responsibility, mergers and acquisitions, and the geography of FDI.

The information in each volume is impressive, extensive, and to some extent original. As the centerpiece of UNCTAD's work on FDI and TNCs, the reports have a symbiotic relationship with a wide array of related activities. Figure 7.1 illustrates how the work of these entities connect to the WIR as well as the underlying organizational structure of the enterprise. UNCTAD's regular publication of the reports is creating a compendium of data on FDI and TNCs. (One prominent newspaper reporter has observed that UNCTAD has cornered the market on FDI.[4]) The data, which is augmented with case studies, annexes, and bibliographies, cover the entire gamut of topics related to FDI and TNCs. WIRs have culled existing scholarly knowledge and wisdom on important themes, adding the enterprise's own interpretation of the relevance of this scholarship to TNCs and economic development. Despite limited resources, the UNCTAD team has been able to maintain high standards and indeed to enhance its reputation as an unequalled source of data on TNCs and FDI. At the same time, the report's authors have recognized the inadequacies and imperfections of FDI data and have sought to refine it in collaboration with other sources that gather primary data, such as the International Monetary Fund and government agencies.

The volumes are unveiled with some fanfare. The release of the WIR has become somewhat of an annual ritual. Utilizing the "invisible college" and regional UN offices and agencies, press kits are customized for each region and advance copies are distributed but embargoed until the official launch date (the press is asked not to report on their contents before the embargo date and hour). These annual launches generate press reports around the world.[5] Simultaneous news conferences are held in major cities throughout the world with the assistance of local UN staff and any available collaborators. These news conferences have been increasingly successful, yielding press coverage and thereby disseminating WIR findings worldwide.

It is impossible to sum up the series—which is encyclopedic—without running the risk of omitting key ideas and findings. Nevertheless, in line with the underlying theme of this book, a look at the contributions of the series to knowledge creation, capacity-building, and policy analysis is warranted.

Synergy between WIRs and Other UN Activities

Each WIR contains summaries of other UNCTAD activities relevant to TNCs and FDI. These can be classified into three types: legal studies, analysis, and data. Legal studies include the division's work on international investment agreements and bilateral investment treaties as well as its ongoing monitoring of legal developments in host countries (and to a lesser extent in home countries) and the impact of such developments on FDI and other TNC activities. These studies are undertaken by the staff of the enterprise with the assistance of outside consultants (often from the country under review) and with financial assistance from the UN Development Fund administered by UNDP. Included also are country investment guides that are produced by UNCTAD to help promote inward FDI, activities of the World Association of Investment Promotion Agencies on investment promotion, and ongoing relevant work in other agencies such as the ILO, the WTO, and the World Bank. Each report also refers to organizations outside the UN orbit, primarily the OECD and the ICC, both of which conduct their own research on the subject. The FIAS, a unit of the World Bank, conducts a diagnostic analysis of countries' investment climates.[6] Unlike UNCTAD's investment policy reviews, FIAS reports are confidential and hence less likely to be politically sanitized. Summaries of such activities by other international organizations are often contained in WIRs.

Themes and Special Features

The themes of WIRs fall into three broad categories. Some are policy oriented, dealing with issues such as the relationship between FDI and competitiveness, employment, or exports. Others cover technical issues such as mergers and acquisitions, research and development, or the internationalization of production. A third category covers trends by country, region, or industry. Since most topics are time sensitive, they may be revisited and updated in later years. The inaugural issue in 1991, for example, mapped out the geography of FDI by highlighting the dominant position of three entities (the United States, the European Community, and Japan) as both suppliers and receivers of FDI. Seven years later, the 1998 WIR contained an update of trends and examined prospects. Similarly the 1999 WIR revisited the interplay of FDI and the challenge of development, a subject the 1992 WIR had addressed.

Some themes have focused on specific issues. World events have undoubtedly played a part in the selection of the theme and the manner of its treatment. For example, as the inaugural issue was in preparation, the Berlin Wall crumbled and the Soviet Union collapsed; uncertainty was in the air. The UNCTC chose the geography of FDI as its theme in its first volume,[7] limiting its analysis to facts.

As the globalization of manufacturing gained greater momentum, the 1993 WIR contained an extensive analysis of the theme of "integrated international production." It was the first volume to claim a place in scholarship by developing and elaborating on this concept as a meaningful measure of cross-national integration of production via FDI.[8]

The series has introduced a number of concepts and ideas helpful to understanding TNC–host country relations and the development process. The conceptual contributions of WIRs have been numerous, and those reported below are meant to serve as examples. The series has also developed a number of special tables, including lists and rankings of the largest TNCs and host countries, the latter based on indices that measure countries' performance and potential with respect to FDI.

The Geography of FDI: The Triad

The 1991 WIR focused on the triad—the United States, the European Community, and Japan and their respective economic partners, mapping the size and direction of FDI between the world's main economic blocs. It presented data to demonstrate the relative balance of FDI inflows and outflows between Western Europe and North America and, by contrast, the dominance of outflows over inflows for Japan. It also focused on the increasing importance of FDI as a mode of international expansion for TNCs. Whereas the concept of the triad predates the WIRs,[9] the 1991 report expanded upon it with detailed data on FDI and TNCs and was clear and precise with respect to foreign investment.

TNCs and Growth

The *World Investment Report 1992* explored TNCs as engines of growth against the background of major new developments in the global economy, such as the enhanced role of private enterprise, major technological breakthroughs, the continued globalization of firms and industries, the ascendancy of the service sector, and the trend toward regionalization of markets.

This volume examined the role of FDI in economic growth and development in an era of increased liberalization, when incentives replaced restrictions and nationalization and expropriation gave way to privatization. It discussed the extent to which TNCs serve as engines of growth through their potential contributions to capital formation, technology transfer, trade, human resource development, and the environment. These five dimensions of TNCs' potential contributions to the development process were well articulated, documented, and graphed.

An informative table summarized the main regulatory changes in investment regimes in host countries in 1991, illustrating that virtually all countries were moving toward a more liberal and FDI-friendly regime.[10] This finding highlighted the trend of the early 1990s, which had begun a decade earlier with the move toward liberalizing trade and investment regimes and lowering barriers to FDI.

Global Manufacturing and TNCs

The theme of *World Investment Report 1993* was integrated international production. The volume provided both documentation and analysis of how the globalization of production has brought about integrated production systems. It included a study of the complex set of parent-subsidiary relationships. This theme was revisited in 2005 with a new focus on the internationalization of research and development. During the intervening years, the international diffusion of technology had accelerated and several emerging markets had become not merely recipients of imported technology but players at the table. This point was further accentuated in the 2006 WIR, which scrutinized the new breed of TNCs from developing and emerging markets.

The 1993 WIR presented a table of the top 100 TNCs for the first time. This became a standard feature of the series, securing a place alongside lists in *Business Week, Financial Times, Forbes Magazine,* and *Fortune Magazine.* The list ranked TNCs by foreign assets and provided information on their sales and employment.

TNCs and Employment

The theme of *World Investment Report 1994* was employment and the workplace. It included discussion of human resource development, the approach of trade unions to international production, corporate social responsibility, and government policies relevant to employment and the workplace. A detailed analysis of the controversy surrounding the contribution of TNCs to job creation and employment yielded no definitive answers. The report acknowledged that TNCs' use of capital-deepening and labor-saving technologies meant fewer TNC-generated jobs. But it also pointed out that the jobs TNCs created tended to be qualitatively better, both in terms of working conditions and human resource development. As a result, countries courted TNCs by liberalizing investment laws, hoping that their entry would generate new employment opportunities.

The identification of TNCs as engines of growth in the 1992 WIR allowed the 1994 report to illustrate the breadth of their role in global production, employment, and trade. The *World Investment Report 1994* highlighted the role of TNCs in accelerating the pace of integrated international production. It pointed out that TNCs accounted for two-thirds of world trade in the mid-1990s, about half of which was between affiliates of the same firm. The report documented another trend: how emerging economies were becoming more integrated into the global economy through aggressive participation in the globally integrated production and distribution system. Examples were transnational corporations such as Acer, Samsung, and LG Industries, which came from newly industrialized and emerging economies.

The report asked how governments could achieve a competitive edge with respect to FDI through human resource development policies and how they could attract TNCs that might substantially contribute to further development of these policies beyond minimum requirements.

TNCs and Competition

By the time the *World Investment Report 1995* was published, the terms "competitiveness" and "globalization" had become buzzwords of the decade. Even the way the term "competitiveness" was measured had become competitive, exemplified by the split between the World Economic Forum and the Institute of Management Development in Lausanne, hitherto collaborators on the annual World Competitiveness Report series.[11]

The 1995 WIR examined how TNC operations and their linkages with domestic firms affect a country's overall economic performance. It published the finding that national competitiveness increasingly depends on links with the rest of the world but which, in turn, hinged on the extent to which TNCs helped countries integrate into the global market, through FDI and nonequity arrangements. The emphasis on maximizing benefits from TNCs was a turning point of sorts for the series; earlier reports had emphasized curtailing the negative effects of TNCs.

The 1995 report also covered outward FDI from developing countries and transition economies, a new and increasingly important phenomenon. This theme was revisited a decade later when the 2006 WIR focused on TNCs from developing countries and provided data on outward FDI from key developing countries that had begun to distance themselves from other developing countries, particularly the least developed countries. The 1995 WIR also introduced a new feature—a table of the top fifty TNCs based in developing countries.

Investment, Trade, and International Policy

The *World Investment Report 1996* came on the heels of the ratification of the Uruguay Round and the establishment of the WTO. It was appropriate that this issue concentrated on the interplay between trade and investment. From the standpoint of traditional economic theory, trade and FDI do not overlap a great deal (except in product life cycle theory). Comparative advantage, the mainstay of trade theory, applies only to trade, and even the Heckscher-Ohlin model and its subsequent refinements dealt only with trade. FDI had generated its own set of theories. The 1996 WIR attempted to bridge the analytical gap between trade and FDI, not through groundbreaking theory, which was outside its scope, but by empirically demonstrating the interlocking relationship between them.

The report explored the idea of a multilateral set of rules of engagement for FDI, an idea that had undergone several reincarnations since originally proposed as a code of conduct in 1974. It speculated on two possible routes toward such rules. One route was deepening and widening existing multilateral agreements so they would organically evolve into a comprehensive FDI regime. The other route would be to negotiate a new comprehensive multilateral framework for FDI.

As the *World Investment Report 1999* later noted, the political climate had changed with the emergence of a backlash against globalization, and the debate had deteriorated from the technical to the political. No less than thirteen substantive issues remained unresolved. The very definition of "investment" became a contentious matter during the Multilateral Agreement on Investments negotiations.[12] Meanwhile, bilateral and regional accords proliferated while the trend toward liberalization continued and hopes for a multilateral regime faded.[13]

TNCs, Market Structure, and Competition

The *World Investment Report* 1997 focused on market structure and competition, expanding on the themes of the two previous years. One of the methodological contributions of the 1997 WIR was a brief discussion of how to estimate "real" FDI; this was intended to address criticism of the WIRs' FDI data. The 1992 WIR had recognized some imperfections in its data;[14] indeed, collecting reliable data has remained a major challenge for the series. The many obstacles include the lack of transparency in equal measure across countries, differences in measurement, and other problems familiar to empirical research at the international level. The quality of data has consistently improved over time because of two factors: the accumulated skill, experience, and perseverance of enterprise staff, and capacity-building within the UN system. As statistics became increasingly more precise and reliable, the WIR became a major reference for FDI-related data. Many private consulting firms rely on UNCTAD's data, which they repackage and sell to their corporate clients.[15]

The report predicted that ensuring that markets functioned efficiently by setting policies regarding competition would become even more important as countries liberalized their FDI policies.

Trends and Determinants of Foreign Direct Investment

In the first half of the 1990s, privatization grew and nationalization declined. Countries that were emerging from the Soviet orbit as well as developing countries sought to infuse technology and capital into their ailing economies while reducing the burden of subsidizing inefficient and politically driven public sector enterprises. The 1993 WIR documented these trends. By 1997, when the Asian currency crisis erupted, other trends had overshadowed this optimism. The 1998 WIR thus took a broader view than the earlier volumes in the series.

The report contended that in years to come, a new configuration of "locational determinants"—human resources, infrastructure, market access, technology, innovative capacity, and "created assets"[16]—would be most attractive to potential foreign investors. The 1998 WIR placed the main responsibility for attracting FDI on host countries.

In its consideration of the Asian economic crisis that had hit several countries in 1997, the 1998 WIR noted that FDI had proven to be more stable and less subject to the effects of this crisis than other private capital flows. While the crisis had improved the cost competitiveness of some countries in the region, some exports had suffered. This was illustrated by case studies of production at Toyota and Honda, export operations in Thailand and Malaysia, and the impact of the Asian financial crisis on Japanese outward FDI.

Foreign Direct Investment and the Development Challenge

Whereas most volumes in the series address specific themes, occasionally the full spectrum has been embraced, as in the case of the *World Investment Report 1999*. It covered the entire landscape of FDI and TNCs and is the longest in the series to date. Its theme was the relationship between FDI and development, a broad topic and one that is central to UNCTAD's mandate. The report expounded on different dimensions of the *problematique:*

- The development of networked oligopolies in the information technology sector
- How to increase financial resources and investment
- How to enhance technological capabilities
- How to increase export competitiveness
- How to generate employment and strengthen the skill base
- How to protect of the environment
- Ways to assess FDI and development in the new competitive context

It then noted four types of challenges developing countries faced:

- Information and coordination failures in the international investment process
- Consideration of infant industries as local enterprises develop so that inward FDI did not crowd them out
- The fact that TNCs offer static advantages when domestic capabilities are low or fail to improve over time or when there is insufficient foreign investment to raise relevant capabilities
- The weak bargaining position and weak regulatory capacity of host-country governments, which can result in unequal distribution of benefits or abuse of market power by TNCs[17]

The 1999 WIR also dealt with the important issue of how to define the corporate social responsibility of transnational corporations and the role of civil society and governments and codes and guidelines in this endeavor. It provided case studies on Royal Dutch/Shell and Mattel to illustrate how various TNCs were approaching this issue.

Mergers and Acquisitions and Development

The theme of the *World Investment Report 2000*, mergers and acquisitions, was timely and more informative and interesting than some earlier volumes. Many of its findings were based on original in-house research that was conducted to provide to a deeper understanding of the recent spate of mergers and acquisitions.

The United Kingdom retained its position as the largest investor in 2000, aided by the UK company Vodafone AirTouch's acquisition of Mannesmann (Germany) and the acquisition of the Atlantic Richfield Company (United States) by BP (UK). In general, investments by European firms in the United States increased through megamergers in 2000.[18]

Foreign Direct Investment and Linkages

The *World Investment Report 2001* explored the well-established theme of linkages that had been articulated by earlier scholars such as Thorstein Veblen, W. W. Rostow, W. Arthur Lewis, and Simon Kuznets. These scholars had argued that development and industrialization cannot occur in isolation and that latecomers must hitch their wagons to forerunners if they are to develop a modern economy.[19] Developing countries may not be able to bypass all of the time-consuming steps toward modernization, but they can shorten the gestation period by linking their nascent industries to more-established global giants.

This volume addressed the role of linkages in maximizing benefits from the bundle of assets that accompany FDI—capital, technology, skills, and market access—thus creating increased income, employment, and domestic capital formation for host countries.

This volume reaffirmed that the impact of inward FDI depends, in part, on the extent to which foreign affiliates establish linkages with local enterprises and integrate into the local economy. It explored promoting more, and deeper, backward linkages between foreign affiliates and local suppliers. It discussed policies that countries might pursue by looking at measures that have been successful and options that deserved special attention, such as Singapore's "local industry upgrading," Welsh Development Agency's "Source Wales," and Malaysia and Ireland's national linkage development programs.

Transnational Corporations and Export Competitiveness

The *World Investment Report 2002* examined the role of TNCs in export competitiveness, reflecting the continuing maturity of many host countries and implying that the ability of a country to export is a litmus test of the impact of FDI and TNC entry on development. This notion entails a sophisticated approach to the relationship between firms and nation-states, as it acknowledges the primacy of the firm as a potential exporter. Nations do not export; firms do. Yet nations set and enforce rules by which importers and exporters must abide. This report also drew attention to the symbiotic relationship between development and competitiveness. This link is important to emphasize, for much of the literature on competitiveness, led by Michael Porter, tends to focus on competitiveness at the level of the firm, occasionally causing a "level-of-analysis" problem.[20]

National and International Policies

The *World Investment Report* 2003 returned to the arena of policy. FDI had fallen for a second year even as the liberalizing trend regarding FDI continued. It was time to investigate the policy environment. The report found that even though FDI was falling globally, not all receiving countries were impacted equally. Whereas such a conclusion can be intuitively obvious, the report identified winners and losers and—more critically—the underlying reasons for their success or failure. Do countries pursue aggressive liberalization policies simply to attract FDI or are these policy changes a subset of a larger and more systemic change at the macroeconomic policy level? The conventional FDI literature tells us that FDI policies do not take place in a vacuum but are a part and parcel of broader economic policies.

The Shift toward Services

The theme of the *World Investment Report* 2004 was another emerging issue— the increasing growth of FDI in service industries. Services accounted for the largest share of FDI worldwide and in developed and developing countries. The most dramatic growth of FDI stock was not in the traditional services such as banking, accounting, and transportation but in electricity, telecommunications, and water services; the cumulative value of the stock of FDI in services was over 60 percent of the total $4.4 trillion. This growth had exceeded the growth in trade, which itself had consistently outpaced aggregate world economic growth.

The Internationalization of Research and Development

The *World Investment Report* 2005 dealt with the internationalization of research and development and the impact of this trend on development. It addressed the international diffusion of technology, the pivotal role TNCs played as the major drivers of internationalization, alternative policy responses available to host countries, and the international policy framework. The report noted that research and development had become a candidate for off-shoring but that only a few developing and emerging countries were active players in this arena. Both push (increasing costs) and pull (availability of alternatives) forces were driving this process. The report argued that if host developing countries took advantage of the opportunity to participate in the global research and development systems of TNCs, it would open the door not only to transfer of technologies developed elsewhere but also to the technology creation process itself. They could engage in targeted investment promotion and the establishment of science and technology parks.

TNCs from Developing and Transition Economies

The 2006 report spotlighted the new breed of TNCs—those based in developing countries. The theme of *World Investment Report 2006* was *FDI from Developing and Transition Economies: Implications for Development*. It noted that whereas FDI from developing countries still accounted for less than 15 percent of world FDI and its share had not gone up significantly over the previous decade or so, a few developing countries were becoming serious players, investing $117 billion outside their borders in 2005. A number of TNCs from selected developing economies were emerging as major actors on the world stage, and they were here to stay. This is a significant change in the global economy and will have substantial consequences for international economic and political relations. TNCs are seeking to improve their competitiveness by expanding in the fast-growing markets of emerging economies and seeking new ways to reduce costs, and a few firms based in developing countries are becoming increasingly attractive partners. These Third World TNCs are multiplying rapidly, and many of them are competing and cooperating with their more traditional counterparts in much the same way. It is noteworthy that many of these firms were based in countries with a high FDI potential, high FDI performance, and a high innovation capability index.

Whereas the last few volumes are, on the whole, bearers of good news for a few developing and emerging economies, not all was rosy for transnational corporations. Over the years, the overwhelming majority of policy changes in the FDI regimes of host countries have been in the direction of more liberalization, but the 2006 report detects somewhat of a reversal of this trend. While most changes in 2005 favored greater liberalization, the number of policy changes unfavorable to FDI went from four in 2000 to forty-one in 2006. One can argue that liberalization of FDI regimes has gone about as far as it can and that a measure of skepticism is beginning to moderate that trend. One can also argue that this portends disturbance ahead. Subsequent volumes dealt with extractive industries (WIR07) and infrastructure (WIR08).

On the Whole

The contribution of the WIR series in its first eighteen years is clear. The series has contributed to knowledge through conceptualizing about FDI and by assembling and refining data on FDI gathered through surveys conducted by staff as they interface with government officials and other guardians or generators of data, data collected by consultants, and data drawn from case studies or other projects. As WIR editors have become more confident about conducting their own independent research, surveys conducted by in-house researchers have become increasingly popular. In later years, the editors have sent questionnaires to TNCs soliciting their views on a variety of issues ranging from the investment climate to changes in mergers and acquisitions activities, determinants of research and development expenditures, and locations.

Given the diversity of circumstances, the series has avoided issuing boilerplate prescriptions on how to attract and benefit from FDI. Instead, the reports have laid out policy options and the associated strategies and risks to enable developing countries to adjust and fine tune their policies within the existing global context. The WIR's policy analysis has consistently addressed the various implications of globalization for developing countries. Early identification of trends and policy options put WIR ahead of the curve much of the time.

Future Challenges

Seventeen years is relatively long in the life of a UN publication series. Over this time, the World Investment Report series improved in quality, accuracy, and relevance, each volume building on the strength of the previous one. They have become more widely used by practitioners, academics, and governments. The material has been used in classrooms and in textbooks. The series is used in graduate and executive training programs. Perhaps most important from the viewpoint of its editors and contributors is the impact the reports have had on host developing countries' policies with respect to FDI.

From the outset, this series has had two objectives, to document and analyze trends in foreign direct investment and transnational corporations and to examine key issues of relevance to developing countries. Although each WIR can stand alone, each also builds on the work of prior years, producing a cumulative body of knowledge. The series has also broken new ground in terms of statistics, new concepts, and ideas.

Impact on Other Literature

Many of the findings, tables, graphs, case studies, and other analyses in the series have been used in other publications. An examination of a dozen international business and management texts revealed that most of them make some use of WIR charts and data. Some of these textbooks provide links to

UNCTAD's Web site, where there is a wealth of information.[21] Less is known about the extent to which the series inspire analysis. The international press also has used the information published in WIRs to update readers on foreign investment issues and related matters.[22]

A survey of academic reviews of the various WIRs reveals that the series is being noted with increasing frequency by academic publications and reviewers have generally been quite positive. Private organizations regularly incorporate the quantitative data contained in WIRs into their own proprietary databases. Although it is difficult to track such citations, these reports have found a useful place alongside the resources of the WTO, the IMF, and the World Bank as a primary source of economic data.

Reviews of WIRs

The WIRs have multiple constituents. The primary constituent is governments, but TNCs, members of academia, the media, research organizations, civil society groups, and the United Nations system itself also use them; each of these entities has unique needs for information. The greatest difference perhaps is between the needs of policymakers and academic audiences. This dichotomy is not merely academic; even within the United Nations, there is occasional rumbling that the WIRs are not sufficiently scholarly. For policy-oriented readers, on the other hand, they may appear too academic. The "Overview" section of each report remedies this problem to some extent. Executives and policymakers can learn much about strategy from reading the text, case studies, and tables.

Some reviews have criticized WIRs for heavily reflecting the views of TNCs and for promoting FDI,[23] while others fault the series for advocating the agenda of developing countries. Still others suspect the series to be an instrument of international civil servants who want to establish a WTO-like bureaucracy on investment.

Although some make suggestions for improvement, academic reviews of WIRs have been generally complimentary. For example, the late Raymond Vernon wrote:

> The series of reports has earned a reputation for evenhandedness and objectivity in the pursuit of the ticklish question of the costs and benefits of foreign direct investment. From the first, it has been the product of the entrepreneurship and planning of Karl P. Sauvant, who has drawn his analytical support not only from the UNCTAD staff but also from a global network of scholars.[24]

Other positive reviewers such as H. Peter Gray have made constructive comments. For instance, Gray noted in his review of the 1998 WIR that the concept of TNC transnationality, while interesting, raised questions. Since it was partly based on the ratio of foreign to total assets and assets are measured by book value of physical assets, the value of technology-intensive firms whose balance sheet asset values are underpriced may be distorted in the transnationality index in favor of the company's home-country assets.[25] However, underpricing of assets should not make a difference because both the numerator and denominator will be affected unless underpricing applies only to the values of assets abroad. Other reviewers such as Loraine Eden have pointed out measurement deficiencies.[26]

Contributions to Knowledge

The most traceable impact of the series has been in knowledge creation, ranging from conceptualization and analysis to data-gathering and measurement. The reports have been innovative in their introduction of new concepts and terminology as well as in making further refinements to existing concepts.

The geography of FDI: Although the concept of the triad was not new, the reports' measurement of the relative and absolute flows of FDI between triad members added precision. The initial work on the geographic aspects of FDI in the 1991 WIR was followed in several volumes.

Integrated international production: By identifying details of integrated international production within TNCs, the reports added to our understanding of this aspect of globalization. The concept was first introduced in the 1993 WIR and was revisited and elaborated upon in various later issues.

Linkages: On more than one occasion but explicitly in the 2001 WIR, the concept of linkages was given detailed treatment. Conclusions and recommendations pointed to the responsibilities of both TNCs and host countries. TNCs need to engage local firms more aggressively, while host countries need to enhance their capacity to absorb technology.

Privileged access: Access to corporate resources TNCs grant to their affiliates by virtue of ownership and management ties and the preferential access these firms grant to suppliers creates an uneven playing field tilted in favor of these affiliates. This in turn entails policy implications for nation-states and strategic policy implications for firms.

Corporate Social Responsibility (CSR): Several issues have encouraged TNCs to integrate CSR into their practices and have encouraged host countries to insert CSR provisions into investment agreements.

Sequential and associated FDI: The focus of the series on development drew attention to the importance of additional investments after the initial investment. Such supplemental investments are made to upgrade, augment, and render more efficient the initial investment that may have been prompted by host-country initiatives such as privatization. The series repeatedly emphasized that conditions in the host country determine the extent to which initial investment may be followed by such sequential investments.

Contestability of markets: This is another concept that the series introduced or adapted to the area of FDI. It refers to conditions under which a global market exists for firms as targets of acquisition in mergers and acquisitions. A market that is created as a consequence of liberalization policies in different countries allows acquiring firms to bid openly for the local firm being sold through privatization or otherwise and will therefore maximize the value of the firm being acquired.

Investment-related trade measures: Inspired by the WTO's trade-related investment measures, the term investment-related trade measures is used in the series to denote the impact of trade-enhancing or trade-curtailing measures on investment and location decisions.

Indices: The WIRs have introduced a number of concepts, including the index of transnationality of firms (TNI) and, in the 2000 WIR, the index of transnationality of countries. In the 2002 WIR, a new concept was added to the list of concepts and phrases—namely, the index of FDI potential (as opposed to an index of FDI performance). The index of inward FDI performance is based on a country's share of world FDI relative to its share of world GDP, while the index of inward FDI potential is an unweighted average of some twelve variables that include growth rate, exports, and expenditures for research and development. The WIRs offer a two-by-two matrix that divides countries into four groups—those with high performance and high potential, those with high performance and low potential, those with low performance and high potential, and those with low performance and low potential. Those with the highest potential and lowest performance need to take heed.[27] Countries high in both potential and performance seem to be more fully integrated into the global economy.

All these innovative measures and indices can increase our understanding of the depth and breadth of globalization. Moreover, they show the extent to which various host developing countries have internationalized their economies. These are useful as analytical tools, as are Transparency International's corruption perception index, the World Competitiveness Forum and Institute of Management Development's respective competitiveness indices, the Heritage Foundation's economic freedom index, and A. T. Kearney/*Foreign Policy*'s globalization index, to name a few. All are useful aggregates.

The series has tried to straddle the line between the academic and policy arenas. As with all such cases, this in-between position has two sides. The series can speak to a wider range of audiences once they are exposed to it. It can also be dismissed by purists, or simply overlooked, for not being sufficiently "academic."

One of the tasks that remains to be accomplished in future issues is the addition of an index by author and subject. Such an addition would help readers navigate through the book-size volumes.

Tracking Policy Developments

By continuously chronicling, monitoring, and summarizing FDI policy developments at national, regional, and international levels, the reports have enabled readers to study, compare, refine, or strategize in a more informed manner. FDI-related policy developments in China are an example.[28] The tracking of other policy issues such as the aborted multilateral agreement on investment, multilateral trade negotiations under the WTO and their impact on FDI, regulatory changes in developing countries with respect to FDI, and policy aspects of particular countries that draw upon UNCTAD's investment policy reviews all exemplify the proclivity of the series toward policy. Straddling the line between a laissez-faire approach to economic activity and an approach that advocates complete government control over such activity, the series and the enterprise that generates it tend to take a middle-of-the-road position, not unlike the conventional wisdom articulated by Robert Wade,[29] the World Bank,[30] and John Dunning, among many others: markets need to be governed, and sometimes the multilateral solution is preferable to unilateral or even regional arrangements, since multilateral treaties provide a better opportunity to create a level playing field for all while giving preferential treatment to the few that deserve and need it. The WIRs have thus exhibited a bias toward some form of multilateral, equitable, and transparent accord and, in any case, for rules of engagement that can serve as guideposts. Throughout its existence, the series has held a mirror to the world, reflecting the realities of the changing global economy and the foreign investment within it. The series has been concerned with how policymakers can capture the benefits of foreign investment to enhance their countries' economic development. Its comprehensive and ongoing review of policy developments is valuable and serves as a historical record as well as a guide for latecomers.

Over time, corporate strategists, government decision makers involved in international economic and investment policies, and scholars have followed the dynamics of global strategy and the business environment presented in the WIR series. The United Nations in general and UNCTAD in particular has had a bias toward development, and the WIRs are meant to guide policy in de-

Figure 7.1 The WIR Series: Linkages with other UNCTAD Activities[1]

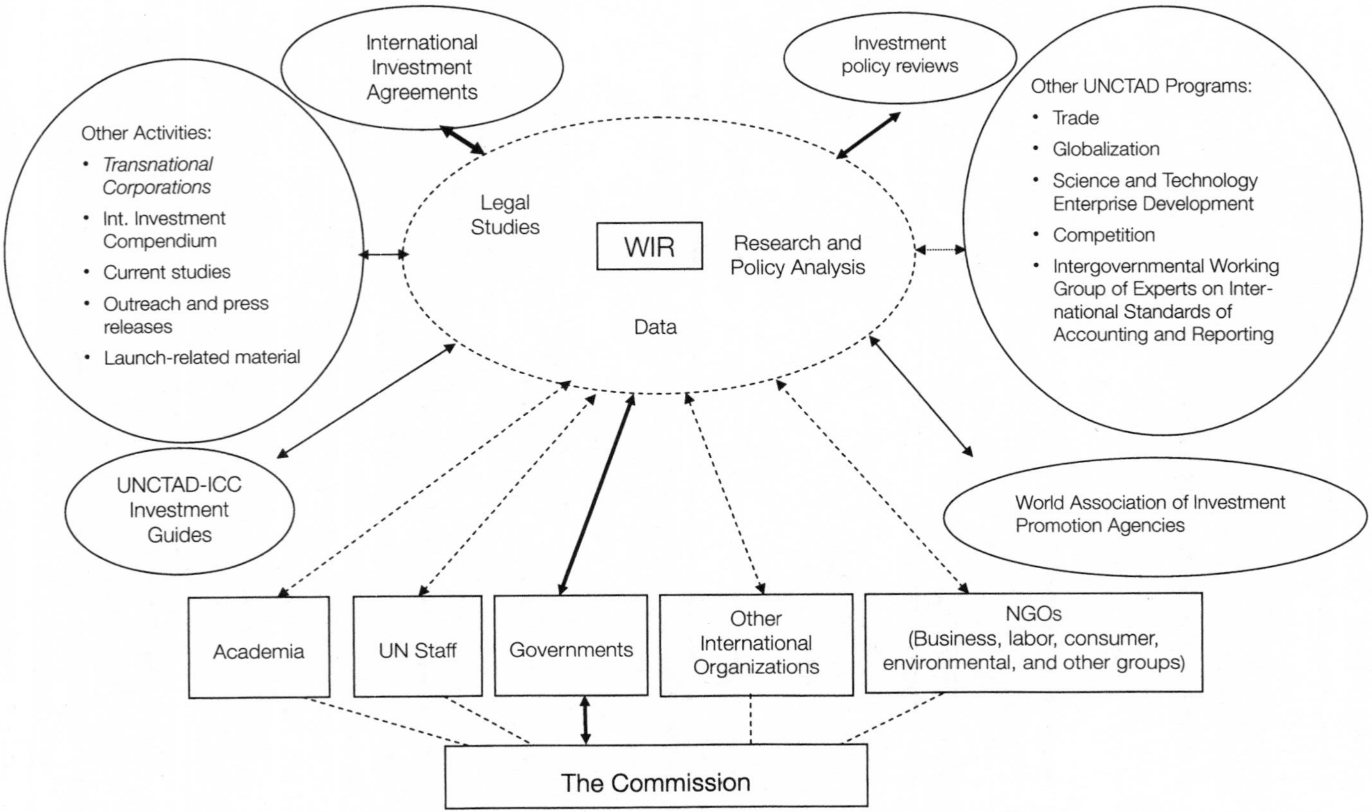

Other UNCTAD Programs:
- Trade
- Globalization
- Science and Technology
- Enterprise Development
- Competition
- Intergovernmental Working Group of Experts on International Standards of Accounting and Reporting

Investment policy reviews

World Association of Investment Promotion Agencies

International Investment Agreements

WIR

Research and Policy Analysis

Data

Legal Studies

Other Activities:
- *Transnational Corporations*
- Int. Investment Compendium
- Current studies
- Outreach and press releases
- Launch-related material

UNCTAD-ICC Investment Guides

NGOs (Business, labor, consumer, environmental, and other groups)

Other International Organizations

Governments

UN Staff

Academia

The Commission

1. Explanation of the figure: As the central intellectual output of the enterprise, the WIR series relates to a number of other activities. Legal studies cover a variety of issues dealing with the legal aspect of FDI and TNCs.

The lines drawn between the contents of the WIRs and other activities signify the intensity of mutual relations. Thus, international investment agreements and WIRs have a symbiotic relationship, as does the World Association of Investment Promotion Agencies and LDC investment guides and investment policy reviews and other publications. Some of the findings contained in one publication may find their way into the other, thus multiplying the distributional and educational benefits. Underlying the production of each WIR is a variety of groups, each with a distinct role. Thus, academics serve as consultants, giving ideas, text, and feedback, while governments provide data and use the publication for their own policy purposes. Staff members at other UN and non-UN international organizations are both consumers of the series as well as contributors to them, as are nongovernmental organizations. The entire series is officially mandated, sanctioned, and authorized by the commission, which consists of member states, and to which the division reports as its governing body.

veloping countries. Its lists of the world's largest TNCs are valuable. The continuous monitoring and documenting of trends—some dramatic, others mundane or gradual—is another important contribution.

The entire series, including full texts and the "Overviews" were put in English on a single CD-ROM. Other languages, such as Spanish, French, Russian, Arabic, and Chinese, are gradually being made available. Executive summaries in some of these languages have been posted on the WIR link on the UNCTAD Web site.

One problem of the series has been the progressive bulk of the reports; they had already quadrupled in size by 1995, and four years later, the 1999 WIR was some 500 pages long. This caused a gradual price rise, and the increased weight made it difficult for readers, including students whose professors used it as a supplementary text.[31] A remedy was to publish an overview separately in a concise pamphlet. These pamphlets, which consist of an executive summary, the volume's table of contents, and some important tables and charts, were welcome and helped disseminate major results more widely.

A more serious challenge facing the series is the inconsistency and lack of reliability of some data.[32] Government-generated data may be exaggerated or inaccurate in that they report investment projects that have been approved but not actually implemented. Since data are aggregated from individual investment projects, missing data cannot be included, causing FDI to be underreported. Even so, governments are the most important source of FDI information in the World Investment Reports. Another issue is that despite meticulous care, errors do occur. Some of the largest Third World TNCs are missing from the WIR list. As the series becomes better known, its data will improve in accuracy. In the meantime, despite its shortcomings, the WIR series is the best that can be had, and UNCTAD, its custodian, has developed the institutional capacity to sustain and nurture it.

It is apparent that the WIR's architects and editors are both leaders and followers of trends. The series follows the realities of the world, but its editors and contributors also devise new concepts. The series has established itself as the primary source in the field and is future oriented. The theme of the 2001 WIR is linkages, both backward and forward. The series had already covered TNCs as engines of growth, competitiveness, employment, and development. Delving deeper into the linkages between FDI and host development, while not an original idea, was nonetheless important and provided an opportunity for deeper analysis. Such analysis was also undertaken in the 2005 and 2006 WIRs, proving the timeliness of certain topics and the need to revisit particular themes. Meanwhile, persistent problems of poverty, disease, security, international migration, and the contending forces of globalization compel the

United Nations to continuously monitor the intellectual and policy landscapes, lest it be blindsided by challenges it has failed to detect.

Major issues that would be useful to cover in future WIRs include:

- The Internet and its impact on TNC strategies and host-country policies
- Third World TNCs, especially the new breed of transnational corporations from developing countries[33]
- Social responsibility and corporate ethics, which have been addressed repeatedly but need continued monitoring
- Transparency of firms and nations regarding policies and practices that impact FDI flows
- Understanding and mitigating risk from the perspective of the firm and the state
- The increasing international mobility of labor and its impact on national policies and corporate strategies
- The role of nongovernmental organizations in the areas of TNCs and FDI
- The trade-off between national autonomy and global interdependence

Some of these themes have indeed been covered in prior issues, but new information warrants a periodic revisiting of key issues, while new challenges will dictate themes for further exploration.

In the increasingly competitive world economy in which the focus is shifting to competitiveness and liberalization, striking the proper balance between enlightened control and overly restrictive policies is complex and challenging. Neither blind faith in the invisible hand nor excessive control rooted in xenophobia will yield an optimal and socially desirable outcome. The WIR series has provided policymakers ample information to guide policy. For scholars, the issues treated by this series are the mainstay of the interaction between the fields of development, international business, and management. Equally important, assembling and analyzing data provides critical nourishment for all readers; they can learn from the past and peer into the future to better understand this increasingly significant area of internationalization of firms, economic activity, and national economies.

The series, in spite of its shortcomings, remains indispensable to international business practitioners and corporate executives who make daily decisions on global operations and strategies, to government officials involved in economic policy formulation and implementation, and to academicians studying international economic issues.

8

Other Members of the UN Galaxy: The Constellation

- *The International Labour Organization*
- *The World Health Organization*
- *Others in the UN Galaxy*
- *The UN Global Compact*
- *Conclusion*

With respect to TNC-host country relations and particularly FDI and the related subject of corporate conduct, two competing institutional paradigms have persisted—one legalistic, the other moralistic. Followers of the legalistic approach have argued that in order to be effective, rules of conduct and behavior must have legal teeth. Moralists, on the other hand, have relied on less formal concepts to create incentive structures, such as mutual benefit, good citizenship, corporate social responsibility, engagement, and dialogue.

The UNCTC and UNCTAD in New York and Geneva have formed a pivotal axis for UN activities on TNCs. However, other UN agencies have played specific and often significant roles. These various agencies have also contributed to our knowledge of TNCs and FDI and have contemplated the relative merits of the legalistic and moralistic alternatives as they discharge their respective duties and add value within their particular mandates. To fully comprehend the magnitude of the system's role in enhancing the understanding about TNCs, a brief review of the pertinent constituent agencies is necessary. If a global compact, accord, convention, or set of rules of engagement for TNC activity is ever to emerge, it will most likely be a result of the confluence of these seemingly disparate efforts.

This chapter surveys TNC-related work undertaken by agencies other than the UNCTC or UNCTAD. Each of the UN entities has left its own indelible mark, reflective of its own mission and culture. Some have seen their relations vis-à-vis TNCs as a practical one; others have been driven by advocacy. A glance at the agenda of each reveals differences in approach, strategy, and tactics but also continuity at the systemic level.

Within the UN system, some thirty UN agencies touch on the activities of TNCs. Nearly a dozen have a more intense interest in TNC and FDI matters, forming what we will refer to as the UN galaxy. Each member of this system has, in some way or other, contributed to our understanding of the interaction between TNCs and their host countries. However, the exact nature of the interface between these agencies and TNCs depends on three contextual parameters—stakeholders, issues, and time. By virtue of its mandate, each agency deals with a set of discrete issues that necessitates certain stakeholders' involvement. For example, pharmaceutical TNCs are more likely to have a stake in health initiatives designed and implemented by the World Health Organization than, say, TNCs in the information and entertainment services, which would likely have a greater stake in policies that impact transborder data flows and information services.

Time, the third element, impacts the relationship between TNCs and host countries and the role each UN agency plays because the actors, issues, agenda, and overall tone and tenor change with time. In addition, interorganizational dynamics and interests may have an impact on policies that emerge from each agency.

After reviewing the roles of a certain number of members of this galaxy, the chapter will end with an analysis of the UN Global Compact, an initiative launched by Kofi Annan in 1999 to bring together TNCs and other organizations to follow a set of voluntary behavioral standards rooted in the UN's many declarations, resolutions, and mandates.

The International Labour Organization

The International Labour Organization was established in 1919 at the Treaty of Versailles. When the United Nations was created in 1946, the ILO became its first specialized agency. Through its unique tripartite structure of governments, workers, and employers, the organization seeks to promote social justice and internationally recognized human and labor rights. The ILO Charter states that universal peace can be achieved only if it is based on social justice. Labor conditions characterized by "injustice, hardship and privation to large numbers of people," it has warned, could produce "unrest so great that the peace and harmony of the world are imperiled." The original charter established that:

· Labor is not a commodity.
· Freedom of expression and association are essential to sustained progress.

- Poverty anywhere constitutes a danger to prosperity everywhere.
- The war against want requires national effort, supported by concerted international effort in which the representatives of workers and employers have equal status with those of governments.

These principles were reaffirmed in the Declaration of Philadelphia on 10 May 1944. The declaration laid the groundwork for the incorporation of the ILO into the newly born UN system.

The ILO formulates international labor standards in the form of conventions and recommendations that set minimum standards for basic labor rights, including the right to organize, collective bargaining, equality of opportunity and treatment, and other standards that regulate conditions across the entire labor spectrum.

According to Francis Blanchard, the longtime director-general (1973–1988), the problem of the multinational corporation was brought up at the ILO, in part at the insistence of the trade union federation. He elaborated:

> In the governing body we have a group of 14 workers representative of major trade unions in the world who became very vocal about the conduct . . . of multinational corporations—a notion . . . which emerged very sharply and dramatically from this economic context, namely the fear expressed on all sides about the future and . . . the problems of the working people. The discussion started in the ILO under extremely difficult circumstances, because the employers group was extremely reluctant to enter this debate; the workers groups were pushing hard and governments were divided.[1]

At its 1971 General Conference, the ILO adopted a resolution on Social Problems Raised by Multinational Undertakings, which set out a program of work, including studies, conferences, and consultations involving its three constituent groups. At the same time, organized labor in the United States and Western Europe began to expand beyond national borders. Trade unions such as the U.S.-based United Auto Workers and its Canadian and European affiliates set out to improve workers' conditions by collectively striving to harmonize labor practices. Under the auspices of trade unions, numerous meetings were held with TNCs such as Philips, General Electric, Shell, Nestlé, and Grace.[2]

At its 185th Session in Geneva in February–March 1972, the ILO's Governing Body decided to convene a meeting on the subject of TNCs and social policy. A group of twenty-four experts drawn from governments, employers, and workers' groups attended this meeting in Geneva in October and November of 1972. In a brief series of seven conclusions, the group recommended that more data be collected and more studies be conducted on the subject. In its penultimate paragraph, the experts requested the Governing Body to instruct the ILO director-general to undertake "a study of the usefulness of international principles and guidelines in the field of social policy relating to the activities of multinational enterprises, and the[ir] elements and implications."[3] It is interesting to note that the ILO expert group's reference to "principles" and "guidelines" and the tone of its recommendations stands in sharp contrast to those of the Group of Eminent Persons that came two years later. The ILO was content with voluntary guidelines with the hope that they would take the form of law once member countries ratified and adopted them.[4]

While ECOSOC and UNCTAD are perhaps the most heavily involved members of the UN galaxy, the ILO has made its own contribution to capacity-building, knowledge creation, and policy with respect to FDI and TNCs, or, in ILO parlance, multinational enterprises. Its work included a number of studies begun in the late 1960s that have continued into the twenty-first century. Abebe Abate, an ILO officer who was involved in the early work, related that even before the General Assembly resolution that led to the creation of the UN Centre, the ILO's International Institute for Labor Studies had studied industrial relations and TNCs. This led to more work on these issues at the ILO.[5]

Workers and governments, especially developing-country governments, were keenly interested in the ILO's work. Employers were more ambivalent but were involved nonetheless. Although Soviet-bloc countries were present during these discussions, there was much more interest from G-77 countries because the latter believed that their political independence was being undermined by their strong economic dependence on former colonizers and their allies. Consequently, these countries viewed TNCs with suspicion, as if they were surrogates for the erstwhile colonial masters. Abate, Blanchard, and other ILO staff saw this as the crux of the problem in the 1970s.

From 1969 to 1974, the ILO conducted a number of studies, established working groups, and held meetings of experts on the subject of multinational enterprises.[6] A consensus emerged to draft a voluntary code and propose a declaration addressed to governments, workers' organizations, and employers, including TNCs. Thus was born the Tripartite Declaration of Principles concerning Multinational Enterprises and Social Policy.

The ILO's first major policy publication, which led to the formulation of the Tripartite Declaration, was the 1973 study *Multinational Enterprise and Social Policy.* This was to the ILO what *Multinational Corporations in World Development,* the 1973 background report for the Group of Eminent Persons, was to ECOSOC in New York. The background report laid the foundation for the UN organizational structure related to TNCs. Similarly, most, if not all, subsequent work on TNCs within the ILO can be traced to this 1973 report on the impact of TNCs on workers.

The ILO report examined the nature and growth of TNCs, their geographic and industrial concentration, their impact on labor and employment, types of headquarters-subsidiary arrangements, technology transfer, and the structure of trade. It attributed the "emotional responses" that TNCs had evoked "in all areas it has touched—political, fiscal, economic and, not least, social" to the complexity of the relationship between them and their detractors.[7] It emphasized both mutuality and conflict of interests between firms and nation-states. The report was succinct and even-handed, devoid of the rhetoric that had spilled into some of the earlier debates.

The 1973 study concluded that more work was needed on how TNCs impacted working conditions and how industrial relations might function in a multinational context. Appended to the report was a 60-page summary and recommendations by the group of experts on the relationship between TNCs and social policy. Eight representatives from each of the three pillars of the ILO—employers, employees, and governments—constituted the expert group. Observers from UN agencies, other international organizations, and employee and employer organizations also participated.

In November 1977, the ILO's Governing Body adopted a statement of principles on TNCs and labor-related issues. The declaration was blessed by governments, workers, and employers. While noting efforts under way within the UNCTC and the OECD, it established a series of guidelines for its stakeholders.

This Tripartite Declaration noted the "substantial benefits" to home and host countries that result from the activities of TNCs, through FDI and other means.[8] It sought to encourage TNCs to make positive contributions to economic and social progress and to minimize and resolve the difficulties the various operations of TNCs might cause. It took note of UN resolutions advocating the establishment of a New International Economic Order.

The declaration addressed other specific and relatively uncontroversial matters pertaining to labor relations, including job creation; equality of opportunity and treatment, employment security, and training for workers; safety regulations on the job; industrial relations; freedom of association and the right of workers to organize; collective bargaining mechanisms; structures to handle grievances; and systems to settle disputes. Each statement was grounded in at least one previous ILO convention or recommendation, thus giving the instrument further legal legitimacy.

The administration and implementation of the declaration proved to be more difficult than generating the document; the organization became caught in political tensions that arose from East-West rivalries. Nevertheless, the ILO began developing a series of training programs to promote and help implement its basic principles. Some provisions of the declaration did find their way into the national legislation of various countries, albeit in varying degrees. Meanwhile, the organization continued the task of fine-tuning internationally acceptable labor standards through capacity-building, dialogue, and research. As with similar initiatives, the declaration took on a life of its own. A review process was initiated to monitor adherence and to report on progress to the ILO Governing Body.

Some two decades after the 1977 declaration, the ILO Governing Body, under the leadership of Juan Somavía, concluded that changed global labor relations required that some issues be revisited. Worsening conditions of work caused by outsourcing, layoffs, and footloose industries that tend to relocate in search of the lowest labor costs demanded that the ILO respond on behalf of labor. Thus, in 1998, the ILO adopted the Declaration on Fundamental Principles and Rights at Work as an update to the original declaration. It reaffirmed the rights of workers to collective bargaining and freedom of association. Noticing the cloud of protectionism hanging over the global economy and the stalled multilateral trade negotiations, it cautioned states against using labor standards as a pretense for engaging in protectionist policies. The rights at work declaration was a commitment by governments, employers, and workers' organizations to uphold the basic rights of freedom of association and collective bargaining, to eliminate forced and compulsory labor, to abolish child labor, and to eliminate discrimination in the workplace.

Since 1998, the ILO has sought to maintain an active interest in areas where TNCs are extensively involved, particularly where this involvement might give rise to conflicts between management and labor. It conducts training for all three stakeholder groups, but more often for developing countries seeking advice on labor-related matters. It also dispatches missions to mediate labor-related disputes or complaints. Mission reports are submitted after the conclusion of an official visit, but due to the sensitivity of the parties to any negative publicity or repercussions, reports on such meetings are usually confidential. Nevertheless, this type of hands-on activity demonstrates areas where theory and policy intersect.

From its establishment in 1919 until 2006, the ILO has adopted nearly 200 conventions, covering the entire spectrum of labor relations. It has been more frequently embroiled in controversy than UNCTAD not only because of its views on labor issues but, more important, because many of these conventions lead to regulatory action at the national level. It was thrust in the midst of a crisis in Myanmar in 2001 when it took on the issue of child labor. A year earlier, two Myanmar activist workers, Aye Myint and Su Su Nwe, had lodged complaints about the practice of forced labor in Myanmar with the ILO and their government. ILO field officers pursued the matter in spite of threats against their lives. Enraged, the government threatened to withdraw from the

ILO. The ILO's Governing Body expressed "grave concern" and "firmly rejected" perceived "attempts to influence the ILO's position through various forms of pressure and intimidation."[9]

After negotiations involving Myanmar's UN ambassador in Geneva and an ILO mission to the country in 2006, the government decided to cooperate rather than withdraw. However, the situation did not change, and the matter was placed on the agenda of the International Labour Conference at its annual general assembly in June.[10] Thus, some five years after the aggrieved workers' complaints, the ILO continues to exercise its soft power on their behalf. The Myanmar case, among others, illustrates the extent to which an international organization can project its limited soft power vis-à-vis nation-states, a power that emanates from its tripartite group of stakeholders.

In summary, while the Tripartite Declaration has proved its staying power, it has also been tempered in accordance with changing times. The Governing Body issued a revised version of the declaration in 2000 that broadened the social content of the original document to take into account changes in the global economy and added and emphasis on social responsibility. In 2004, the ILO established a committee to oversee implementation of the declaration. The organization has spearheaded other proactive initiatives, including the establishment in 2002 of a World Commission on the Social Dimensions of Globalization. To be sure, the organization has had to navigate a delicate path, given its tripartite structure and the diversity within each of these three groups. A member of one of these groups, Jill Murray, a critic of TNCs, who worked within the ILO system at the Bureau of Workers' Activities, observed:

> In an important decision in 1988, the Committee on MNE[s] clarified the "balance" which the Declaration seeks to strike between the interests of MNEs and member states. . . . To take the view that minimizing negative social repercussions *per se* fulfils the overall purpose of the Declaration is therefore not correct. . . . Such action must also . . . contribute to economic and social progress.[11]

Murray concluded that the ILO declaration cannot be used to redress misuse of the power of multinational enterprises even when such power is used in breach of the declaration.

Director-General Juan Somavía has summed up the contributions of the ILO:

> In many respects, the whole ILO convention system on workers' rights, which is negotiated here because we have legislative capacity . . . is adhered to on a voluntary basis because you have to ratify a convention for it to become a commitment—it is a mixture of international decision-making plus national decision-making . . . [and it] has been very successful because it is the basis of most labor legislation in the world.[12]

On the structure of the ILO, Somavía believes:

> The strength of the ILO structure [lies in the fact that] the people sitting in the governing body for the employers represent the international organizations of employers, which . . . [are] active in [more than] 130 . . . countries. . . . And the fourteen workers, most of them come from the International Confederation of Free Trade Unions (ICFTU), and the World Confederation of Labor, who represent in total about 220 million organized workers throughout the world. So these are real democratic structures in . . . that the people who get here are elected by their peers.[13]

The World Health Organization

As the global guardian of public health, the WHO has wrestled with TNC issues on a number of occasions. This UN organization, established in 1948, has targeted tobacco companies in its efforts to raise awareness of the risks of smoking, a global health matter. It has also challenged the marketing practices of manufacturers of substitutes for breast milk, thereby bringing about changes in how TNCs market their products to poor rural inhabitants of Third World countries. Although there are other examples of the interface between the WHO and TNCs, these two deserve particular attention.

It has been long recognized that smoking tobacco is a serious health hazard. The thousands of deaths associated with tobacco-related illnesses and the staggering cost of providing health care for smokers demonstrate tobacco's deleterious health effects in unequivocal terms. Extensive research by the U.S. National Institutes of Health and the World Health Organization and court rulings in several countries provide further confirmation. The history of efforts to control tobacco consumption and advertising of, production of, manufacture of, and trade in tobacco is lengthy and amply documented.[14]

The hundreds of millions of individual smokers constitute the main stakeholders. Next are the producers, manufacturers, and traders of tobacco. As guardians of public health, national governments and international agencies must also be included as stakeholders, as their mandates are to protect the health and welfare of their constituents. Ancillary groups—consumer associations, civil society organizations, and other interest groups—are active at the margins. Each of these groups, in one way or another, has a stake in the outcome of the WHO's tobacco initiatives. These affect the livelihood of tobacco producers and their workers, governments that bear the costs of health care and forgo tax revenues lost when consumption declines, and tobacco users, whose health is almost certainly at risk.

Although the harmful effects of tobacco have long been known,[15] the attack on the tobacco industry began in earnest when individuals, groups, and states brought suit against U.S. tobacco companies in U.S. state and federal courts, seeking reimbursement for health care expenditures incurred in treating citizens' tobacco-related diseases. In 1985, a subcommittee of the U.S. House Committee on Energy and Commerce held hearings on the harmful health effects of tobacco. Ten years later, Dr. Jeffrey Wigand, who had worked for the multinational tobacco manufacturer and distributor Brown and Williamson, became a celebrated whistle-blower when he revealed that over the years, tobacco companies had withheld information from the public and had "spiked" their products to render them more addictive, and in the process, more carcinogenic.[16]

In 1997, tobacco manufacturers and a group of state attorneys-general in the United States reached a nationwide settlement of all claims against the tobacco companies called the Tobacco Resolution. It contained some of the same elements that ultimately found their way into the later master settlement, namely consent by tobacco companies to refrain from certain behavior deemed harmful to citizens' health, including advertising. A year later, a Master Settlement Agreement was reached between forty-six states, the District of Columbia, and Puerto Rico and several major tobacco companies, including Philip Morris, R. J. Reynolds Tobacco Company, Brown & Williamson Tobacco Corporation, and Lorillard Tobacco Company. The companies agreed to pay $246 billion over the ensuing twenty-five years in exchange for release from liability for past and future damages. Tobacco manufacturers unsuccessfully challenged the constitutionality of the Master Settlement, but the U.S. Supreme Court affirmed its legality in 2002.

It was not long before the issues raised by litigations in the United States percolated into the international arena. In 2000, following the recommendations of a UN interagency task force, the World Health Organization took up the challenge of investigating and publicizing the harmful effects of tobacco at the global level. The organization's objective was to seek a global solution to a worldwide health hazard. Armed with its own studies and those of numerous medical researchers around the world, the WHO warned smokers, governments, and tobacco companies that smoking had become "the single biggest preventable cause of death." It estimated that in 2003, there were 1.3 billion smokers worldwide, half of whom were expected to die prematurely of a tobacco-related disease.[17]

Efforts by the WHO to develop global rules to curb the advertising, promotion, sales, and smuggling of tobacco products soon bore fruit. In May 2003, WHO member nations unanimously adopted the Framework Convention on Tobacco Control (FCTC) during the 56th World Health Assembly in Geneva.

It was the first international legal instrument negotiated under the auspices of the WHO, and it was aimed at curbing the global spread of tobacco products. By the 29 June 2004 ratification deadline, 88 percent of the member nations had become signatories to the convention. Of these, thirty became parties to the treaty when they completed the subsequent steps of ratification, acceptance, approval, formal confirmation, or accession.[18]

The tobacco industry was united in its opposition to the WHO initiative. When the 191 nations of the WHO began negotiations in 2000 on FCTC, the world's seven largest global tobacco companies, including Philip Morris and Japan Tobacco[19], were attempting to preemptively develop a voluntary pact. However, this pact was superseded by what transpired under the WHO. The Web site[20] of the Tobacco Manufacturer's Association, a UK organization, does not explicitly refer to the WHO or the FCTC. Instead, it focuses on tax revenues collected by governments from sales of tobacco products. The companies' response to the FCTC was a resilient and positive one that included a complex mixture of strategies, akin to their behavior after the Master Settlement. Remarkably, no tobacco companies went bankrupt. On the contrary, the industry enjoyed an above-average profit margin that resulted in an industry performance on a par with, or better than, the manufacturing industry as a whole.[21]

Philip Morris, the U.S. largest tobacco company, pursued a twin strategy of diversifying its products and diversifying geographically. It aggressively diversified its product portfolio by acquiring food, beverage, and other companies while also restructuring into Philip Morris International and Philip Morris USA to more effectively expand in the global market. Even as it diversified its product profile away from tobacco, the company expressed its agreement with some objectives of the FCTC. In its own words:

> Among the areas where we share common ground with the WHO are the prevention of youth smoking; reasonable restrictions on marketing; efforts to continue to inform the public about the health consequences of smoking and the benefits of quitting; regulation of the content of tobacco products; package labeling requirements; reduction and elimination of cigarette smuggling; and reasonable restrictions on smoking in public places.[22]

Other major companies pursued similar strategies.[23] Although R. J. Reynolds Tobacco Company (not to be confused with R. J. Reynolds, Inc.) was silent with respect to the FCTC, other companies including British-American Tobacco (BAT) and Japan Tobacco faced the convention head on. Japan Tobacco, which traces its origins to 1898, was reconstituted after it purchased R. J. Reynolds, Inc. in 1999. As the manufacturer of three of the world's most rec-

ognizable brands of cigarettes (Camel, Salem, and Winston), Japan Tobacco
controlled three-quarters of the Japanese tobacco market in 2004.[24] The company testified and provided documentation to challenge the premises of the
FCTC:

> We represent not only our 45,000 employees worldwide, but also millions of
> people who depend on us for their livelihoods—tobacco growers, suppliers, and
> retailers. . . . While we are willing to cooperate and work with the WHO, the
> principle of "proportionality" demands that the impact of a proposed regulation
> needs to be proportional to its expected benefit. The FCTC fails to meet this
> key test.[25]

BAT echoed many of the sentiments expressed by others in the industry:

> As the producers of a legal product we assert the right to communicate with adult
> consumers and also the right to participate in international trade. We take issue
> with the notion that the world in the 21st century is faced with a tobacco "epi-
> demic" that is "spreading across national borders" . . . that international tobacco
> companies are . . . "spreading the epidemic" and that advertising is claimed to
> be the "tool" to do so. . . . [T]obacco use was widespread in all countries in the
> world for centuries, well before the advent of either international tobacco com-
> panies or mass market advertising. . . . [W]e do recognise the role of the WHO
> in supporting governments with health policy advice based on sound science . . .
> [and] it is appropriate for the WHO to advise on tobacco control measures within
> its field of expertise.[26]

In this statement, BAT recognized that the WHO had a role to play, but argued that the role was more limited than that envisioned by the FCTC. The
industry was steadfast in its belief that it had rights and that only governments
can regulate, so therefore any international accord cannot be more than voluntary. These arguments have the echo of similar debates a quarter-century earlier, when codes of conduct were being crafted for TNCs under the auspices
of the UNCTC. In the case of the WHO, the path to regulation emanated
from national (and even subnational) governments, percolated up to the international level, and upon ratification took the form of a convention. This process, in turn, worked its way down to the national level and took the form of
national legislation; the process had come full circle and ended in a tangible
instrument with legal teeth. This stands in contrast to voluntary guidelines or
codes that lack the enforceability of the law of the land.

While the tobacco companies appeared to have accepted the underlying
premise of the FCTC—namely, that tobacco is harmful to health—and have
shown some willingness to move toward fulfilling the convention's goals, it is
clear that disagreement remains within the industry as to how far the FCTC
should go in curbing companies' production, marketing, and distribution, tradi-

tionally the domain of private enterprise. Most, if not all, tobacco companies oppose the binding international instrument proposed by the FCTC. Many prefer to invoke the widest possible spectrum of stakeholders or individual choice or stress basic rules of competition in a free market system. Thus there is no "intra-stakeholder unanimity" among tobacco companies on how to meet this external challenge. This was especially evident during the litigation process, when some companies broke rank with the others.

The uneasy, if not hostile, environment continued to cast its shadow over the tobacco companies. In 1999, the U.S. Justice Department began preparations to file a massive suit in U.S. federal court, again charging tobacco companies with conspiracy to defraud consumers by denying the dangers of smoking and by deliberately marketing cigarettes to underage youth even though the companies were aware of the causal link between smoking and disease. After five years, federal prosecutors brought this action for damages in September 2004, demanding that the companies "disgorge" $280 billion in "ill-gotten gains."[27]

Tobacco companies responded vigorously, denied the charges, and went on the attack, as they had in earlier court battles. It is noteworthy that press coverage of this case did not mention the WHO or the FCTC. A federal appellate court later reversed the decision. While the tobacco industry fought various court battles in the United States and other countries, the WHO continued to seek ratification of the convention by its member states.

Two decades earlier, the WHO was embroiled in a well-publicized controversy involving the marketing and distribution of infant food products. In the 1970s, Nestlé, the giant Swiss TNC, was accused of unfair and unethical marketing practices in developing countries, primarily Africa, where it sold its powdered milk and other infant food products. Critics claimed that the company engaged in deceptive marketing practices by dressing its sales personnel to look like doctors and nurses, giving the impression that formula food was medically acceptable. Some doctors, at the instigation of the company, also tried to convince mothers and hospitals to switch to powdered milk after allegedly being bribed by Nestlé to do so. Critics also charged that Nestlé gave free samples to induce mothers to stop nursing their babies and begin feeding them infant formula.

Activists, primarily in Western Europe and North America, mobilized and initiated a worldwide consumer boycott of all Nestlé products, spearheaded by Douglas A. Johnson at the Newman Center in Minneapolis, Minnesota, who organized the Infant Formula Action Coalition. Organizers argued that children fed infant formula had an infant mortality rate three times higher than babies who were breast-fed. They also argued that breast-feeding may serve as a natural contraceptive. Moreover, they said, poor and illiterate mothers who diluted the milk to stretch their meager income unwittingly caused diarrhea and other diseases in their infants.

Nestlé vehemently rejected these accusations at first and asserted that it was producing a product that was inherently healthy and safe and was encouraging economic development in developing countries by promoting hygiene, scientific dairy farming, and education and creating jobs.[28] Under pressure, however, Nestlé reversed its position and, with the assistance of the World Health Organization and the nongovernmental organizations that had championed the boycott, worked toward change.

In 1981, the WHO, in cooperation with UNICEF, Nestlé, and other manufacturers of breast milk substitutes, crafted a voluntary code of conduct that established a number of parameters for marketing these products, especially in developing countries. As a gesture of good will, Nestlé agreed to establish an independent auditing committee that would monitor its compliance with the agreement. U.S. senator Edmund S. Muskie—who had just stepped down from the Senate and from a short stint as U.S. secretary of state—headed the committee. Some key provisions of the agreement are set out in Box 8.1

Box 8.1. Key Provisions of the 1981 WHO Code on the Marketing of Baby Food

Corporations that manufacture baby food and infant formula may not

- Promote their products in hospitals or shops or to the general public
- Give free samples to mothers or free or subsidized supplies to hospitals or maternity wards
- Give gifts to health workers or mothers
- Promote their products to health workers: any information companies provide to health workers must be limited scientific facts
- Promote foods or drinks for babies
- Give misleading information
- Contact mothers through sales personnel of companies that manufacture infant formula
- Produce labels that use language mothers do not understand and that do not include clear health warnings
- Show baby pictures on labels for infant formula
- Produce labels with language that idealizes the use of the product

Source: WHO/UNICEF International Code of Marketing of Breastmilk Substitutes, available at http://www.babymilkaction.org/regs/thecode.html (accessed 12 June 2006).

Critics seemed to be satisfied by these steps, at least at first, although they insisted on Nestlé's continued adherence to these marketing restrictions. Soft power seems to have hit Nestlé hard, proving that results can be achieved this way, a route perhaps less difficult than through national legislation. In 2005–2008, a new wave of protest, albeit not as vociferous as the earlier wave, was gaining momentum, adding more fuel to the antiglobalization fire.

Others in the UN Galaxy

The UN Food and Agriculture Organization

From its headquarters in Rome, the FAO has dealt with TNCs in matters involving the production and distribution of food and agricultural products and the use of fertilizers, pesticides, and herbicides. The FAO has been at the forefront of global food security since its inception. It works with private-sector partners across the agricultural and food chains as well as fertilizer manufacturers and big grain commodity trading companies. The organization can have a potentially significant role in helping to achieve the Millennium Development Goals (MDGs), which aim to eliminate hunger by 2015. Most notable among its partnerships is the Codex Alimentarius,[29] under which the WHO, governments, and the private sector work to establish food standards. Another FAO initiative was the International Treaty on Plant Genetic Resources for Food and Agriculture, which was approved in 2001 and entered into force on 29 June 2004.[30]

Box 8.2. United Nations Food and Agriculture Organization

Program	Corporate Partnerships	Activities
AGORA (Access to Global Online Research in Agriculture)	Founding publishers of AGORA are Blackwell Publishing; CABI Publishing; Elsevier; Kluwer Academic Publishers; Lippincott, Williams & Wilkins; Nature Publishing Group; Oxford University Press; Springer Verlag; and John Wiley and Sons.	Provide free access to more than 400 key journals in food, nutrition, and agriculture and related biological, environmental, and social sciences to professionals in developing countries where resources are not available to purchase subscriptions.

Program	Corporate Partnerships	Activities
Codex Alimentarius	FAO/WHO. Private-sector organizations participate in meetings as part of government delegations and often include consumer groups and industry representatives.	Develop food standards and guidelines and related texts such as codes of practice under the Joint FAO/WHO Food Standards Program. Codex standards are now the benchmarks against which national food measures and regulations are evaluated.
Program on Assistance to School Milk Promotion	Tetra Pak; DeLaval (Sweden)	Facilitate the exchange of information about implementing school milk programs.
Manual on Good Practices for the Meat Industry	Carrefour (France)	Implement in a practical way the Code of Practice on Meat Hygiene of the Codex Alimentarius

Source: FAO Web site, www.FAO.org

These activities bring the FAO in direct contact with a number of TNCs who operate in a functionally specific, practical, and vital area of economic activity, namely the production, distribution, and sales of food.

UNESCO

In the 1970s, a group of developing countries called for a New International Economic Order. About this same time, some in this group pursued a parallel demand for a New International Information Order. The United Nations Educational, Scientific and Cultural Organization became the forum for discussions relevant to this new demand. Many developing countries believed that many (if not most) information systems were biased toward developed countries and therefore these global information and media corporations were the primary targets of the New International Information Order. Attacks on cultural imperialism and cultural pollution were commonplace in developing countries, and some of the more radical governments believed that state control of national media was necessary to guide the development process without external pressures. Nondemocratic leaders are known for their disdain of a free press, but, further emboldened by the success of their OPEC brethren and the passage of the NIEO declaration, potentates seized the moment to attempt to curb the press and exercise more control over the media. This early reaction against globalization was done in the name of national sovereignty to protect their people from foreign influence. Mass media was blamed for encouraging "consumptive emulation" and a revolution of rising expectations.

Western countries were understandably unenthusiastic about the demands of less developed countries to establish a New International Information Order, as were members of the global media. The idea soon lost steam, the movement fizzled, and the term New International Information Order was relegated to a brief footnote in the history of rebellion against the encroachment of globalization.

UNECSO, like other UN bodies, gradually adopted a more accommodating style and joined hands with the international business community. Its collaborative work included corporate partnerships with U.S., Western European, and other global companies.

Box 8.3. UNESCO's Corporate Partnerships

Program	Corporate Partnerships	Activities
Life Sciences	L'Oréal	L'Oréal-UNESCO Award singles out remarkable female scientists from the five continents of the world. The L'Oréal-UNESCO Fellowship program encourages young scientists to pursue their research in Life Sciences in the laboratory of their choice.
Amdapha and West Kemeng area of Arunachal Pradesh	MacArthur Foundation	Promotion of the Apatani landscape and adjoining areas as a natural cultural world heritage site under the UNESCO's World Heritage; a research-based synthesis volume entitled *Shifting Agriculture and Sustainable Development: Tradition in Transition*; a policy document that is rele-

Program	Corporate Partnerships	Activities
		vant to the northeast of India in general and for the state of Arunachal Pradesh in particular; an audiovisual documentary on the Apatani cultural landscape entitled *When the Mist Is Lifted*; UNESCO–Center for Environment Education outreach publication, *One Sun, Two Worlds—An Ecological Journey.*
Mondialogo	DaimlerChrysler	Promotion of intercultural dialogue and exchange. A School Contest, an Engineering Award, an Internet Portal.
School project for children in difficult circumstances	Hans Christian Andersen ABC Foundation	Classes follow a specially elaborated curriculum and use teaching methods adapted to the needs and problems of at-risk children. They complement government efforts to reinsert the children into the school system. The children are also given lunch and clean clothes, further encouraging school attendance.
SpaceForScience	Alcatel Alenia	SpaceForScience provides telecommunication and multimedia satellite services to education and research institutes in Southeastern Europe.
Social and economic development around the world	Microsoft	Areas of Cooperation: Education and learning, community access and development, cultural and linguistic diversity and preservation, digital inclusion and capacity building, exchange and promotion for best practices on the use of Information and Communication Technology (ICT) for socio-economic development programs, fostering web-based communities of practice, including content development, knowledge sharing and empowerment through partici-

Program	Corporate Partnerships	Activities
		pation, facilitating exchange and strategies.
		The Next Generation of Teachers Project
Intangible cultural heritage	Samsung	Production of audiovisual contents on the intangible cultural heritage by BBC World Ltd. (UK). Financing of a Manual on the implementation of the Convention for the Safeguarding of the Intangible Cultural Heritage. Development of a photo series of Masterpieces of the Oral and Intangible Heritage of Humanity Renovation of the Intangible Heritage Homepage in the UNESCO website.

Source: Information available at www.UNESCO.org.

These partnerships drew UNESCO closer to the international business community and not only helped it shed its image from earlier years but also brought it into a collaborative ambit consistent with the sentiments of the times.

Bretton Woods Institutions

The Bretton Woods institutions are specialized agencies of the United Nations that have dealt in one form or another with FDI and TNCs. The IMF works closely with governments as well as private international financial institutions on a wide range of financial policies, procedures, and transactions that impact international financial flows. Among TNCs, its primary constituents are international banks and financial intermediaries. The IMF has played a key role by serving as a receptacle for the collection of data on FDI as part of its role as the global monitor of financial flows. The World Bank has played a somewhat different, albeit complementary, role in this same arena; it provides financial and technical assistance to developing countries. Over the past six decades, it has financed many large and small economic projects throughout the world. Through affiliated organizations, it has also contributed equity capital in partnership with private investors. The International Finance Corporation (IFC), the World Bank subsidiary most directly involved with private investment, has worked in partnership with TNCs to establish manufacturing plants and other productive enterprises. Unlike the World Bank, the IFC is permitted to lend money for private projects and take equity positions in them. This brings the World Bank, through the IFC, in direct contact with transnational corporations. The IFC has also advised developing countries on FDI matters through its consulting and research arm, Foreign Investment Advisory Services, which conducts studies similar to UNCTAD's investment policy reviews. As these FIAS studies are confidential, they can be more blunt in their assessment.

Another arm of the bank, International Centre for the Settlement of Investment Disputes, has provided a settlement mechanism for FDI-related disputes. Although it began in a lethargic mode, some disputes have been brought to it in recent years, and it works now as it was envisioned to.

Although not part of the UN, the mandate of the World Trade Organization is important here because trade agreements negotiated under its auspices deal with four investment-linked areas: national treatment, transparency of rules and regulations, protection of investors, and dispute settlement. Each round of trade negotiations has resulted in an expanded role for WTO, thanks to the increasing interrelationship between trade and FDI. This became particularly evident during the Uruguay Round in 1995, when FDI was included as an item on the agenda. The Doha Round, launched in 2002, has further expanded the overlap.

UNIDO and the Lima Declaration

The United Nations Industrial Development Organization was created to promote industrialization in developing countries. This focus has brought it in direct contact with TNCs, although there is scant reference to TNCs in the documents of the organization. The focus, instead, is on industrialization, industrial development, the acquisition and development of science and technology, and programs with similar goals. The need to take action to facilitate industrialization in developing countries was made clear in the Lima Declaration of 1976, which mandated that UNIDO, an arm of the UN, promote developing countries' acquisition, absorption, and development of technology. Its location in Vienna, Austria, on the front line between East and West, has made an indelible impact on the organization.[31] Often pulled by one or the other superpower, it has nevertheless managed to develop programs that it considered appropriate to the needs of developing countries.

Think Tanks: UNITAR and UNRISD

The United Nations Institute for Training and Research (UNITAR), initially based in New York and now based in Geneva, has been active, as its name implies, in the areas of training programs and research. The institute produced a series of case studies on technology transfer in the 1970s, including an overview by Walter Chudson.[32] Later it became a base for scholars such as Sidney Dell, who had earlier been the director of the UNCTC. In more recent years, the institute has become a center for a variety of intellectual contributions, including work on codes of conduct and other facets of TNC activities. Research activities at UNITAR have ebbed and flowed depending on personalities, issues, and funding.

The United Nations Research Institute for Social Development (UNRISD) in Geneva is still another autonomous UN agency engaged in multidisciplinary research on the social dimensions of contemporary problems that affect development. Working with a network of national research centers, UNRISD has conducted research on civil society and social movements; democracy, governance, and human rights; identities, conflict, and cohesion; social policy and development; and technology, business, and society. Its recent publications have dealt with TNC regulation and include an annotated list of recent initiatives on this at the corporate, national, and international levels.[33]

The International Trade Institute, a partnership of the WTO and UNCTAD, conducts training programs for developing countries on trade issues. This is yet another example of interagency collaboration and one that has had a certain degree of success. Although it is autonomous, the institute has drawn on expertise from both its parent institutions. It has conducted many workshops, particularly for countries seeking entry into the WTO or are in the early stages of their participation and need training and expertise.[34] It also maintains databases on trade and related topics.

World Intellectual Property Organization

The industrial revolution created a need for a regime to protect artistic and literary works and promote entrepreneurship. In the knowledge-intensive global economy of the twenty-first century, the World Intellectual Property Organization (WIPO), whose genesis goes back to the 1883 Paris Union,[35] has become important for the technology and intellectual property activities of TNCs. The protection of these intangible but strategically important assets must be assured and their flow across national boundaries must be facilitated to encourage technological development and innovation by TNCs.

Host countries and local firms seek the same protection of these assets in their own quest for development and growth. The raison d'être of WIPO is to promote an international regime to protect intellectual property that strikes a balance between the producers and users of technology and between encouraging innovation and discouraging abuse of the monopoly power of the holder of that right; this focus has remained essentially unchanged over the last century.

One of the organization's most significant contributions has been the drafting of "model laws." Many of its nearly 100 member states have incorporated some of these laws into their national legislation. Adoption of WIPO's model laws by a country can have cumulative consequences at the multilateral level. As more countries adopt these model laws, the ultimate result may well be the emergence of a global convergence on specific intellectual property issues. An example of convergence is the similarity between WIPO's work on intellectual property protection and that of the World Trade Organization on trade-related aspects of intellectual property.

WIPO is critically important to both TNCs and developing countries, for it is in the interest of all to have a level playing field. When other international rule-making bodies like the WTO and WHO contemplate drafting multilateral rules in their fields of expertise and action, they are aware of WIPO's precedent.

Protecting intellectual property has always been a major issue in the area of technology transfer. During the debates and negotiations on a code of conduct for technology transfer in the mid-1970s to early 1980s, TNCs insisted on receiving guarantees for their patents, trademarks, trade names, and copyrighted technology before agreeing to transfer them. No code emerged because the gap on key policy issues between the United States and its western allies and the G-77 could not be bridged. During this period, WIPO was largely sidestepped while UNCTAD assumed a dominant role.

How do the various members of this constellation relate to one another and what do they contribute to the common cause? The answer is mixed and changes with time and political climates. Each member of the UN galaxy, nevertheless, has reason to claim a role in TNC–host country relations and economic and social development. Are the scattered agencies complementary or redundant? Do they duplicate one another's work or do they augment and reinforce each other? An example of complementarities is the work on the marketing of breast milk substitutes by WHO and UNICEF and on the tobacco industry by WHO and the World Bank. When the World Health Organization was championing the "tobacco initiative," research at the World Bank in 2002 documented the economic impact of tobacco control, reinforcing WHO's arguments.[36] Complementarities exist with respect to data collection, for example, between UNCTAD and IMF and between FIAS and UNCTAD case studies, each of which are diagnostic and policy oriented but differentiated by the scope of dissemination.

The UN Global Compact

As the new millennium approached, UN Secretary-General Kofi Annan saw the transformations in the economic and social structure wrought by globalization and its discontent as both a warning and an opportunity. The warning was the violent reaction of a coalition of formerly disparate groups against globalization and the international trading system that was typified by the demonstrations in Seattle in 1999. The opportunity was the possibility to aim for a general consensus on the fundamental conditions under which all forms of global commerce might be peacefully and productively conducted.

In 1999 at the World Economic Forum in Davos, Switzerland, the Secretary-General challenged world business leaders—the elite of global capitalism—to rise to meet their social and ethical responsibilities. He invited TNCs and other large firms to join a UN-headed partnership mission called the Global Compact. The compact would promote "responsible" global capitalism[37] and respond to basic needs in the areas of human rights, labor, and the environment. Annan advocated the principle that corporations can do well by doing good.[38] The original nine principles of the Global Compact in these three areas were grounded in one or more of the fundamental principles that constituted the raison d'être of the 1948 United Nations Universal Declaration of Human Rights. A tenth principle,[39] which addressed the problem of corruption, was added in June 2004 after the United Nations adopted the Convention against Corruption.[40] These ten principles are listed in Box 8.4.

Box 8.4. Global Compact: The Ten Principles

The Global Compact asks companies to embrace, support, and enact, within their sphere of influence, a set of ten principles in the areas of human rights, labor, the environment, and anti-corruption. These principles were derived from:

- The Universal Declaration of Human Rights
- The International Labour Organization's Declaration on Fundamental Principles and Rights at Work
- The Rio Declaration on Environment and Development
- The United Nations Convention Against Corruption

Human Rights
  · Principle 1: Businesses should support and respect the protection of internationally proclaimed human rights; and
  · Principle 2: Businesses should make sure that they are not complicit in human rights abuses.

Labor Standards
  · Principle 3: Businesses should uphold the freedom of association and the right to collective bargaining.
  · Principle 4: Businesses should eliminate all forms of forced and compulsory labor.
  · Principle 5: Businesses should effectively abolish child labor.
  · Principle 6: Business should eliminate discrimination in employment and occupation.

The Environment
  · Principle 7: Businesses should support a precautionary approach to environmental challenges.
  · Principle 8: Businesses should undertake initiatives to promote greater environmental responsibility.
  · Principle 9: Businesses should encourage the development and diffusion of environmentally friendly technologies.

Anti-Corruption
  · Principle 10: Businesses should work against all forms of corruption, including extortion and bribery.

Source: UN Global Compact Web site: http://www.unglobalcompact.org/AboutTheGC/TheTenPrinciples/index.html (accessed 13 June 2006).

In furtherance of the compact, a special section of the Secretary-General's office was established, with a small staff and modest budget, to provide general information, nurture new partnerships, develop studies, and arrange dialogues throughout the world. Georg Kell, the director of this office, reported directly to Kofi Annan. Kell has zealously championed the compact since its inception.

The compact's operational phase was launched at UN headquarters in New York on 26 July 2000. Chaired by the Secretary-General, the meeting brought together senior executives from some fifty major TNCs and other leaders of labor, human rights, environmental, and development organizations.[41] The compact, undertaken in partnership with each of the UN agencies, NGOs, and other stakeholders, is based on dialogue and discourse. It is also linked to the

UN's broader Millennium Development Goals, a "global partnership for development," that was enunciated in September 2000. These aim to eradicate poverty and hunger, establish universal primary education and gender equality, reduce child mortality, improve maternal health and environmental sustainability, and combat HIV/AIDS, malaria, and other diseases.[42] Some of the means for achieving these goals include trade and foreign direct investment because both contribute to the economic development of less-developed states.

Once the Global Compact was launched, UN staff encouraged companies to participate. In its 2001 pilot phase, companies were asked to describe their strategy for conforming to the compact's tenets by submitting specific examples of their business operations that included one or more of its principles. Forty-two companies submitted statements that indicated that they were addressing one or more of the principles of the Global Compact. For example, British Telecom stated that it was addressing all the principles, while Indian Oil Corporations, Ltd. indicated that it had implemented several of the principles through its community development activities in health care. Global companies such as BASF, DaimlerChrysler, Deloitte Touche Tohmatsu, DuPont, Royal Dutch/Shell, SAP, UBS, and Unilever described their corporate involvement.

Since the compact's first progress report in 2001, the program has continued to gain support. Hundreds of companies and organizations—from business, labor, and civil society associations to members of academia, cities, and even stock exchanges—have signed on to the compact. The list of companies on the compact's Web site (unglobalcompact.org) shows its diverse nature; these TNCs are from both developed and developing countries and from emerging market economies.

As the Global Compact has gained momentum, it has developed monitoring and reporting mechanisms for companies and other organizations that have endorsed its tenets. One such instrument is a self-reporting system. Critics of this approach argued that companies might be quick to endorse but slow to implement the ten principles, perhaps driven by a desire to gain publicity, or what *The Economist* has described as "blue-washing," a reference to the UN's association with the color blue.[43] The Global Compact Office responded by instituting a reporting system called "grey-listing." The UN's grey list named companies that had signed on but failed to report on exactly what they were doing to comply with the terms of the compact. A public report of such noncompliance could serve as an instrument of moral suasion, and champions of the compact at the UN have employed its power through this means. While this is an interesting approach to the exercise of soft power, the jury is still out on its efficacy. More research is necessary to accurately gauge the effects of these efforts. The incorporation of compact tenets into the company practices of TNCs is a welcome and positive development, and time will tell whether these changes will influence corporate conduct in the long term.

Box 8.5. Pitching the Global Compact to Companies

To convince companies to join the Compact, the Global Compact office stated these benefits:

- Working directly with UN agencies, labor and nongovernmental organizations, and other groups on partnership projects
- Participating, in a climate of mutual respect, in action-oriented "Global Policy Dialogues" that address key issues related to sustainable development and corporate citizenship
- Sharing good practices and learning with other companies
- Having confidence that the Global Compact's principles are endorsed and universally supported, thus providing a robust and widely recognized platform for issues of corporate citizenship
- Leveraging the UN's global reach and convening power with governments and other bodies
- Accessing the UN's deep knowledge and expertise related to development issues, key country information, and facilitation of other broad multi-stakeholder partnerships
- Building goodwill in communities where companies operate
- Receiving recognition for substantive company action and change (corporate reputation)
- Having higher employee morale and productivity, an improved risk profile, and increased operational efficiencies

Source: UN Global Compact, available at http://www.unglobalcompact.org

---

Since the original aim of the Global Compact was to create a consensus among the major players in the global network of economic activities, the UN has reached out to organizations beyond TNCs, including civil society organizations interested in human rights, labor, and the environment. Proponents might argue that the Global Compact provides a response to some of the negative consequences of global capitalism that cannot be remedied by legal means. The compact's aims are parallel to the same noble goals that underlie the existence of the United Nations[44]—the betterment of humankind. Moreover, the compact is a multi-stakeholder initiative that is consistent with the exigencies of today's global economy.[45]

Conclusion

This chapter has reviewed the galaxy of organizations that constitute the UN system, insofar as they have some relevance to TNC or FDI matters. Each of the organizations mentioned in this chapter has played a role in capturing the benefits of private enterprise for the benefit of humankind. Several institutions have played a role in devising rules of engagement that can contribute to the global commons. The Framework Convention on Tobacco Control, spearheaded by the World Health Organization, is intended to be binding; it covers details from advertising and labeling to illicit trade and even sponsorship. The UN Global Compact, on the other hand, appeals to good corporate citizenship and action and persuades by arguing that good behavior often means a good bottom line. Earlier efforts under the aegis of the ILO set global standards regarding working conditions and labor rights. Other organs have drawn TNCs into their respective orbits toward common objectives. The cumulative results of these efforts have yet to be fully realized. There is, more realistically, splatterings on the canvas with a vague concept of how they amount to a whole. The UN Global Compact comes closest to a unified system, but it lacks sufficient legitimacy and acceptance; perhaps in time it will gain its rightful place as an overarching system of values.

One must view the alternative approaches of binding international agreements and voluntary agreements that rely on moral suasion in light of seven parameters of legitimacy: 1) the desirability of the approach or instrument; 2) the feasibility of the approach or instrument; 3) the extent to which there is consensus among members of a stakeholder group about desirability and feasibility; 4) the degree of clarity with which stakeholder groups perceive one another; 5) the extent of trust between stakeholder groups; 6) whether each group concedes a legitimate role for the others in the process; and, perhaps most important, 7) the legal status of the proposed regime.[46]

A comparison of the Framework Convention on Tobacco Control and the Global Compact reveals certain distinguishing features. The first is intended to be binding, the second voluntary; one has created a clear delineation between adversaries who think the other fails to view issues from its perspective; the other aims to build on commonalities between groups. Similarly, the ILO approach—a tripartite declaration and convention—is only as effective as members who ratify it want it to be.

Unilateral and binding rules can also ascend to the global level. It was, after all, the massive anti-smoking campaign and extensive litigation in the United

States that provided the momentum for global rule-making with respect to tobacco. It is conceivable that multilateral rules that emanate from national roots are more likely to ultimately be adopted at the global level than rules contemplated in the insularity of international organizations.

While the original Tripartite Declaration of the ILO served as a foundation for the policies, guidelines, and national laws that followed, reference to the declaration itself seems to have waned with time. The 1998 statement regarding the right to work was ambitious and declarative in tone, but it lacked legal teeth. Although ILO leaders wanted to set standards and serve as a moral compass with respect to labor relations and working conditions, the ultimate proof must come from the reality on the ground, that is, through corporate action or inaction. This cannot be determined until a rigorous international study can establish a link between corporate behavior, national legislation, and ILO declarations and proclamations. Such a study on the efficacy of the efforts of the ILO and other international bodies is needed. This is not to say that efforts such as the Global Compact or other voluntary or "soft power" instruments are ineffective. However, research also needs to be done to determine the opportunity costs and unintended consequences of pursuing soft power in the face of hard realities. Declaring murder against the law has not stopped homicide; merely declaring corporate (or any other) conduct illegal is not a sufficient condition for eliminating it. The UN galaxy can bring us together toward a consensus on a desirable, feasible, and multilateral (and thus legitimate) regime.

9

The Legacy and the Future

- *The UN Galaxy*
- *The Enterprise and Its Legacy*
- *Other Members of the Galaxy*
- *Contributions and Shortfalls*
- *Changing Context and Swinging Pendulum*
- *Recommendations for Unmet Challenges*
- *Alternative Scenarios: Fission, Fusion, or Confusion? Fertile, Fragile, or Fatal?*

This book has studied the UN galaxy's intellectual contributions to the study of the role of transnational corporations in developing countries. It has addressed the impact of TNCs on economic development and international relations and the attendant national and international policy issues. The book began with an analysis of FDI, the main vehicle through which TNCs expand into and impact developing countries. This final chapter discusses whether, and in what respect, the UN has been ahead of or behind the curve in understanding the enlarging role of TNCs in the global economy.

The relationship between countries that need capital, management skills, and technology and TNCs, the primary creators, transferors, and users of these assets, has changed over time. This relationship was largely harmonious during the period from the end of World War II to the late 1960s. However, in the decade that followed, discontent, disillusionment, and discord dominated international relations, including FDI- and TNC-related matters. Flashpoints and crises followed one another in rapid succession. The breakdown of the Bretton Woods system of fixed exchange rates, together with energy emergencies, the Vietnam war, the Chilean episode, and corporate bribery scandals and indictments caused these to be called the leaden years.[1]

In turn, these events produced vociferous demands by some developing countries, primarily in Latin America, to reshape the international economic order and the role and influence of FDI. Developing countries perceived the global reach of TNCs as a symbol of their lingering exploitation and dependence.

This hue and cry led some countries to urge the UN to take action to ensure that TNCs better met the needs of developing countries. It was against the backdrop of the stormy 1970s, that, in 1973, ECOSOC appointed a Group of Eminent Persons to study the impact of TNCs on economic development and international relations and to advise the UN on this issue. This group, discussed in detail in Chapter 4, engaged in an extensive process of inquiry and presented its recommendations in 1974. Among the most important recommendation was that the UN establish a permanent commission and a permanent research center on TNCs to assist the UN and national governments on matters pertaining to TNCs and FDI. In particular, the enterprise was to study the feasibility of producing a multilateral agreement on TNCs, perhaps in the form of a code of conduct.

In subsequent years, dramatic political, economic, technological, and cultural changes altered the context and the tenor of the debate on TNCs away from confrontation and toward collaboration. The UN shifted from designing codes of conduct to curb the influence of TNCs to inviting TNCs to join a global compact to further the common good. As a world debating society, the "parliament of man" (a term used by Paul Kennedy), or the ultimate "born global"[2] organization, the UN has the potential to play a pivotal role in steering a "fragile" world toward a more "fertile" future.[3] The growth of new technologies, epitomized by the Internet, cellular telephony, and the digital revolution, have underpinned this transformation.

This final chapter examines the intellectual contributions to the study of transnational corporations in developing countries spawned within or filtered through the galaxy of disparate units of the United Nations. We have studied the impact of TNCs on economic development and international relations and the attendant national and international policy issues. The chapter discusses whether, and in what respect, the UN has been ahead of or behind the curve in understanding the enlarging role of transnational corporations in the global economy. We begin with a brief analysis of the phenomenon of foreign direct investment, the main vehicle through which TNCs expand into and impact developing countries.

The UN Galaxy

The UN is an amalgam of organizations and institutions, each tasked with a specific mandate. Some parts of this galaxy are more concerned with TNC/FDI issues than others. Many parts of the UN galaxy have made contributions to the study of TNCs and FDI in development.

It is also an organization made up of women and men with both expertise and dreams who are most often driven by motives that transcend national boundaries. To determine the organization's accomplishment with respect to TNC–host country relations, one can view the organization as both an arena—with nations as primary players—and as an organic entity comprised of such men and women. With this perspective, it is not difficult to concur with Paul Kennedy and Louis Emmerij, Richard Jolly, and Thomas G. Weiss[4] that more successes have emanated from the professional staff than from its membership of nation-states. Applying the Emmerij-Jolly-Weiss dichotomy of the UN as both arena (with nation-states as players) and actor (through the actions of secretariats, staff, and experts) to UN intellectual contributions on TNCs and FDI, the UN system has met expectations and occasionally exceeded them. The UN has often had a moderating and constructive influence in its role as an actor rather than as an arena. The zealous champions have worked as actors to produce change, cognizant of their limitations in matters of hiring and, especially, firing.[5] The proverbial 80/20 rule—where 80 percent of the work is performed by 20 percent of the employees—seems too often at play in the offices of this august institution.

The Enterprise and Its Legacy

The enterprise was designed in 1974 to help developing countries bolster their technological and managerial capacities and to constrain unacceptable behavior by TNCs in those countries. In recent years, more emphasis has been placed on the former than on the latter. Over a period of nearly two decades, the enterprise produced an impressive array of studies, reports, and publications that contributed to the creation, assembly, and diffusion of knowledge and information about TNCs and FDI. Important examples are the annual World Investment Report series, the 20-volume library of scholarly research on TNCs, and the journal *Transnational Corporations*. Capacity-building took a variety of forms, including workshops and training seminars on FDI and TNCs to strengthen governments' capacities to formulate and implement pertinent national policies and negotiate with TNCs. The UNCTC also conducted surveys of university curricula on FDI and TNC topics, compiled industry and topical case studies, and consulted with officials of developing country governments to help them streamline their FDI policies and associated institutions.[6]

The work of the enterprise during the New York years also included a number of analyses pertinent to policy formulation. Most notable were the efforts of the enterprise to draft an international agreement, a code of conduct to guide and/or regulate the behavior of TNCs, a task built into the mission of the UNCTC from its inception. The continuation of this task was spurred on by a small but vocal group of developing countries. However, the Centre's strong effort drew opposition from other stakeholders that helped to bring the New York years to an end.

The end of the UNCTC in New York provided an opportunity for a new beginning at UNCTAD in Geneva, a UN organization whose specific mandate was to advocate on behalf of developing countries. During the UNCTAD years, from 1993 to the present, the enterprise continued its mission and activities and matured. UNCTAD demonstrated resilience in adapting to, and even influencing, the shifting international economic landscape.

As TNCs and host countries became more accommodating toward each other, the posture of the enterprise swung more toward pragmatism, with a stronger focus on assisting developing countries through knowledge creation and capacity-building and less focus on championing institutional policy change. Nevertheless, work continued on international investment agreements, international accounting and reporting standards, and bilateral investment and double-taxation treaties.

As the world economic environment changed, flexibility was needed to craft rules of engagement on TNC-related issues. Such rules were more likely to endure if they met certain parameters of legitimacy, that is, a) if they were the result of multilateral negotiations with a broad consensus on the desirability and feasibility of such rules; b) if there was clarity of perception among stakeholders on the nature of the problem; c) if there was mutual recognition of legitimate self-interests of all stakeholders; and d) if there were commensurate enforcement mechanisms.[7] The proposed code of conduct failed to meet these parameters of legitimacy, and it was abandoned in 1992 (see Box 9.1). But many of the ideas and concepts in the draft code proved viable and resurfaced in other forms. That many of these ideas endured illustrates that the enterprise was sometimes ahead of the curve in sensing the concerns of its stakeholders.

Most of the contributions of the enterprise to knowledge creation have been through data collection and the application of existing concepts and theories rather than through producing ground-breaking new paradigms. This is appropriate for an organization whose charge does not call for such theoretical work. However, the enterprise has on occasion ventured into more abstract paths, as noted in the review of WIRs in Chapter 7. Furthermore, it has been a catalyst for the dissemination of data and facts.

The annual World Investment Report series has become an important and expanding inventory of knowledge and information related to FDI and TNCs and a highly visible contribution of the enterprise. This series, born in New York in 1991 and transferred to UNCTAD in 1993, was ahead of the curve in its ability to provide careful and detailed examination of TNC-related topics through a thorough and multilevel process of peer review involving scholars engaged in frontier research. The series, which has successfully straddled scholarship[8] and policy,[9] has earned respect in academic and government circles and, albeit to a lesser extent, in the business world.

The continued relevance of the enterprise, and indeed of the entire UN system, will be determined by the extent of its contributions in the three critical areas identified in this book—building capacity, creating knowledge, and shaping policy. These contributions, in turn, will depend on the degree to which its capabilities can be directed toward issues of survival and growth in a world still suffering from hostility, poverty, overpopulation, pollution, and other ills.

Other Members of the Galaxy

Whereas this book has devoted much attention to "the enterprise"—the totality of the work by the UNCTC and UNCTAD on TNCs and FDI—other stars in the UN galaxy have made valuable contributions to knowledge on these subjects, as discussed in Chapter 8. Two, notably WIPO and the ILO, predated the creation of the UNCTC and even the UN itself. The ILO began to focus attention on TNCs in the late 1960s, well before the UN Department of Economic and Social Affairs spotlighted the subject. Concurrently, and consistent with its tripartite structure of labor, management, and government, the ILO also focused on labor relations and the employment effects of what it called multinational enterprises. Its tripartite structure gave it a unique trajectory and legitimacy.

The ILO's work led to a major policy instrument, the 1977 Tripartite Declaration of Principles concerning Multinational Enterprises and Social Policy. Its aim was "to encourage the positive contribution which multinational enterprises can make to economic and social progress and to minimize and resolve the difficulties to which their various operations may give rise, taking into account the United Nations resolutions advocating the Establishment of a New International Economic Order."[10] Two decades later, the ILO augmented this declaration with its Declaration on Fundamental Principles and Rights at Work, which placed new emphasis on issues of corporate discrimination against workers and child labor.[11]

Chapter 8 also considered the work of the WHO and other agencies, concluding with the Global Compact, the latest UN initiative to engage TNCs. The WHO's tobacco initiative illustrates the interface between an international organization and its member governments. This organization seized on the public outcry about the deleterious effects of tobacco use to negotiate the 2003 Framework Convention on Tobacco Control, a binding international instrument on the marketing and sale of tobacco. In this instance, the UN had been behind the curve; the anti-tobacco campaign was a result of the coalescence of grassroots movements and government agency activism at the national level. However, the WHO was able to capitalize on evidence accumulated through national litigation and public health research to craft an international instrument which is binding after a government has ratified it. Similarly, the WHO served as an international forum when a controversy over infant formula pitted Nestlé against consumer and other activist groups.

WIPO, a descendant of the oldest international economic accords, has worked with TNCs to protect intellectual property rights. It has also facilitated the transfer of technology to developing countries through training and technical assistance.

During the 1970s, UNESCO, based in Paris, became an arena for North-South confrontation when some developing countries, riding the wave of demands for a New International Economic Order, sought a New International Information Order. These were aimed at reducing some of the asymmetries in access to information between them and industrial nations. However, this effort proved futile and was eventually abandoned. The new UNESCO of the twenty-first century has adopted a more conciliatory posture vis-à-vis TNCs and has developed a working relationship with global media and publishing industries.

UNIDO, too, has shed its former image as an organization strongly influenced by the economic philosophy underpinning central planning. This perception may have sprung from its close working relationship with former eastern bloc countries and their state-owned enterprises. The post-1989 UNIDO has a permanent presence in many developing countries, extensive institutional expertise, and knowledge of the industrialization process and continues to play an active role in developing countries. UNIDO initiatives, such as technical assistance and industry, country, and FDI studies, have contributed to knowledge and information creation, capacity-building, and policy formulation in these countries.

The WHO approach to tobacco control—mandating corporate behavior through a binding multilateral convention fortified with legal teeth—is in stark contrast to the use of the soft power of moral suasion employed by the Global

Compact, an initiative by former Secretary-General Kofi Annan. The compact attempts to convince TNCs that they can do well by doing good—that is, by voluntarily adhering to certain ethical principles anchored in the common heritage of humankind. The ten principles of the compact are grounded in prior UN proclamations, conventions, and declarations and embrace issues relating to human rights, labor standards, the environment, and anti-corruption. Many TNCs and other entities have accepted the principles, although cynics have accused companies of using the UN to "blue-wash" their images by signing on but not following through with serious action. A major argument of proponents of the Global Compact is that corporate social responsibility is good business, and some evidence has proved this to be so.[12] The contrast between these two approaches demonstrates the range of alternatives open to the UN.

In 2005, the Global Compact office, in collaboration with the Swiss government and the International Finance Corporation, organized a conference that focused on the positive relationship between good social conduct and profitability. It held a similar leadership summit in Geneva in summer 2007. In addition to these highly visible events, the office has participated in numerous workshops and seminars around the world to spread its new gospel.

The topic of corporate social responsibility has thus come to the fore once again. In this rejuvenated discussion, advocates present mounting evidence that good deeds often mean a better bottom line. This notion has taken hold in the financial planning industry, where there now are a variety of funds comprised of stocks of socially responsible corporations that are said to be at least as profitable as other funds, if not more so. The compact is comprehensive in nature as it brings together under one umbrella many issues that had been addressed in a piecemeal fashion earlier. Global Compact advocates believe its effectiveness and influence will depend on its ability to fashion and sustain productive partnerships and alliances, not only between TNCs and other actors, but within the UN and with NGOs and national governments. Similarly, members of the UN galaxy have developed organizational capabilities and competitive advantages that can be parlayed into a collective strength.

Contributions and Shortfalls

UN contributions to a greater understanding of and knowledge about TNCs and FDI have issued from many sources but primarily, though not exclusively, from the enterprise. The UN's capacity-building activities and its monitoring and formulation of policy at national and international levels with respect to TNC–host country relations have been impressive and influential. It has contributed in many ways to a better understanding of issues and trends and has also served as a canary in a mineshaft, detecting signs of strain in the global economy. More often than not, the UN and its constituent agencies have been ahead of the curve, although the path has been strewn with obstacles, particularly in the stormy 1970s.

The UN system's greatest strength lies in the core competencies and institutional relationships that its component agencies have honed over the years. UNCTAD and the UNCTC together clock more than thirty years of knowledge and best practices experience on matters dealing with TNCs and FDI and on ways that TNCs and host countries can cooperate to meet the development needs of the latter and the legitimate wealth-seeking objectives of the former. Providing appropriate jobs and the best quality of goods and services at reasonable prices can benefit both TNCs and the countries in which they operate. As learning organizations with the ability to tap into resources, capabilities, and markets throughout the world, TNCs have also transformed themselves in the process, abandoning many of the nationally oriented and sometimes distorting strategies of the 1970s to pursue more productive global-oriented and socially responsible strategies instead.

The enterprise has straddled a fine line between being proactive and reactive. In the years leading up to the creation of the enterprise, UN staff played a proactive role. This was particularly so at the outset, since the desire to establish such an entity was intense among a few member countries and equally intense inside the UN. But once the atmosphere became more temperate and settled, the enterprise reacted to the change in the FDI climate and adapted accordingly. On the whole, evidence has shown that on issues such as transborder data flow and services, investment promotion, and technical assistance to small- and medium-sized enterprises, the enterprise has been ahead of the curve. On earlier issues such as TNCs in South Africa and the more recent issues of labor rights and globalization, the UN has been proactive.

Another important contribution of the enterprise has been the development of indigenous human resources through its many training programs and seminars and through curricula development. Participants in these programs have gained new empirical knowledge and analytical tools.[13]

The greatest achievements of the UN's involvement in matters relating to FDI and TNCs have consisted of assisting its primary beneficiaries—developing countries—through knowledge creation, capacity-building and human capital development, and policy formation and institution-building. Its approach to TNC–host country relations has been nuanced by its attention to the quality of capital and the complementary roles of TNCs, governments, and markets. As times change, there will be questions about how the interests, strategies, and operations of TNCs can be more successfully reconciled with those of national governments.

Changing Context and Swinging Pendulum

The sweeping changes brought on by globalization, the dramatic increase in all forms of international exchange (trade, FDI, capital flows, cross-border mergers and acquisitions) and a renewed push for greater corporate social responsibility are among the major changes between the 1970s when the enterprise was born and today. Comparing the totality of circumstances in earlier times and now, it is clear that there are new opportunities and greater challenges. Earlier attention to ideology has been gradually replaced with a more pragmatic approach to FDI and economic development. Most developing countries have now embraced their own brand of a market-based economic system and seek to use each others' best practices, to coordinate policies and institutional mechanisms when feasible, and to take full advantage of services that the international system can provide.

In the interim, the enterprise had been an agent of change, helping with a gradual paradigm shift in the thinking of developing countries in the 1980s. This trend was bolstered by the accelerated tempo of globalization, the collapse of the communism and the subsequent surge in international capital investment in Central and Eastern Europe, and the progression of an increasing number of erstwhile "developing" countries into the ranks of "emerging" economies.

This changed context is evident in many other ways. In the 1970s, the discussions were dominated by the demand for a new economic order and a more aggressive advocacy role at the UN. The decade saw scandals involving ITT, Gulf, and dozens of other companies as well as some government officials. By contrast, more recent years have seen the rise of Third World TNCs from China, India, South Korea, Mexico, Brazil, and Taiwan. These TNCs have come to resemble their western counterparts by increasing their economic prowess and foreign presence and by beginning to tread where no developing-county firm had gone before by bidding for and buying western companies and challenging global giants on their own turf.[14] These new economic powers engage in their own form of global expansion through mergers and other partnerships. Examples are India's Mittal Steel Company's acquisition of Luxembourg-based Arcelor (and its incursions into Asian and African oil businesses) and Brazil's Companhia Vale do Rio Doce's $17.6 billion bid on a Canadian nickel-mining company, primarily to acquire its management skills.

There have been, nonetheless, recent signs that the pendulum may be swinging again. The earlier era of relative prosperity and optimism was punctuated by the Asian currency crisis in 1997 and the wave of antiglobalization demonstrations that erupted in Seattle in 1999. More turmoil followed after September 11, 2001. Wars and invasions and the rise of cross-border terrorism have become the order of the day as Afghanistan, Iraq, and some African countries, including Somalia and Sudan, are plagued with domestic armed conflict. Radicalism has swept Venezuela, Iran, Peru, Ecuador, Argentina, and even Mexico.[15] Far from being universally embraced, globalization and its primary symbol, the TNC, have come under fire once again. Paradoxically, aside from some targeted attacks on American oil facilities, hotels, resorts, and retail food chains, TNCs seem to have evaded direct assault. Globalization has become the new galvanizer of protest and discontent.

While a few developing countries are becoming hostile to western economic systems and values, the majority of developing countries are pursuing policies of accommodation, institution-building, and market-based economic development in order to further integrate into the global economy and partner with TNCs.

As the context of international economic relations changed, so did the role and influence of the United Nations. As a creature of its constituent member states, it could not deviate far from the views and values of its stakeholders. Constrained by its path-dependency, the UN's attitude toward TNCs, and thus its recommendations to developing-country governments, has undergone a major shift. As an aggregator of a multitude of opinions, the UN has neither promoted TNCs nor advocated radical action against them. Rather, it has acted as a catalyst and, to some extent, a balancer of views as well as a moderator of stakeholders' reactions. Figure 9.1 is a stylistic representation of how the UN can be placed vis-à-vis its member states with respect to the issues relating to TNCs and in relation to an imaginary median of neutrality. It straddles a median between extremes.

In the 1970s, governments' views toward FDI and TNCs spanned a wide spectrum, from those slightly to the right of the neutral line (certain countries in Southeast Asia) to those at the far left (Latin American countries, including Brazil, Chile, and Mexico).[16] Major transformations in the global economy resulted in a gradual global swing to the right, with some countries still at one or another extreme vis-à-vis the rest. In the early twenty-first century, the overall climate placed the majority of countries to the right of the median, with a scant minority (such as Venezuela, Iran, Cuba, and North Korea) still at the left of center.

Figure 9.1 positions the UN closer to the line of neutrality throughout the

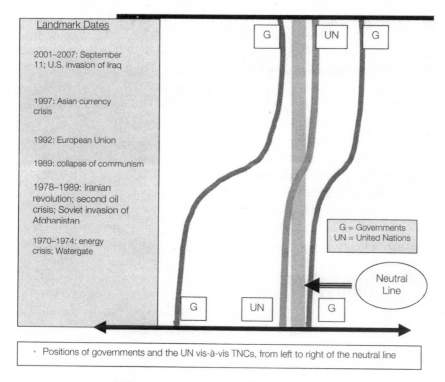

Landmark Dates

2001–2007: September 11; U.S. invasion of Iraq

1997: Asian currency crisis

1992: European Union

1989: collapse of communism

1978–1989: Iranian revolution; second oil crisis; Soviet invasion of Afghanistan

1970–1974: energy crisis; Watergate

G = Governments
UN = United Nations

Neutral Line

· Positions of governments and the UN vis-à-vis TNCs, from left to right of the neutral line

Figure 9.1 Nation-States and the UN System:
A Stylized Representation of Shifts in Position/Perspective since the 1970s

period between the early 1970s and today. The organization has always tended to gravitate toward the center while member countries have swung to the right. Of course, at any given time some countries are at one extreme or the other, depending on the issue at hand. The same is true of the members of the UN galaxy; some are farther to the right, others are closer to the left. On the whole, however, the model posits that the UN has swung to the right over the past forty years and that the system has been both an anchor, keeping the international community steady, and a gravitational force, pulling it toward the center.

Recommendations for Unmet Challenges

In this concluding chapter, we offer a set of suggestions for improvement and further work that aims to bring new players on board and address new and unmet challenges. The triadic relationship between the United Nations, nation-states, and TNCs has changed as nations and firms have evolved. Thus, there is a need for a strategic realignment at the UN in tandem with changing contexts and circumstances. The UN has amply demonstrated the unabated deepening of globalization through FDI and more intense TNC involvement in international economic relations. Various signs point in different directions for the enterprise and the entire UN galaxy.

As the march toward the further globalization of markets, production, and people continues, the world economy could be headed for another stormy period. In the first decade of the twenty-first century, economic and political fractures and heightened cultural and religious tensions have threatened the stability and continuity of global capitalism, which was triumphantly celebrated at the fall of the Berlin Wall. As the epitome of this global capitalism, the TNC has undergone profound transformation, metamorphosing from the predominantly western ethnocentric model to a geocentric one, from a symbol of mistrust and exploitation to an instrument of wealth creation with the potential for doing good, and from an entity to be tamed to one that possesses strengths that should be co-opted. Meanwhile, corporate scandals have produced self-correcting mechanisms within firms as well as a tightening of government oversight and penalties.[17]

The 2000 Millennium Summit brought representatives from 189 countries (including 150 heads of government) and 1,350 NGOs to the UN in New York. At that summit, the world community pledged to launch a concerted attack on poverty, child mortality, illiteracy, hunger, unsafe water, gender discrimination, HIV/AIDS, malaria and other diseases, and the degradation of the environment. The MDGs adopted at that summit seek to achieve universal primary education, improved maternal health, and new global partnerships for development.

The last of the Millennium Development Goals—new global partnerships for development—could well involve TNCs. The UN's Global Compact Office instituted a number of positive incentives to encourage TNCs to participate in that effort. The compact office encourages TNCs to sign onto the compact, arguing that their association with it will burnish their image as good corporate citizens and thereby enhance their value. Cynics have called such positive inducements "blue-washing."

The compliance-reporting instrument of the compact office devised in 2006 is an illustration of the UN's use of soft power and a rebuttal to the charges of blue-washing. It publishes on its Web site a list of companies that have signed the compact but have not reported the specific details of their compliance. It would be appropriate to investigate the impact of such a practice, if any, on corporate strategy to determine whether moral suasion is a better incentive than legal teeth.[18]

As the global economy showed signs of strain and some predicted a possible backlash against globalization and its concomitants, FDI and TNCs, the United Nations system came under scrutiny again. Many stakeholders continued to view it with ambivalence and many felt that it needed to be rejuvenated. Ideas for reform have ranged from tinkering to radical surgery[19] and even abandonment.[20]

Faced with such demands to restructure, reform, or streamline and challenged to collaborate within the system, members of the UN galaxy are on a quest for legitimacy and a scramble for relevance. In addition, at least two high-level panels have recently drafted versions of how the institution can be reconfigured to bring it in concert with the changing times.

Although organizational lethargy often trumps action toward change, some members of the galaxy have risen to the occasion. UNIDO is a case in point. Under a recent restructuring, it cut its staff from 1,600 to 650 while still remaining faithful to its mission of advising developing countries on industrialization and technology transfer strategies. Other UN organs have engaged in similar reconfiguring.

There is little doubt that there is duplication, redundancy, and waste within the UN system. Some large plenary UN meetings are reminiscent of the Chinese People's Congress, with rituals and ceremonial gestures that can stifle open debate and real dialogue. Dignitaries gather, make declarations, and leave chronic problems unresolved. Often projects materialize only at the insistence of an enthusiastic champion who is able to sell the idea to those who control the agenda or the purse strings. Issues can become muddled and agendas can become self-serving.

Nevertheless, this book has demonstrated that the institution's cumulative contributions to our understanding of issues related to international economic relations, particularly TNCs and FDI, have been impressive. If the galaxy did not exist, we would have to invent it. Yet improvements are in order. Below are recommendations that might create a more efficient and cooperative environment in which the UN galaxy can continue its important work.

Emerging Issues on TNCs and FDI: Social, Environmental, and Security Concerns

New and broader issues are beginning to change the direction of discourse on TNCs and FDI. UN studies should institute a more interdisciplinary (for example, sociological, economic, environmental, and ethical) and multifaceted approach to these issues. This kind of approach lends itself to cooperative and consolidated work by the various UN agencies with overlapping interests and agendas. Another issue is related to the new players in the global arena, such as India and China and TNCs from emerging markets, and the impact of their entries on the landscape of TNCs and FDI. As urban areas in India and China have very high pollution levels, these countries will bring the broader issues of environmental protection into the global arena. Environmental protection is already a part of the UN Global Compact and the Millennium Development Goals and is therefore of special interest to the organization.

Strategic Internal Partnerships to Reduce Redundancy

The problems of redundancy and duplication of work might be solved by strategic partnerships among members of the UN galaxy. A new architecture might develop in which a strategic partnership is built among these members that is based on the competitive advantage of each. The 2006 UNCTAD panel also stressed the need to identify comparative advantages and competitive strengths and for partnerships within the UN system and beyond it. The panel urged greater focus, fewer projects, closer contact on the ground in developing countries, and closer ties with NGOs and private business, thereby enhancing UNCTAD's competitive advantage.

Consolidation can also be a solution to duplicative work. For example, some matters related to the international intellectual property regime recently shifted from WIPO to the WTO. And a comparison of the work of UNCTAD on the social dimensions of TNCs and FDI such as employment with that of the ILO on globalization and the right to work shows both a conceptual affinity and an interest and skill overlap between the two organizations. The challenge is to determine the extent to which these two specialized agencies are redundant or complementary. Attempts to consolidate, streamline, and create partnerships between UN agencies can be hamstrung when UN organizations cannot agree on the means of cooperation, even though there is agreement about ends.[21]

Similarly, UNCTAD's work on trade and enhancing the export competitiveness of developing countries is in concert with the WTO's goal of helping developing countries integrate into the global economy. UNIDO has traveled a similar road in promoting industrial development in developing countries. These entities could consult and parse the same concept or issue into its different aspects for each to work on. This would produce a more comprehensive whole and would avoid duplication and save both time and money. Similarities of mission, views, and expertise can combine to create a more powerful force that is greater than the sum of its parts. This kind of cooperation is one of the most promising yet most daunting challenges facing the UN system in its economic development work.

It is a challenge because UN staff, like others, is wary of any incursion onto their turf. Replacing turf battles with true dialogue and the exchange of ideas would ultimately be a benefit, not the least of which would be to the developing countries that many UN agencies are committed to help. Clash of cultures is often one of the key obstacles to successful mergers and strategic partnerships. Some members of the galaxy may see things in a different light. Even within the same UN agency different divisions may not be in full concordance. Organizational lethargy and vested interests may prove the greatest obstacles to strategic partnerships. Some may want sole control of an idea. An example is when two UN agencies cooperate to produce a country report but then cannot agree to jointly publish the results.[22] Dissension among stakeholders within an agency may also hinder synergy, as in the trade and investment divisions of UNCTAD. These obstacles can be overcome by the shared vision, idealism, and common language of development that bind members of the UN galaxy.

External Strategic Partnerships

One shortcoming of the enterprise has been its inability to bring TNCs more fully on board by, for example, creating a stronger link between them and the issues and information covered by the WIR series. The evocative and divisive issue of the code notwithstanding, the enterprise engaged with representatives of TNCs more consistently during its New York years than it has in more recent years. Perhaps because the UN is comprised of governments, nonstate actors are relegated to a second tier. The UN should rededicate itself to creating a special focal point on TNCs within the UN (like the UNCTC in New York) to interface with TNCs about their relations with home and host countries on matters of good corporate citizenship and their impact on the development process. With concomitant authority and responsibility, a reconstituted new enterprise could succeed.

The UN galaxy should strive for stronger bonds with academia. Agencies could send representatives to the most relevant and important academic gatherings. The UN could institute an annual lecture series and have regular meetings with academics to seek their input, as it does successfully in the context of WIRs. There should more opportunities for regular interchanges with representatives from academia, transnational corporations, and NGOs. There might also be an advantage to establishing collaborative relations between small- and medium-sized domestic companies and transnational firms. Both of these could take the form of advisory councils.

Updating Data

Data and information is an area that is ripe for improvement. The enterprise has been very successful in collecting data on FDI and TNCs but has been less successful in the area of refining and widely disseminating that data. The enterprise needs to update the World Investment Directories, which have proven to be a useful information source for investors and host countries alike. There should be more data on geographical as well as sectoral distribution of FDI stocks and flows and changes in them. In addition, some unique data that was painstakingly collected by enterprise staff continues to be underutilized. This includes data about the subsidiaries, sales, and employment of TNCs and other attributes. The enterprise has yet to claim perfection in the reliability of some of its data, but the quality of the statistical information continues to improve and to demand increasing transparency of TNCs.[23]

More Publicity on Work in Progress at the UN

More work is needed to market various UN initiatives. The UN could learn about this from the OECD and World Association of Investment Promotion Agencies, who do it well. One way to market more effectively is to make greater use of its Web site. Another is to make its material more readily available for use in colleges, universities, and executive education programs.

Streamlining and Eliminating Redundancies

A number of blue-ribbon panels, committees, and task forces are deliberating on various reforms and how to implement them and are also making constructive recommendations. For example, in June 2006, UNCTAD's new secretary-general, Supachai Panitchpakdi, appointed a Panel of Eminent Persons to advise him on challenges facing UNCTAD and how best to meet them. This eight-person panel, which included current and former presidents of countries, presented twenty-one recommendations on how to enhance UNCTAD's development role and impact and made significant recommendations relevant to TNC-related activities. One of the panel's recommendations was that all UN agencies sign a compact in which each agency agreed to adhere to the core competency of the other agencies.

The recommendations of UNCTAD's 2006 Panel of Eminent Persons could be beneficial to other members of the galaxy as they interface, to a greater or lesser degree, with governments, TNCs, and NGOs. Thus in structure, strategy, and culture, the United Nations of the twenty-first century is analogous to other global organizations. Both the Bretton Woods institutions and the UN were products of the hegemonic world system that emerged from the ashes of World War II. But whereas the former reflected the power structure epitomized by the dollar standard in a fixed-exchange-rate regime, with all other currencies pegged to it, the latter was global in scope and membership from its beginning. This legacy gives the UN and its constituent parts a competitive advantage over existing and yet-to-be-crafted institutional configurations.

The panel's recommendation of a thorough inventory of UN agency mandates to identify the core competencies in each agency relative to FDI and TNC matters implied that it is not uncommon for the activities of agencies to overlap. This is arguably the case with UNCTAD, the ILO, UNIDO, and WIPO, as well as the Bretton Woods institutions and the WTO. In 2007, the leadership of the IMF and the World Bank were also struggling with restructuring to bring the institutions into better alignment with new global realities.[24] One can point to the WTO's Trade Policy Review series, case studies that analyze the international trade policy framework of countries. Although limited to trade in name, in substance, most cover FDI policies as well.[25] The same is true, to a lesser extent, of UNCTAD's investment policy reviews, which are intended to be limited to FDI but by necessity have expanded into trade.

Some research and capacity-building work of the World Bank and its affiliates the Multilateral Investment Guarantee Agency (MIGA) and the FIAS also overlap with FDI work at UNCTAD. For example, UNCTAD's investment policy reviews are similar to the diagnostic case studies done by the FIAS. A similar overlap in mandate or function is becoming evident between UNCTAD's work on FDI and that of the World Trade Organization. As the WTO's agenda expands to include an increasing array of FDI-related issues, redundancy may increase. The WTO has a solid dispute resolution and enforcement mechanism. This kind of capability eluded the enterprise when it ended its quest for binding rules in the form of code of conduct on TNCs.

An institutional reconfiguration might incorporate FDI-related matters, including ongoing work at the OECD,[26] into an expanded WTO, thereby extending its mandate beyond a negotiating and dispute-settling forum on trade issues to capacity-building and knowledge creation with regard to investment and trade. The World Bank's International Centre for the Settlement of Investment Disputes, which plays a complementary dispute-resolving role, could be folded into this newly agglomerated setup.

What Host Developing Countries Can Do

Developing countries could also do more by overcoming confrontational attitudes and becoming more active partners in "shared success," where FDI, trade, and globalization have benefited firms and nations. They could do a great deal more, too, to collect data. Much of the UN information comes from host countries, many of whose bureaucracies are somewhat frugal in sharing information and providing basic data. Much has been made of the relative softness of the data the enterprise publishes on FDI stocks and flows, mergers and acquisitions, repatriated profits, and the like. Data on sales, employment, and assets on the tables published in WIRs see regular improvement but are still far from ideal.

Alternative Scenarios: Fission, Fusion, or Confusion? Fertile, Fragile, or Fatal?

These recommendations are intended to help bring about a more optimistic future. Reconciling the differences between national interests and those of TNCs and developing a broad consensus on how to meet the daunting challenges ahead will be a function of the interplay of forces that bring all stakeholders in the system together—fusion—and the forces that pull them apart—fission. The outcome may be eventual convergence or perpetual confusion. Perlmutter has used the terms fertile, fragile, and fatal to describe alternative futures. We postulate that as the best available mechanism for building consensus, the UN galaxy can have a decisive role in helping humankind reach for a fertile future and achieve it.

Although members of the UN galaxy have developed along functional lines, each of them dealing with a number of related issues, the multidimensional nature of many real-world challenges requires new organizational configurations. One might be a matrix structure, a networked organizational design that builds on competencies of erstwhile autonomous or even independent entities.[27] Using the TNC model of alliance formation, the UN could develop a structure to deal with the challenges of development. In such an alliance formation, TNCs, NGOs, and governments would each play a role. UNCTAD's expertise and knowledge of FDI and TNCs could combine with those of UNIDO in the area of industrialization for the benefit of both organizations and ultimately for developing countries, the primary intended beneficiary. In May 2006, the World Health Organization was charged by its governing body, the World Health Assembly, with developing a global strategy for intellectual property, health research and development, new medicines for disease that especially affect developing countries, and related intellectual property matters. The WHO could partner with the World Intellectual Property Organization, whose charge is to oversee intellectual property issues. The commission and the UNCTC was originally devised in this matrix configuration; deliberations concerning TNCs during the New York years (1974–92) were conducted by engaging TNCs, other UN agencies, NGOs, and national governments. That the enterprise relocated to UNCTAD is due less to the efficacy of this kind of structure than to the intractability of the problems it was then charged with—in particular, a code of conduct. Failure to enact the code on TNCs stood in contrast to its many successes in knowledge creation and capacity-building.

The World Trade Organization, which was established in 1995 to replace GATT, was empowered to investigate and enforce rules to punish violators. Its viability and utility is fortified with a kind of power UNCTAD does not have.[28] During the previous rounds of international trade negotiations, the agenda had progressively expanded to include, in the Seventh Round, matters related to investment. The dispute settlement mechanism empowered the WTO to mediate and settle disputes and to authorize punishment. It might be appropriate in this time of reassessment to revive the debate on whether FDI/TNC issues fit better under UNCTAD or the WTO. If the UN system were to commission a new Group of Eminent Persons to focus on TNC-related issues and devise a mandate, how would its recommendations differ from those made in 1974? That such an idea has not been put forth suggests that the *problematique* itself has changed from a focus on TNCs to the broader phenomenon of globalization and from confrontation and control to cooperative work and harnessing; now more hands are extended than swords drawn. To this we must add the proliferation of instruments—the web of controls—that TNCs must navigate, from self-imposed instruments to those that are industry-based, NGO-initiated, governmental, regional, and international and from narrowly focused instruments to sweeping instruments. Thus a new blue-ribbon council similar to the 1973–1974 Group of Eminent Persons might now question the need for a binding global contract, seeking instead a mechanism whereby the disparate, conflicting, or suboptimal arrangements can be brought into harmony. Advocates of the UN Global Compact forcefully argue that it comes closest to such an arrangement.

Meanwhile, most countries seek the assets, technology, management skills, market access, and global scope of TNCs and encourage their involvement in the quest of developing countries for economic development. Over the past few decades, empirical evidence has provided ample support for market-based solutions to problems of promoting efficient and sustainable economic development. At the same time, there is near-consensus that the market must be properly "governed" through simple and transparent formal rules, trust-based commercial relationships, a balance of encouragements and penalties, and an understanding of, and general agreement on, the basic rules of engagement.

A new blue-ribbon group would envision such a rule-based scenario as portending an optimistic future. The UN, of course, has made and held countless declarations, goals, and summits. Despite these, the global economy continues to grapple with the Janus face of globalization. There are centrifugal forces that pull its constituent parts away from each other; these include growing income gaps within and between nations and the apparently uncontrollable waves of conflict and migration fueled by such gaps. On the economic front centrifugal forces include the stalemate over global trade talks, persistent protectionism in developed countries, misaligned currencies, and the specter of another round of stagflation similar to those that accompanied the 1973–1974 and 1978–1979 oil crises. Other forces that threaten the fragile system are religious fundamentalism, the tension between faith and reason, and global terrorism.

As the UN system engages in another round of soul-searching, hope remains that the centripetal forces that drive globalization and the universal human quest to seek better lives, fueled by revolutions in telecommunication and transportation, will overcome the monumental obstacles posed by these centrifugal forces.[29] In the torturous path toward global civilization or "first or last global civilization"[30] as Howard Perlmutter calls it, the outcome of the interplay of these centrifugal forces of fission and the centripetal forces of fusion may be nothing but confusion.[31] In Perlmutter's typology, there are three alternative futures, fertile, fragile, and fatal. What James Coleman has called "social capital"—that which is embodied in relationships among persons—and the UN galaxy are mighty valuable global assets.[32] If, as the ultimate "born-global" institution, the UN can combine the collective knowledge and expertise of its constituent parts on TNCs/FDI together with its unique capabilities as a "consensus-builder," to borrow from Joseph Stiglitz, and capture value from the enormous potential it has amassed, a fertile future can materialize.[33] Such a future would combine the technological and organizational assets of TNCs with the UN's social capital. Navigating the future will be far easier if the UN can overcome the centrifugal forces that tend to pull galaxy members away from each other and instead build on their complementarities. A 2006 report of deliberations by some forty foreign policy experts on the future of the UN observed that the organization was merely a sum of its parts, the nation-states that constitute it, which are subject to different and perhaps conflicting expectations. It concluded that the organization can play to its strengths as a provider of humanitarian assistance—what we have called "common cause."[34] The danger this group saw was that the organization might get caught in the tensions that divide developed, emerging, and developing countries.

Thus, the UN is facing external as well as internal pressures. Should the organization fail to rise to internal challenges, it will only muddle through external ones, and confusion will reign. Recall, however, that the United Nations is driven by dreams and visions that can transcend national boundaries. It was built on ideals by idealists and survives on the shoulders of new generations of idealists. The fertile future is there for the taking.

Notes

Series Editors' Foreword

1. Craig N. Murphy, *The UN Development Programme: A Better Way?* (Cambridge: Cambridge University Press, 2006).
2. D. John Shaw, *The UN World Food Programme and the Development of Food Aid* (New York: Palgrave, 2001).
3. Maggie Black, *The Children and the Nations* (New York: UNICEF, 1986); and Maggie Black, *Children First: The Story of UNICEF* (Oxford: Oxford University Press, 1996).
4. For details on the forty books in the Global Institutions Series, edited by Thomas G. Weiss and Rorden Wilkinson, see http://www.routledge.com/politics/ series_list.asp?series=1.
5. Thomas G. Weiss and Sam Daws, eds., *The Oxford Handbook on the United Nations* (Oxford: Oxford University Press, 2007).
6. United Nations Intellectual History Project, *The Complete Oral History Transcripts from UN Voices* (New York: Ralph Bunche Institute for International Studies, 2007).
7. Louis Emmerij, Richard Jolly, and Thomas G. Weiss, *Ahead of the Curve? UN Ideas and Global Challenges* (Bloomington: Indiana University Press, 2001), xi.

Introduction

1. In the literature, the terms transnational corporations (TNCs), multinational corporations (MNCs), and multinational enterprises (MNEs) are often used interchangeably, except where explicit distinction is made. In the mid-1970s, the terminology was debated at some length within the UN and the term transnational corporation was adopted; however, various UN agencies and scholars have employed different terms at different times. Where necessary, differences between these terms will be pointed out. See Box 0.1 for a review of terms and definitions.
2. Foreign direct investment (in contradistinction to other types of investment outside one's national boundaries) is a somewhat slippery concept and has a longer intellectual history than the study of TNCs. Long before preoccupation with the enterprises that invest abroad, scholars had been studying FDI. One critical difference between FDI and other forms on investment abroad has to do with control. Using control as the determining criterion, the contemporary literature defines it as owner-

ship of a controlling interest in the equity of a foreign firm. The concepts of FDI and TNCs have become increasingly intertwined in the literature and in policy debates. The former deals with financial flows, while the latter deals with organizational configuration and legal ownership and control.

3. This is their particular term for TNCs. See Box 0.1.

4. The Framework Convention on Tobacco Control was adopted by the World Health Assembly on 21 May 2003. Its impact has already been felt by tobacco and other TNCs.

5. These scandals are well publicized, and many of the culprits associated with them have been fined, humiliated, and even incarcerated. It was reported on 15 May 2003 that Bernard Ebers, former chairman and CEO of WorldCom, had failed to pay a $25 million installment on a $400 million loan received from WorldCom. See "Report: WorldCom Wireless & Pentagroup Financial LLC," Ripoff Report #28481, available at http://www.ripoffreport.com/reports/0/028/RipOff0028481.htm. A slew of corporate crooks headed for prison; others were forced to give up the helm in humiliation. Such is the magnitude of corporate malfeasance that may give wind to the next hurricane.

6. See Louis Emmerij, Richard Jolly, and Thomas G. Weiss, *Ahead of the Curve? UN Ideas and Global Challenges* (Bloomington: Indiana University Press, 2001).

7. See United Nations, *The Impact of Multinational Corporations on Development and on International Relations* (New York: United Nations, 1974). The volume includes the report of the Group of Eminent Persons.

8. See Raymond Vernon, *In the Hurricane's Eye: The Troubled Prospects of Multinational Enterprises* (Boston: Harvard University Press, 1998).

9. See *World Investment Prospects to 2010: Boom or Backlash?* (New York and London: Economist Intelligence Unit and Columbia University Program on International Investment, 2006).

1. Ideas and Institutions Relevant to Foreign Investment and TNCs Prior to World War II

1. John A. Cantwell, "The Changing Form of Multinational Enterprise Expansion in the Twentieth Century," in *Historical Studies in International Corporate Business*, ed. Alice Teichove, Maurice Lévy-Leboyer, and Helga Nussbaum (Cambridge: Cambridge University Press, 1989).

2. John H. Dunning, *Multinational Enterprises and the Global Economy* (Reading, Mass.: Addison-Wesley, 1993), 99. This early history is documented at length in Dunning, *Multinational Enterprises*; and Raymond M. Jones, *Strategic Management in a Hostile Environment: Lessons from the Tobacco Industry* (New York: Quorum Books, 1997).

3. Dunning, *Multinational Enterprises*, 600.

4. Ibid.

5. John M. Keynes, "Foreign Investment and the National Advantage," *The Nation and Athenaeum* 35 (August 1924): 584–587; Carl Iverson, *Aspects of International Capital Movements* (London and Copenhagen: Levin and Munksgaard, 1935); Royal

Institute of International Affairs, *The Problem of International Investment* (London: Cass, 1937).

6. Dunning, *Multinational Enterprises*, 600.

7. Mira Wilkins, *The Maturing of Multinational Enterprise: American Business Abroad from 1914 to 1970* (Cambridge, Mass: Harvard University Press, 1974).

8. John H. Dunning, *Studies in International Investment* (London: George Allen & Unwin Ltd., 1970), 2–3.

9. See Dunning, *Multinational Enterprises*, Tables 5.1 and 5.2, pp. 117–118.

10. This is not to suggest a lack of studies on the subject. See Alfred D. Chandler, Jr., "The Growth of Transnational Industrial Firms in the U.K. and U.S.: A Comparative Analysis," *History Review* 33, no. 3 (1980): 396–410; Mira Wilkins, *The Emergence of Multinational Enterprise: American Business Abroad from the Colonial Era to 1914* (Cambridge, Mass.: Harvard University Press, 1970), and Douglass North, *Structure and Change in Economic History* (New York: Norton, 1981); and Dunning, *Multinational Enterprises* (and the extensive bibliography therein) point to a few early studies. But most writings related to foreign direct investment came later.

11. This legal concept originated in Latin American jurisprudence. American companies invoked the power of the United States when a dispute arose with Latin American host countries. The Calvo clause, which eventually found its way into all judicial systems of the region, maintains that "aliens are not entitled to rights and privileges not accorded to nationals, and that therefore they must seek redress for grievances only before the local authorities." A. A. Fatouros, "International Law and the Third World," in *International Law: Cases and Material*, ed. Louis Henkin, Richard C. Pugh, Oscar Schachter, and Hans Smit (St. Paul, Minn.: West Publishing, 1980), 699.

12. See Thomas Gladwin and Ingo Walters, *Multinationals Under Fire: Lessons in the Management of Conflict* (New York: John Wiley & Sons, 1980), 9–27.

13. Ibid., 26.

14. See, for example, Cleona Lewis, *America's Stake in International Investment* (Washington, D.C.: Brookings Institution, 1938); Wilkins, *The Emergence of Multinational Enterprise*; and Dunning, *Multinational Enterprises*, chapters 5, 20, 21, and 22.

15. Lee C. Nehrt, J. Frederick Truitt, and Richard W. Wright, *International Business Research: Past, Present, and Future* (Bloomington: Indiana University Press, 1970).

16. Eugene Stanley, for example, addressed such questions as which services private foreign investors and their governments could provide to one another and "the role of international private investment in the origin and development of international political friction and war." Quoted in David Burtis, Farid Lavipour, Steven Ricciardi, and Karl P. Sauvant, *Multinational Corporation-Nation-State Interaction: An Annotated Bibliography* (Philadelphia: Foreign Policy Research Institute, 1971), 239.

17. Edward Hallett Carr, *The Twenty Years' Crisis, 1919–1939* (London: Macmillan, 1939), 210.

18. Ibid., 224

19. Ibid., 226.

20. This was the dream of the League's founding fathers, including Woodrow

Wilson. But the United States failed to join, thus helping to guarantee the League's demise.

21. The Covenant of the League of Nations, available at http://www.yale.edu/lawweb/avalon/leagcov.htm (accessed 22 January 2003).

22. Ibid.

23. "The Members of the League agree that the manufacture by private enterprise of munitions and implements of war is open to grave objections." Ibid., Article 8.

24. League of Nations, *Commercial Policy in the Post-War World* (Geneva: League of Nations, 1945), 21.

25. See ibid.

26. See D. H. MacGregor, *International Cartels* (Geneva: League of Nations, 1930); and Mira Wilkins, *The Maturing of Multinational Enterprise: American Business Abroad from 1914 to 1970* (Cambridge, Mass.: Harvard University Press, 1974).

27. League of Nations, *Commercial Policy in the Post-War World*, 210.

28. In *The Theory of Economic Development*, originally published in 1911, Joseph Schumpeter put forth the argument that growth in a private enterprise economy was caused by entrepreneurs seeking to appropriate revenue from their invention or innovation. Schumpeter argued that they should be granted temporary monopoly over the use of this intellectual property so that their new invention, innovation, or process could lead to new industries and markets and thus to economic development. Economists refer to this as "Schumpeterian rent."

29. Trade-related intellectual property rights were negotiated as part of the 1986–1994 Uruguay Round agreements in an attempt to streamline the way these rights are protected around the world and to bring them under common international rules.

30. Originally a loose coalition of developing countries when UNCTAD was established in 1964, the G-77 grew to some 130 countries but retained its original name. It seeks to promote the interests of developing countries, primarily within UNCTAD, but the group's influence ebbs and flows depending on the issue and the time. For a comprehensive history, see Odette Jankowitsch and Karl P. Sauvant, eds., *The Third World without Superpowers: The Collected Documents of the Non-Aligned Countries*, 4 vols. (Dobbs Ferry, N.Y.: Oceana, 1978).

31. The debate over the code of conduct for technology transfer was one of the arenas in which North-South confrontation played itself out. See Tagi Sagafi-nejad, Richard Moxon, and Howard V. Perlmutter, eds., *International Technology Transfer Control Systems* (New York: Pergamon, 1981); and Surendra J. Patel, Pedro Roffe, and Abdulqawi Yusuf, eds., *International Technology Transfer: The Origins and Aftermath of the United Nations Negotiations on a Draft Code of Conduct* (The Hague: Kluwer Law International, 2001).

2. The Early Post–World War II Era

1. Colonial relationships that had prevailed for a century or more between Great Britain, France, the Netherlands, and Spain and other powers and their colonies gradually gave way to arm's-length relations between independent countries. This ground shift continued its swing to the extreme and helped explain the tumult witnessed in the 1970s. This theme will be explored further in Chapter 3.

2. As World War II was drawing to a close, finance ministers, politicians, and economists (including John Maynard Keynes) from some forty-four countries gathered in Bretton Woods, New Hampshire, and devised a tripartite system for the postwar capitalist world: the World Bank, the IMF, and the ITO.

3. It is significant that the International Trade Organization, the third leg of the Bretton Woods institutions, failed to include foreign investment explicitly in its mandate, although the subject had been included in its original formulation under the 1944 Havana Charter.

4. See UN, *Multinational Corporations in World Development* (New York: UN Department of Economic and Social Affairs, 1973), Table 9, pp. 144–145. Note the discrepancy between total inflows and outflows, a measurement problem that continued to persist in subsequent publications that built on this pioneering study.

5. See World Bank, *World Development Indicators 2002* (Washington, D.C.: World Bank, 2002).

6. In fact the average annual rate of growth of the world economy during this decade was about 5.3 percent, while world trade grew at a rate of around 7.9 percent. See World Bank, *World Development Indicators 2002*. For the growth of membership in the number of independent states, see John Naisbeth, *Global Paradox: The Bigger the World Economy, the More Powerful Its Smallest Players* (New York: W. Morrow, 1994).

7. See Osvaldo Sunkel, "Big Business and 'Dependencia': A Latin American View," *Foreign Affairs* 50 (April 1972): 517–534. See also UN, *Multinational Corporations in World Development*, 42 and passim.

8. See John Dunning, *Explaining International Production* (London: Allen and Unwin, 1988), Tables 3.1 and 3.2, pp. 74–75. Figures are in nominal dollars.

9. See John H. Dunning, *Multinational Enterprises and the Global Economy* (Reading, Mass.: Addison-Wesley, 1993), 555 and passim. Dunning sees the relationship between host countries and TNCs in three phases: honeymoon, confrontation, and reconciliation. See also Tagi Sagafi-nejad, "Transnational Corporations–Host Country Relations and the Changing Foreign Direct Investment Climate: Toward 2000," *International Trade Journal* 9, no. 1 (1995): 85–106.

10. See Mira Wilkins, *The Emergence of Multinational Enterprise: American Business Abroad from the Colonial Era to 1914* (Cambridge, Mass: Harvard University Press, 1970).

11. See Sidney Dell, *The United Nations and International Business* (Durham, N.C.: Duke University Press for UNITAR, 1990), 8–13.

12. See Dunning, *Multinational Enterprises*.

13. See UNCTAD, *Proceedings of the United Nations Conference on Trade and Development*, vol. 1, *Final Act and Report* (New York: UN, 1964), 49–50.

14. See UNCTAD, *Trends in International Investment Agreements: An Overview* (Geneva: UN, 1999), 16.

15. See Richard W. Cottam, *Nationalism in Iran* (Pittsburgh, Pa.: University of Pittsburgh Press, 1964); Michael Tanzer, *The Political Economy of International Oil and the Underdeveloped Countries* (Boston: Beacon Press, 1969); Neil H. Jacoby, *Multinational Oil: A Study in Industrial Dynamics* (New York: Macmillan, 1974). Reports of this coup continued to surface over the years, haunt U.S.-Iran relations, and serve as an example of the interference of covert operations in the internal af-

fairs of other countries. See "The Oily Americans," *Time Magazine*, 19 May 2003, 53, for a discussion of the role the CIA played in Iran during the oil nationalization episode.

16. The developing countries' demand for a NIEO in 1974 spawned a burgeoning cottage industry and a large volume of publications. For a comprehensive chronicle of the activities of the G-77, see Odette Jankowitsch and Karl P. Sauvant, eds., *The Third World without Superpowers: The Collected Documents of the Non-Aligned Countries*, 4 vols. (Dobbs Ferry, N.Y.: Oceana, 1978). Volume 1 in this series contains the UN General Assembly resolutions pertaining to the NIEO.

17. Driven by a desire to control the flow of information and in the guise of preventing "undesirable Western influences" from creeping into media reports, many developing countries also sought to devise a New International Information Order, complete with Third World news agencies and South-South collaborations beyond the reach of western media. The forum for this drive was UNESCO, and the effort failed.

18. The Andean Common Market (ANCOM) was a regional subgroup within the Latin American Free Trade Agreement in 1969 between Bolivia, Chile, Colombia, Ecuador, and Peru. Venezuela joined in 1973. ANCOM's 1971 "Decision 24" was designed as a comprehensive foreign investment code hailed by developing countries beyond the group as a symbol of Third World solidarity and activism. The decision was assailed by advanced-market-economy countries and by TNCs as overly restrictive and counterproductive. Although subsequently modified and rendered less onerous, it remained unpopular and was eventually abandoned in practice. See Karl P. Sauvant and Hajo Hasenpflug, eds., *The New International Economic Order: Confrontation or Cooperation between North and South?* (Boulder, Colo.: Westview Press, 1977). For an English translation of Decision 24, see *Journal of Common Market Studies* 10 (June 1972): 339–359.

19. See Howard V. Perlmutter and Tagi Sagafi-nejad, *International Technology Transfer: Guidelines, Codes and a Muffled Quadrilogue* (New York: Pergamon Press, 1981).

20. See Dunning, *Multinational Enterprises*, 117–126.

21. See John H. Dunning, *Studies in International Investment* (London: George Allen & Unwin Ltd., 1970), 37. See also Anthony Sampson, *The New Europeans* (London: Hodder and Stoughton, 1968).

22. See Robert Gilpin, *U.S. Power and Multinational Corporations: The Political Economy of Foreign Direct Investment* (New York: Basic Books, 1975).

23. See U.S. Department of State, unpublished mimeo, 1969.

24. See Jean-Jacques Servan-Schreiber, *Le Defi Americain* (Paris: Edition Denoel, 1967); and Servan-Schreiber, *The American Challenge*, trans. R. Steele (New York: Atheneum, 1968). This volume drew attention to the perception among Europeans that American takeovers of European companies were imminent.

25. Jack N. Behrman, *National Interests and the Multinational Enterprise: Tensions among the North Atlantic Countries* (Englewood Cliffs, N.J.: Prentice Hall, 1970).

26. See Kari Levitt, *Silent Surrender: The Multinational Corporation in Canada* (New York: St. Martin's Press, 1970); and A. E. Safarian, *Foreign Ownership of Canadian Industry* (Toronto: University of Toronto Press, 1966).

27. "McDonaldization" was a similar term that became popular many years later. See Benjamin Barber, *Jihad vs. McWorld: How Globalism and Tribalism Are Reshaping the World* (New York: Ballantine Books, 1996).

28. See Inter-American Development Bank (IDB), *Multinational Investment, Public and Private, in the Economic Development and Integration of Latin America* (Washington, D.C.: IDB, 1968), 19.

29. The liberalization of capital markets and removal of restrictions on outward FDI was not universal across the West, but most of the restrictions on capital exports were gradually lifted.

30. See Hans Singer, "The Distribution of Gains between Investing and Borrowing Countries," *American Economic Review* 40, no. 2 (1950): 473–485; G. C. Allen and Audrey G. Donnithorne, *Western Enterprise in Far Eastern Economic Development: China and Japan* (New York: Macmillan, 1954); Edith T. Penrose, "Foreign Investment and Growth of the Firm," *Economic Journal* 66 (1956): 220–235; John H. Dunning, *American Investment in British Manufacturing Industry* (London: George Allen and Unwin, 1958); John H. Dunning, *Studies in International Investment* (London: George Allen & Unwin Ltd., 1970); and William Brian Reddaway with S. J. Potter and Christopher Thomas Taylor, *Effects of U.K. Direct Investment: Final Report* (Cambridge: Cambridge University Press, 1968).

31. See L. E. Fouraker and John M. Stopford, "Organizational Structure and Multinational Strategy," *Administrative Science Quarterly* 13 (1968): 47–64; and John M. Stopford and Louis T. Wells, Jr., *Managing the Multinational Enterprise: Organisation of the Firm and Ownership of the Subsidiaries* (London: Longman, 1972).

32. As evident from the writings of such prominent international business scholars as Jack Behrman, Richard Farmer, Endel Kolde, Howard Perlmutter, Barry Richman, Richard Robinson and as documented by Sanjaya Lall, *Foreign Private Investment and Multinational Corporations: An Annotated Bibliography* (New York: Praeger, 1975); and Tagi Sagafi-nejad and Robert Belfield, *Transnational Corporations: Technology Transfer, and Development: A Bibliographic Sourcebook* (New York: Pergamon, 1980). See Jack N. Behrman, *National Interest and Multinational Enterprise: Tensions among the North Atlantic Countries* (Englewood Cliffs, N.J.: Prentice Hall, 1970); Richard D. Robinson, *Internationalization of Business* (Hindsdale, Ill.: Dryden Press, 1984); Endel J. Kolde, *International Business Enterprise* (Englewood Cliffs, N.J.: Prentice Hall, 1968); Howard V. Perlmutter and Tagi Sagafi-nejad, *International Technology and Transfer: Codes, Guidelines, and a Muffled Quadrilogue* (New York: Pergamon, 1981).

33. See Dell, *The United Nations and International Business,* 12–19.

34. Ibid., 13.

35. N. T. Wang, interview with the author, New York, 22 August 2000.

36. Other volumes in this series have devoted sufficient attention to these aspirations and attendant targets. See, for example, Louis Emmerij, Richard Jolly, and Thomas G. Weiss, *Ahead of the Curve? UN Ideas and Global Challenges* (Bloomington: Indiana University Press, 2001).

37. During ECOSOC deliberations on restrictive business practices, for instance, the representatives of the USSR, Czechoslovakia, and Poland asserted that the U.S. proposal was "designed to camouflage the objectives of U.S. monopolies which were seeking to dominate world markets, exploit underdeveloped countries, and discrimi-

nate against the socialist countries." Dell, *The United Nations and International Business*, 15.

3. The 1970s

1. The demand for a new order, the roots of which went back to 1959, if not earlier, was inspired primarily by OPEC actions and was given wings by successive UN resolutions concerning permanent sovereignty over natural resources. These demands led to an intense if ephemeral round of "global negotiations" to implement the goals of the NIEO. After several years of futile to-and-fro, they were abandoned. Other initiatives have continued to come both from within and without the UN system, and to the extent they relate to ideas concerning TNCs, they will be discussed in later chapters. For a comprehensive review of the NIEO literature, see Linus A. Hoskins, "The New International Economic Order: A Bibliographic Essay," *Third World Quarterly* 3, no. 3 (1981): 506–527.

2. The term "Sovereign State of ITT" was coined by Anthony Sampson; see *The Sovereign State of ITT* (New York: Stein and Day, 1973). Other writings on these corporate scandals include books by Ovid Demaris, *Dirty Business: The Corporate-Political Money-Power Game* (New York: Harper's Magazine Press, 1974); Fredrick Warren-Boulton, *Vertical Control of Markets: Business and Labor Practices* (Cambridge, Mass.: Ballinger Publishing, 1978); and John T. Noonan, Jr., *Bribes* (New York: Macmillan, 1984).

3. See Charles Kindleberger, ed., *The International Corporation: A Symposium* (Cambridge, Mass.: MIT Press, 1970); Raymond Vernon, *Sovereignty at Bay: The Multinational Spread of U.S. Enterprises* (New York: Basic Books, 1971); and Raymond Vernon, "The Product Cycle Hypothesis in the New International Environment," *Oxford Bulletin of Economics and Statistics* 41 (1979): 255–267; Robert Black, Stephen Blank, and Elizabeth C. Hansen, *Multinationals in Contention: Responses at Governmental and Intergovernmental Levels: A Research Report* (New York: The Conference Board, Inc., 1978); Thomas Gladwin and Ingo Walters, *Multinationals Under Fire: Lessons in the Management of Conflict* (New York: John Wiley & Sons, 1980).

4. Originally published in Paris by Edition Denoel in 1967, *Le Defi Americain* became a symbol of European resentment toward U.S. foreign investments in Europe. See Jean-Jacques Servan-Schreiber, *The American Challenge* (New York: Atheneum, 1968).

5. Richard J. Barnett and Ronald E. Muller, *Global Reach: The Power of the Multinational Corporations* (New York: Simon and Schuster, 1974), 213.

6. Kari Levitt, *Silent Surrender: The Multinational Corporation in Canada* (New York: St. Martin's Press, 1970).

7. Stephen H. Hymer, "The Multinational Corporation and the Law of Uneven Development," in *Economics and the World Order: From the 1970s to the 1990s*, ed. Jagdish Bhagwati (New York: Macmillan, 1972).

8. See Stephen Hymer, "The Efficiency Contradictions of Multinational Corporations," *American Economic Review* 60, no. 2 (1970): 441–448; and Hymer, "The Multinational Corporations and the Law of Uneven Development," in *Economics of the World Order: From the 1970's to the 1990's* Jagdish Bhagwati, ed. (New York: Mac-

millan, 1972); Miguel Wionczeck, "Mexican Nationalism, Foreign Private Investment and Problems of Technology Transfer," in *Private Foreign Investment and the Developing World*, ed. P. Ady (New York: Praeger, 1971), 191–206; and Constantine V. Vaitsos, "The Process of Commercialization of Technology in the Andean Pact," in *International Firms and Imperialism*, ed. Hugo Radice (London: Penguin, 1975); Osvaldo Sunkel, "Big Business and 'Dependencia': A Latin American View," *Foreign Affairs* 50 (April 1972): 517–534.

9. The Watergate affair exposed incidents of corruption in the Nixon White House. It was revealed, for instance, that "Northrop had contributed $150,000 (some of it laundered) to Nixon's re-election campaign; although company officials did not know it, the money went to a secret fund to defend the Watergate burglars"; LeRoy Ashby and Rod Gramer, *Fighting the Odds: The Life of Senator Frank Church* (Pullman: Washington State University Press, 1994), 458. Northrop was among the companies that was later indicted.

10. Ashby and Gramer, *Fighting the Odds*, 412.

11. See ibid., 416. See also Josephine Alexander, "Chile: The Anderson Intervention," *The Nation* 214, no. 17 (24 April 1972).

12. See U.S. Congress, Senate Committee on Foreign Relations, Subcommittee on Multinational Corporations, *Multinational Corporations and United States Foreign Policy: Hearings Before the Subcommittee on Multinational Corporations of the Committee on Foreign Relations* (Washington, D.C.: Government Printing Office, 1973–1976).

13. Ashby and Gramer, *Fighting the Odds*, 416.

14. Ibid., 419.

15. Ibid.

16. In the Netherlands, Prince Bernhard was implicated in the Lockheed and Northrop bribery scandals. Elsewhere, high government officials in Bolivia, Iran, Japan, Saudi Arabia, and South Korea were implicated, as were Lockheed, Northrop, Exxon, and Gulf. The last two signed "voluntary disclosures" about payoffs abroad. See Ashby and Gramer, *Fighting the Odds*, 453 and passim.

17. In the course of amending the 1934 Securities Exchange Act in 1977, the House of Representatives praised the SEC's work and its unique role and mandate.

18. The SEC division that investigated these scandals was headed by Stanley Sporkin, "the son of a judge, and a dedicated investigator"; Ashby and Gramer, *Fighting the Odds*, 457.

19. U.S. House of Representatives, *Unlawful Corporate Payments Act of 1977*, Report No. 95-640, available at http://www.usdoj.gov/criminal/fraud/fcpa/history/1977/houseprt.html (accessed 1 November 2007).

20. Ashby and Gramer, *Fighting the Odds*, 457.

21. Ibid., 457–458; see also Fredrick-Warren Boulton, *Vertical Control of Markets: Business and Labor Practices* (Cambridge, Mass.: Ballinger Publishing Co., 1978), 255–257; Anthony Sampson, *The Arms Bazaar: From Lebanon to Lockheed* (New York: Viking Press, 1977), 271–273.

22. See Committee on Banking, Housing, and Urban Affairs, *Foreign Corrupt Practices and Domestic and Foreign Investment Improved Disclosure Acts of 1977*, U.S. Senate Report No. 95-114 (1977), available at http://www.usdoj.gov/criminal/fraud/fcpa/history/1977/senaterpt.html (accessed 1 November 2007).

23. See Gladwin and Walters, *Multinationals Under Fire*, 323.

24. Corporate scandals, including "slush funds" and bribes, were pervasive not only in U.S. companies but in European (Siemens) and Asian (Hyundai) companies in the post-9/11 era.

25. The background to these resolutions, including ECOSOC resolution 1359 (XLV), is discussed in Sidney Dell, *The United Nations and International Business* (Durham, N.C.: Duke University Press for UNITAR, 1990), 55–72.

26. See United Nations, *Report on the Panel on Foreign Investment in Developing Countries* (Amsterdam, 16-20 February 1967), E.69.II.D.12. See also Dell, *The United Nations and International Business*, 175.

27. Ibid.

28. Unlike the first meeting, which generated an agreed-upon text, this meeting produced only a rapporteur's report. See United Nations, *Panel on Foreign Investment in Latin America* (Medellín, Colombia, 8–11 June 1970), E.71.II.A.14. See also Dell, *The United Nations and International Business*, 56–62.

29. Dell, *The United Nations and International Business*, 61.

30. Ibid., 62.

31. Ibid.

32. After leaving the post of under-secretary-general, de Seynes reflected:

> After thousands of encounters and millions of words, the so-called dialogue on transnational corporations is still more evocative of adversary court proceedings than a Socratic cognitive process. . . . All parties should appreciate the true value and usefulness of United Nations institutions, the rationalizing and mediating influence which it can exert through a continuous debate, through searching studies and analyses and through practical programs of action and through the definition of broad guidelines, morally binding. . . . Some of us have not given up all hope of seeing the emergence of quasi judiciary international instances which were once visualized [but] broad consensus is unlikely, as long as a climate of mutual confidence has not emerged. . . . Yet they may gradually appear more acceptable when it is realized that coalitions and oligopolistic behavior not only are liable to create very unstable and turbulent conditions, but that they may also lead to situations where all the parties involved are losers.

Philippe de Seynes, "Transnational Corporations in the Framework of a New International Economic Order," *CTC Reporter* 1, no. 1 (December 1976): 15.

33. For two comprehensive bibliographies on FDI, see Sanjaya Lall, *Foreign Private Investment and Multinational Corporations: An Annotated Bibliography* (New York: Praeger, 1975); and David Burtis, Farid Lavipour, Steven Ricciardi, and Karl P. Sauvant, *Multinational Corporation–Nation-State Interaction: An Annotated Bibliography* (Philadelphia, Pa.: Foreign Policy Research Institute, 1971). For technology transfer, see Tagi Sagafi-nejad and Robert Belfield, *Transnational Corporations, Technology Transfer, and Development: A Bibliographic Sourcebook* (New York: Pergamon, 1980).

34. Jean-Jacques Servan-Schreiber's *Le Defi Americain* (Paris: Edition Denoel, 1967) is one of the earlier books critical of U.S. TNCs. It was received with much enthusiasm when first published in French. Its English title, *The American Challenge*,

became synonymous with the enormous power that American TNCs were perceived to possess.

35. *Business International* ceased publication in 1993. It was briefly succeeded by *Crossborder Monitor*, which was eventually bought by *Economist* and absorbed into its research unit, the Economist Intelligence Unit.

36. It was first published by the United Nations as *World Economic Survey 1949–50* in 1951. It has been continued annually since, having changed its title to *World Economic and Social Survey* in 1994.

37. ECOSOC resolution 1721 (28 July 1972). Emphasis added.

38. Department of Economic and Social Affairs, *The Impact of Multinational Corporations on Development and on International Relations* (New York: United Nations, 1974), 3.

39. The Bureau of Intelligence and Research and the Policy Planning Council at the U.S. Department of State organized the conference.

40. National Association of Manufacturers, *U.S. Stake in World Trade and Investment: The Role of the Multinational Corporation* (New York: The Association, n.d.).

41. Senators Thomas A. Burke (D-Ohio) and Vance Hartke (D-Indiana) proposed the bill.

42. *International Affairs*, published in Moscow by the All-Union Society Znaniye, which was associated with the Soviet Academy of Sciences, was among the most ardent critics of multinational corporations. It published several highly critical articles in the 1970s. See, for instance, G. Skorov, "The 'Transfer of Technology' and Neocolonialist Manoevres," *International Affairs* 5 (May): 55–62. For other critical views of multinational corporations, see Paul A. Baran and Paul Sweezy, "Notes on the Theory of Imperialism," *Monthly Review* 17, no. 10 (1966): 15–31; and Benjamin J. Cohen, *The Question of Imperialism: The Political Economy of Dominance and Dependence* (New York: Basic Books, 1973).

43. A study of Singapore showed that in 1966, affiliates from the main investing countries contributed one-third of the value added in manufacturing. See Helen Hughes and You Poh Seng, eds., *Foreign Investment and Industrialization in Singapore* (Canberra: Australian National University Press, 1969), 192.

44. See Tagi Sagafi-nejad and Howard V. Perlmutter, "Perception Gaps and Mistrust as Obstacles to Multilateral Solutions: Some Empirical Evidence," in *International Technology Transfer: The Origins and Aftermath of the United Nations Negotiations on a Draft Code of Conduct*, ed. Surendra J. Patel, Pedro Roffe, and Abdulghawi Yusuf (The Hague: Kluwer Law International, 2001), 247–256, for an empirical study that demonstrates areas of consensus and dissent regarding technology transfer control systems such as national laws, corporate codes, or international guidelines from the perspectives of home and host-country governments and firms.

4. The Group of Eminent Persons

1. De Seynes served as a diplomatic emissary under French prime minister Pierre Mendès-France in several European capitals before coming to the United Nations in 1955. His interest in foreign investment issues was evident as early as 1944, when he became involved in the drafting of investment provisions of the Havana

Charter, which envisioned the creation of an International Trade Organization but was never ratified. A progressive French Foreign Service officer, de Seynes was a brilliant intellectual who wrote his own speeches. In one such speech at ECOSOC, he emphasized that the misdeeds allegedly perpetrated by TNCs must cease. In 1976, he left as UN under-secretary-general for economic and social affairs and joined the United Nations Institute for Training and Research (UNITAR) as a senior special fellow. He died in April 2003.

2. Director-general of the International Labour Organization since 1998.

3. Somavía's father-in-law, Hernan Santa Cruz, was the first Chilean ambassador to the UN. He was active in the formation of the UN Economic Commission for Latin America and was the president of the Economic and Social Council in the late 1960s and early 1970s. When Santa Cruz was ambassador in Geneva, Somavía was working on foreign investment issues within the Andean Group. See "The Oral History Interview of Juan Somavía, 2 October 2001," in *The Complete Oral History Transcripts from UN Voices*, CD-ROM (New York: UNIHP, 2007).

4. The Allende government's actions drew strong criticism from the United States and praise, albeit subtle, from the Soviet-bloc countries. The democratic election that brought Allende to power was touted by the Soviets and their sympathizers as a victory of socialism over capitalism. For U.S. foreign policy, this outcome could not be allowed to stand. A combination of domestic forces, CIA intervention, and support from ITT brought down the Allende regime and installed the pro-western regime of Augusto Pinochet. In the process, the Nixon administration incurred the wrath of domestic as well as international critics. For details of the ITT affair, see U.S. Senate, Select Committee to Study Governmental Operations with Respect to Intelligence Activities, *Covert Action in Chile 1963–1973* (Washington, D.C.: Government Printing Office, 1975), available at http://www.derechos.org/nizkor/chile/doc/covert.html. See also Anthony Sampson, *The Sovereign State of ITT* (New York: Stein and Day, 1973).

5. Franklin Root pointed out that "the attempt by the International Telephone and Telegraph Company (ITT) to get the U.S. government to exert economic pressure on the Allende government of Chile reinforced allegations throughout Latin America that the U.S. multinational enterprises pose a threat to national economic independence." Franklin R. Root, *International Trade and Investment*, 5th ed. (Cincinnati, Ohio: South-Western Publishing, 1984), 514.

6. See Philippe de Seynes, "Transnational Corporations in the Framework of a New International Economic Order," *CTC Reporter* 1, no. 1 (December 1976): 15. Emphasis added.

7. His staff initially included, among others, Jacob Muzak, Gustave Feissel, Sidney Dell, N. T. Wang, and Sotirios Mousouris.

8. The twenty members included ten from developed and ten from developing and socialist countries. Careful attention was paid to ensure balanced representation, both geographically and politically. See Box 4.1 for the list of members of the group. Some, including John Deutsch of Canada, had dual roles or had traversed between private, academic, and government sectors during their careers.

9. See Richard Jolly, Louis Emmerij, Dharam Ghai, and Frédéric Lapeyre, *UN Contributions to Development Thinking and Practice* (Bloomington: Indiana University Press, 2004), 57–58.

10. Senator Jacob Javits of the United States was the sole member of the GEP who was a government representative. Organizers later explained that the main players were TNCs and developing-country governments. Although American academics, many of whom had pioneered the study of FDI and TNCs, were notable by their absence, the views of European, Japanese, and developing-country academics played a moderating role.

11. See UN Department of Economic and Social Affairs, *Summary of the Hearings Before the Group of Eminent Persons to Study the Impact of Multinational Corporations on Development and on International Relations* (New York: United Nations, 1974), 19.

12. The UN staff provided a number of other detailed studies on the transfer of technology, taxation, and investment codes.

13. In both format and content, it became a model for several studies that followed, including UNCTAD's annual World Investment Report, which was started in 1991 and is still published annually.

14. At its 1971 General Conference, the International Labour Organization adopted a resolution on the social problems raised by "multinational undertakings." This served as a springboard for the ILO's work, which is discussed later. Note the terminology used in the ILO (MNCs), in contrast to what was used in the Secretariat and other bodies (TNCs) and in contradistinction to the terminology adopted later.

15. This resolution deals with the sovereign right of developing countries to regulate foreign investment in order to ensure that foreign capital operates in accordance with their national development needs.

16. According to the late N. T. Wang, the DESA staff, himself included, asked a number of academics from Harvard University, the University of Pennsylvania, and elsewhere to draft portions of the text without attribution. The UN staff edited the manuscript and issued it as a UN document. Contributors included Raymond Vernon, who had authored pioneering studies on multinational corporations, and some of his younger collaborators including Louis T. Wells and John Stopford.

17. The choice of the word "dimensions" is interesting. The word "impact" would have implied a more rigorous treatment and evaluation of the work of TNCs, while the word "dimensions" dilutes this emphasis.

18. See United Nations, *Multinational Corporations in World Development* (New York: United Nations Department of Economic and Social Affairs, 1973), 87.

19. Scholars whose work was incorporated into the analysis are too numerous to list, but they include Raymond Vernon, Frederick T. Knickerbocker, Jack Behrman, Pierre Uri, John Dunning, Daniël Van den Bulcke, John Stopford, Louis T. Wells, Franklin Root, Howard Perlmutter, Raymond Mikesell, Gerald Helleiner, W. B. Reddaway, Constantine Vaitsos, Robert Stobaugh, A. E. Safarian, Lawrence Franko, Joseph Nye, Osvaldo Sunkel, Arghyrios Fatouros, Jean-Jacques Servan-Schreiber, Harry Johnson, Stephen Hymer, Walter Chudson, Gary Hufbauer, Raúl Prebisch, Albert O. Hirschman, Charles Kindleberger, and George Ball.

20. UN, *Multinational Corporations*, 2.

21. Ibid., 3; emphasis added.

22. Ibid.

23. This is an interesting assumption. It was another decade before the term "Third World multinationals" entered the parlance. The first major conference to

deal with this new breed was held in 1979 at the East-West Center in Honolulu. Among its participants were the present author and Richard Moxon from the University of Washington. Contributors to the edited volume produced after the conference included Edward Chen, John Dunning, Donald Lecraw, Louis Wells, and Eduardo White. See Krishna Kumar and Maxwell G. McLeod, eds., *Multinationals from Developing Countries* (Lexington, Mass.: Lexington, 1981). See also Louis T. Wells, Jr., *Third World Multinationals: The Rise of Foreign Investment from Developing Countries* (Cambridge, Mass.: MIT Press, 1983).

24. The report contained forty-three tables in its Annex III. The format of the tables subsequently became the template for the database on TNCs maintained and updated within the UN system. See Chapter 5.

25. UN, *Multinational Corporations*, 3.

26. The battle lines were being drawn already as two adversarial groups promoted their own approaches. This conflict is encapsulated in disagreement over language; for example, "codes" versus "guidelines."

27. UN, *Multinational Corporations*, 77.

28. Established in 1949, the International Confederation of Free Trade Unions is comprised of unions in some 156 countries. Its priorities are employment and international labor standards; dealing with multinationals; trade union rights; equality for women, people of color, and migrants; and trade union organization and recruitment. See www.icftu.org.

29. UN, *Multinational Corporations*, 87.

30. A general agreement on international investment akin to the General Agreement on Tariffs and Trade had been proposed by Paul Goldberg and Charles Kindleberger in 1970. See Paul Goldberg and Charles Kindleberger, "Toward a GATT for Investment: A Proposal for Supervision of the International Corporation," *Law and Policy in International Business* 2 (Summer 1970): 295–325. The Soviet Union was a major supporter of the aborted International Trade Organization and wanted it resurrected. These political undertones undoubtedly had a dampening effect on the discussions.

31. UN, *Multinational Corporations*, 102.

32. Gustave Feissel, special assistant to de Seynes, traveled to Washington to learn from congressional aides about the details and mechanics of how hearings should be conducted. Personal communication with the author.

33. This explanation was provided by Gustave Feissel in a personal communication.

34. See UN Department of Economic and Social Affairs, *Summary of the Hearings Before the Group of Eminent Persons*.

35. Ibid., 41.

36. Ibid., 296.

37. Ibid., 375.

38. Ibid., 381–384.

39. Ibid., 432–440.

40. Ibid., 441–445.

41. Because of the company's dual nationality, Woodroofe was chairman in Great Britain, Klijnsra in the Netherlands.

42. UN Department of Economic and Social Affairs, *Summary of the Hearings Before the Group of Eminent Persons*, 445.

43. Ibid., 356.

44. Ibid., 168–170.

45. Ibid., 11.

46. Ibid., 327. The practices of off-shoring, outsourcing, setting up tax haven subsidiaries, "domestic international sales corporations," and "foreign sales corporations" did not exist in the 1970s or were just beginning. In subsequent years, subsidiaries and tax havens similar to those predicted by Nye became a commonplace tax evasion scheme. These practices finally incurred the wrath of the WTO and the OECD, which intensified their investigation of these practices.

47. UN Department of Economic and Social Affairs, *Summary of the Hearings Before the Group of Eminent Persons*, 341.

48. Ibid., 342.

49. Ibid., 345.

50. Vagts was referring to the recent Chilean nationalizations of foreign investments that had led to what subsequently became known as the "Chilean Affair," which provided much of the steam for U.S. congressional hearings and the UN initiative to establish the GEP. Given that Juan Somavía was a Chilean national and a member of the GEP, his silence during this testimony is noteworthy. More likely, he was not present during this particular session. Otherwise, given his overall position—sympathy for Third World causes—he might have spoken up. His silence, or absence, may have helped him; he was later appointed as the rapporteur of the GEP.

51. UN Department of Economic and Social Affairs, *Summary of the Hearings Before the Group of Eminent Persons*, 405.

52. Ibid., 199.

53. Ibid., 23.

54. A year earlier, at the Third UNCTAD conference, Mexico's president had introduced the basic elements of a Third World manifesto, which was later to be enshrined, together with its twin National Sovereignty over Natural Resources, at the UN General Assembly as the Charter of Economic Rights and Duties of States These documents gave some developing countries justification for expropriating or nationalizing foreign assets.

55. UN Department of Economic and Social Affairs, *Summary of the Hearings Before the Group of Eminent Persons*, 126–134.

56. Vaitsos had earlier done a study of U.S. pharmaceutical companies in Latin America that revealed evidence of excessive prices and transfer pricing. Vaitsos attributed these practices to imperfect markets and lack of competition. This was one of the studies that gave wind to the critics of TNCs. See Constantine V. Vaitsos, "The Process of Commercialization of Technology in the Andean Pact," in *International Firms and Imperialism*, ed. Hugo Radice (London: Penguin, 1975).

57. Hymer died in an automobile accident before the report was completed. In part to honor his memory but also because they were deemed useful, his entire written and oral statements were reproduced in the report.

58. UN Department of Economic and Social Affairs, *Summary of the Hearings Before the Group of Eminent Persons*, 216.

59. Ibid., 218.

60. Ibid., 220.

61. Melville Watkins, *Foreign Ownership and the Structure of Canadian Industry* (Ottawa: Privy Council, 1968).

62. Ibid., 235.

63. Ibid., 349. This point was examined in an edited volume by John Dunning thirty years later; see John H. Dunning, *Making Globalization Good: The Moral Challenges of Global Capitalism* (Oxford: Oxford University Press, 2003).

64. UN Department of Economic and Social Affairs, *Summary of the Hearings Before the Group of Eminent Persons*, 350–353.

65. Notably John Dunning and Juan Somavía.

66. According to Dunning, Jha was scrupulously fair and as objective as he could be, a man of considerable experience and first-rate judgment—and a good joke teller as well!

67. Prior to coming to New York, Jha had been governor of Jammu and Kashmere, India's ambassador to the United States, and governor of the Reserve Bank of India.

68. The report may not have delved into the testimony thoroughly enough. They were seen as sufficiently important, nevertheless, to warrant separate publication in full (455 pages). See UN Department of Economic and Social Affairs, *Summary of Hearings Before the Group of Eminent Persons*.

69. UN Department of Economic and Social Affairs, *Summary of the Hearings Before the Group of Eminent Persons*, 15.

70. Ibid., 25.

71. Ibid., 26. Emphasis added.

72. Ibid., 35.

73. This was a particularly prescient observation; in the early twenty-first century, cultural imperialism became perhaps the main concern regarding the negative aspects of globalization.

74. The International Development Strategy for the Second Development Decade was articulated under the auspices of the United Nations on UN Day, 24 October 1970. It followed a similar UN initiative launched in 1961 that was known as the First Development Decade. This had been proposed by John F. Kennedy in 1961 and was embodied in General Assembly resolution 1710 (XVI). The International Development Strategy of the Second Development Decade called for a number of new measures to combat poverty and help developing countries in their quest for economic development. It set priorities and targets for the 1970s, one of which was an increase in development assistance to 0.7 percent of donor countries' GNP by the end of the decade.

75. UN Department of Economic and Social Affairs, *Summary of the Hearings Before the Group of Eminent Persons*, 39.

76. Ibid., 40.

77. Ibid., 46. Emphasis in original.

78. Ibid., 47.

79. Ibid., 48. Emphasis added. This resolution represented a slight departure from the UNCTAD's position, which asserted that the sovereign power of each state

allowed it to fix the amount of compensation and be the sole jurisdiction for dispute settlement.

80. This recommendation no doubt referred to South Africa's apartheid regime, although both "human rights" and "racism" have been hotly debated and contested terms within the UN.

81. From 1972 to 1974, UNCTAD undertook a number of country case studies on the topic of the transfer of technology. Subjects included Spain, Chile, and Hungary. A series of background papers, including *Guideline for the Study of the Transfer of Technology to Developing Countries* (1972), were prepared by Charles Cooper, Amartya K. Sen, Frances Stewart, and others under the leadership of Surendra Patel, an UNCTAD economist.

82. These, too, relate to UNCTAD's work to establish multilateral rules on restrictive business practices. See Chapter 6 for details.

83. UN Department of Economic and Social Affairs, *Summary of the Hearings Before the Group of Eminent Persons*, 86.

84. Ibid., 104.

85. Ibid., 105.

86. Ibid., 110.

87. The issue of corruption was mentioned more than once in the course of GEP deliberations. Hans Matthoefer, a West German federal minister associated with a German trade union, was one of the most outspoken critics of corrupt practices of multinational corporations. In an ironic twist, he was implicated in a corruption scandal in Germany several years later. Gustave Feissel, interview with the author, Santa Rosa, California, 22 September 2005.

88. Reflecting on his 1971 book *Sovereignty at Bay* and the 1977 sequel, *Storm over the Multinationals*, Raymond Vernon observed in 1981 that "in 1971, the advocates and the opponents of multinational enterprises were already locked in furious combat" but by 1981 "the tumult of the 1970s over the multinational issue has lost some of its stridence." Raymond Vernon, "Sovereignty at Bay: Ten Years After," *International Organization* 35, no. 3 (1981): 517–529, reprinted in *Multinational Corporations: The Political Economy of Foreign Direct Investment*, ed. Theodore Moran (Lexington, Mass.: Lexington Books, 1984), 247–259.

89. John H. Dunning and Rageish Narnla, *Multinationals and Industrial Competitiveness* (Cheltenham, UK, and Northampton, Mass.: Edward Elgar, 2004).

90. Dunning, personal communication with the author.

5. The Commission and the Centre

1. Never as extreme in its collective position as the few vocal members at its fringes, the UN system has, on the whole, represented the aggregate position of its constituent parts. See the concluding chapter for elaboration of this point.

2. For names of government representatives, see "The Commission on Transnational Corporations," *The CTC Reporter* 1, no. 1 (December 1976): 4–5.

3. The term "nucleus Centre" was the forerunner to the name "UNCTC." Center staff used this creative term because its executive director had yet to be appointed and the Centre had not officially started its work. See "Background and Ac-

tivities of the Commission and the Centre on Transnational Corporations," *The CTC Reporter* 1, no. 1 (December 1976): 6.

4. Originally titled Information and Research Centre on Transnational Corporations, the name was simplified to UNCTC.

5. Before being appointed executive director of the UNCTC, Sahlgren had served in the Finnish Foreign Ministry in Europe, Egypt, and China and had been Finland's permanent representative to the United Nations in Geneva and chairman of the Council of the GATT for 1974–1975. After his term as executive director of UNCTC ended in 1982, he served until 1985 as executive secretary of the UN Economic Commission for Europe. See "The Oral History Interview of Klaus Sahlgren, 19–22 July 2002," in *The Complete Oral History Transcripts from UN Voices*, CD-ROM (New York: UNIHP, 2007). See also Klaus A. Sahlgren, "Scenes from My UN Journey," in *Finns in the United Nations*, ed. Kimmo Kiljunen (Helsinki: The Finnish United Nations Association, 1996), 196–214.

6. In a 2002 interview with the UN Intellectual History Project, Sahlgren asserted that he would not have taken a position with a rank lower than assistant secretary-general. The political and high-profile nature of the UNCTC warranted that its head have direct access to the Secretary-General; "The Oral History Interview of Klaus S. Sahlgren," 31.

7. In the same interview, Sahlgren stated that Juan Somavía (appointed as director-general of the International Labour Organization in 1998) was the other contender for the post. Ibid.

8. The annual budget, which started at about $35 million, was augmented by extra-budgetary contributions from governments, the first being a $600,000 donation from Holland. The Dutch government faithfully continued its financial support to the enterprise, well into the Geneva years, as did governments of Scandinavia, Switzerland, Japan, France, and the United Kingdom. The European Union and UNDP also contributed. These extra-budgetary funds, which accounted for about a quarter of the budget, provided flexibility. During the UNCTAD years, the annual budget ranged between $64 million and $75 million, about a fourth of which came in the form of extra-budgetary contributions.

9. UN document E/5655, May 1975.

10. As discussed in Chapter 4, the major differences had already surfaced during the GEP hearings, as reflected in individual remarks included in the report. Comments by Jacob Javits, for instance, stood in contrast to views expressed by Mexican and other developing-country representatives.

11. UN document E/C.10/12, 28 January 1976.

12. UN document ST/CTC/3, 1976.

13. UNCTC, *Transnational Corporations: A Selected Bibliography 1988–1990* (New York: UN, 1991).

14. UNCTC, *University Curriculum on Transnational Corporations*, 3 vols. (New York: UN, 1991). Vol. 1: *Economic Development*; Vol. 2: *International Business*; Vol. 3: *International Law*.

15. UN document ST/CTC/38, 1983.

16. UN document ST/CTC/39, 1986.

17. They contained FDI-related information on Asia and the Pacific (vol. 1), Central and Eastern Europe (vols. 2 and 8), developed countries (vol. 3), Latin America

and the Caribbean (vols. 4 and 9), Africa (vol. 5), West Asia (vol. 6), and Asia and the Pacific (vol. 7). See http://www.unctad.org/templates/Page.asp?intItemID=3204&lang=1.

18. See UNCTC, *Transnational Corporations in the International Semiconductor Industry* (New York: UNCTC, 1986).

19. UNCTAD's *World Investment Report 2005* addressed the developmental impact of technology transfer to developing countries by focusing on internationalization of research and development and its impact on host developing countries. The following year, the report went further by identifying and analyzing Third World TNCs, entities that perhaps best exemplify the coming of age of developing countries. Third World TNCs are arguably the finest manifestation of the absorption of technology by former recipients; no longer merely at the receiving end of the technology flow, these entities burst on the scene in full force in the first decade of the twenty-first century. See also proceedings of the International Conference on the Rise of TNCs from Emerging Markets: Threat or Opportunity? Columbia Program on International Investment, New York, 24–25 October 2006.

20. UN Department of Economic and Social Affairs, *Multinational Corporations in World Development* (New York: UN Department of Economic and Social Affairs, 1973), 90, document ST/ECA/190.

21. See *CTC Reporter* 1, no. 3 (December 1977): 15.

22. See UNCTAD, *World Investment Report 2001: Promoting Linkages* (Geneva: UNCTAD, 2001).

23. UNCTC, *Transnational Corporations in World Development: A Re-examination* (New York: UN, 1978).

24. This table's basic format remained essentially unchanged over the years. In its original form, data was reported on foreign sales as a percentage of total sales, with similar figures for production, earnings, and employment. In subsequent reports, as better and more comprehensive data became available, similar figures were presented for assets and employment and were combined to construct a "transnationality index" (TNI).

25. UN, *Transnational Corporations in World Development*, 5.

26. Ibid., 10.

27. UNCTC, *Transnational Corporations in World Development: The Third Survey* (New York: UN, 1983), 1.

28. Ibid., 15.

29. From New York to Geneva, the enterprise remained cautious about unbridled liberalization, favoring always the balance that host countries and the international community needed to strike between laissez-faire and state control. We will return to this theme in the concluding chapter.

30. UNCTC, *Transnational Corporations in World Development: Trends and Prospects* (New York: UN, 1988), i.

31. At 623 pages, it was a record-breaker for the UNCTC.

32. The top fifty in the 1985 "billion dollar club" of the largest mining and manufacturing TNCs included three Third World TNCs and oil companies from Mexico, Brazil, and Kuwait.

33. UNCTC, *Transnational Corporations in World Development*, 9.

34. Ibid., 353.

35. The list included Jagdish Bhagwati, Sidney Dell, Norman Girvan, Arghyrious

Fatouros, Guy de Jonquieres, Sanjaya Lall, Robert Lipsey, Charles-Albert Michalet, Goran Ohlin, Dorothy Riddle, Osvaldo Sunkel, Louis Turner, Constantine Vaitsos, Raymond Vernon, and Louis Wells. See ibid., iii–iv.

36. The UNCTC distributed its publications among developing countries at reduced cost.

37. Some of the studies were requested by the commission while others were initiated by UNCTC staff. It is difficult to gauge precisely whether the driving force for these resided with the former or the latter. Good ideas have many parents; bad ones are orphans.

38. See UNCTC, *Transnational Corporations in the International Semiconductor Industry* (Geneva: UN, 1986).

39. Ibid., 360.

40. See "Selected Publications of the United Nations Centre on Transnational Corporations" (New York: United Nations, n.d.), available at UNCTAD.

41. See UN Commission on Transnational Corporations, *Research on Transnational Corporations: Preliminary Report of the Secretariat*, ECOSOC document E/C/10/1, 28 January 1976. This 219-page report is a comprehensive review of research on the political, economic, and social aspects of TNCs.

42. See UNCTC, *University Curriculum on Transnational Corporations*, 3 vols. (New York: UNCTC, 1991).

43. See UNCTC, *Transnational Corporations: A Selected Bibliography* (New York: UNCTC, 1993).

44. See John H. Dunning and Karl P. Sauvant, eds., *The United Nations Library on Transnational Corporations* (London: Routledge, 1992–1993), 20 volumes.

45. *Research on Transnational Companions: Preliminary Report of the Secretariat* (ECOSOC document E/C.10/12, 28 January 1976) was prepared for the second session of the Commission on Transnational Corporations, which met in Lima, Peru, on March 1976.

46. See UNCTC, *Survey of Research on Transnational Corporations* (New York: UNCTC, 1977).

47. See John H. Dunning and John C. Cantwell, eds., *IRM Directory of Statistics on International Investment and Production* (London: Macmillan, 1987).

48. See UNCTAD, *World Investment Directory 1992*, Vol. 1, *Asia and the Pacific* (Geneva: UNCTAD, 1992); *World Investment Directory 1992*, Vol. 2, *Central and Eastern Europe* (Geneva: UNCTAD, 1992); *World Investment Directory 1992*, Vol. 3, *Developed Countries* (Geneva: UNCTAD, 1992); *World Investment Directory 1994*, Vol. 4, *Latin America and the Caribbean* (Geneva: UNCTAD, 1994); *World Investment Directory 1996*, Vol. 5, *Africa* (Geneva: UNCTAD, 1996); *World Investment Directory 1996*, Vol. 6, *West Asia* (Geneva: UNCTAD, 1996); *World Investment Directory 2000*, Vol. 6, *Asia and the Pacific* (Geneva: UNCTAD, 2000); *World Investment Directory*, Vol. 8, *Central and Eastern Europe 2003* (Geneva: UNCTAD, 2003); *World Investment Directory*, Vol. 9, *Latin America and the Caribbean 2004* (Geneva: UNCTAD, 2004). All are available at http://www.unctad.org/templates/Page.asp?intItemID=3204&lang=1.

49. For a report of some of these seminars, see John H. Dunning and Don Lecraw, "The UNCTC Curricula on TNCs: A Contribution to International Business in Developing Countries," *Journal of Teaching International Business* 6, no. 3 (1995): 1–15.

50. See UNCTC, *Transnational Corporations: A Selective Bibliography, 1983–1987*, 2 vols. (New York: UN, 1988); UNCTC, *Transnational Corporations: A Selective Bibliography, 1988–1990* (New York: UN, 1991); UNCTC, *Transnational Corporations: A Selective Bibliography, 1991–1992* (New York: UN 1993).

51. Examples of the shift in orientation can be seen in title of a 1996 ESCAP/UNCTAD monograph: *Foreign Investment in Asian Stock Markets* (New York: United Nations, 1996).

52. UN, *Transnational Corporations and Their Impact on Economic Development on Asia and the Pacific* (Bangkok: ESCAP, 1982).

53. ECA/UNCTC Joint Unit, *Transnational Corporations in the Copper Industry in Zaire*, UN document E/ECA/UNCTC/5, October 1979.

54. ECA/UNCTC Joint Unit, *Transnational Corporations in Africa: Some Major Issues*, UN document E/ECA/UNCTC/21, January 1983.

55. For a report on the activities of some of these joint units, which seem to have peaked in the mid-1980s, see "Activities of the Joint Unit," *CTC Reporter* 15 (Spring 1983): 21–29.

56. See Paul Goldberg and Charles Kindleberger, "Toward a GATT for Investment: A Proposal for Supervision of the International Corporation," *Law and Policy in International Business* 2 (Summer 1970): 295–325.

57. It is also conceivable that de Seynes was influenced by the Havana Charter discussions of the 1940s, which he attended, and was sympathetic to the idea of including FDI matters in a global trade regime, as the proposed Havana Charter had done when it called for the establishment of an international trade organization. The omission of investment from the mandate of the more narrowly focused 1947 GATT assured its survival as the third Bretton Woods institution, whereas the inclusion of investment doomed the international trade organization.

58. UN Department of Economic and Social Affairs, *Summary of the Hearings Before the Group of Eminent Persons to Study the Impact of Multinational Corporations on Development and on International Relations* (New York: United Nations, 1974), 101.

59. Ibid., 54.

60. See George W. Ball, "Cosmocorp: The Importance of Being Stateless," *Columbia Journal of World Business* 25 (November/December 1967): 25–30.

61. UN Commission on Transnational Corporations, *Preliminary Report of the Secretariat*, ECOSOC document E/C/10/1, 28 January 1976.

62. See Juliana Geran Pilon, "Just When U.N. Is in Range," *Wall Street Journal*, 18 September 1986. Pilon was employed by the Heritage Foundation.

63. See Peter Hansen, "The U.N. Code for Multinationals," Letter to the Editor, *Wall Street Journal*, 28 October 1986, 32.

64. For a detailed analysis of such instruments at the corporate, industry, national, regional, and international levels—from the Paris Union of 1883 to the aborted code on technology transfer in the 1980s—see Tagi Sagafi-nejad, Richard Moxon, and Howard V. Perlmutter, eds., *International Technology Transfer Control Systems* (New York: Pergamon, 1981). See also Jill Murray, *Corporate Codes of Conduct and Labour Standards* (Geneva: Bureau of Labour Activities, ILO, 2006), available at http://www.ilo.org/public/english/dialogue/actrav/publ/codes.htm (accessed 1 November 2007).

65. In the early 2000s, the Consus Group, an organization of attorneys and man-

agement consultants, was positioning itself to provide information on the corporate codes of a multitude of companies. See www.Consusgroup.com.

66. This section draws on the 1986 hearings: UNCTC, *Transnational Corporations in South Africa and Namibia: United Nations Public Hearings*, 4 vols. (New York: United Nations, 1986–1987).

67. Pressure to end apartheid and bring down the racist regime of South Africa gained momentum in the 1980s as civic organizations rallied to the cause in Europe and North America. Candlelight vigils and demonstrations propelled governments and the international community into action. The United Nations provided a number of forums for such pressure. The UNCTC hearings, discussed here, were one such forum.

68. In 1920, the League of Nations entrusted South Africa with the administration of Namibia. In 1966, the United Nations revoked that mandate, and in 1971, South Africa's occupation was formally declared illegal under international law. This discussion will emphasize the interrelationship between multinational corporations and apartheid in South Africa, not South Africa's illegal occupation of Namibia.

69. That deadline was in accord with those suggested by Bishop Desmond Tutu and Rev. Leon Sullivan.

70. Both laws can be traced to the establishment in 1914 of the National Party in South Africa, which began implementing the apartheid these laws had legitimized. They prohibited nonwhites from living in or owning property in areas reserved for whites. Using these laws, the apartheid regime forcibly relocated urban residents. These laws were officially repealed in 1991. Today, the District 6 Museum in downtown Cape Town, South Africa, is dedicated to preserving some of the evidence of this practice.

71. See UNCTC, *Transnational Corporations in South Africa and Namibia*, 1:16.

72. See Ibid., vol. 2.

73. Debates on economic sanctions to effect change in regime or its behavior have generally pitted two sides against each another. Advocates argue that it strangles the economy and increases discord among the populace, thus precipitating regime change. Opponents argue that the elite are immune from any hardship that an embargo may cause and that the general public, whose goodwill is essential for regime change, are the ones likely to suffer the most. Peter Hansen, under whose leadership these South African hearings took place, referred to "smart" sanctions in his 2001 interview with the author, suggesting that if they are crafted smartly, sanctions can indeed be an effective means of bringing on pressure and causing change in behavior if not regime. The art of designing such "smart" sanctions had not yet been perfected in the 1980s. Nevertheless, together with the massive public outcry, sanctions must have had some impact, although the exact magnitude can never be measured. Peter Hansen, interview with the author, UNRWA office, Gaza, 13 May 2001.

74. See UNCTC, *Transnational Corporations in South Africa: Second United Nations Public Hearings, 1989*, vols. 1 and 2 (New York: UN, 1990).

75. These were BMW, British Petroleum, Cadbury Schweppes PLC, Colgate-Palmolive Company, Loctite Corporation, The National Mutual Life Association of Australasia Ltd., Rank Xerox Ltd., Salzgitter AG, Shell International Petroleum Co., Ltd., and The Upjohn Company.

76. The Statement of Principles of United States Firms with Affiliates in the Re-

public of South Africa was articulated in 1977 by Reverend Leon Sullivan, a black minister in Philadelphia and a member of the Board of Directors of General Motors. The statement laid out codes of conduct to provide racial equality in employment and social equality outside the workplace.

77. At the time of the hearings, the ICFTU had members in ninety-eight countries.

78. See David Albright, "South Africa's Secret Nuclear Weapons," *ISIS Report* (May 1994), available at http://www.isis-online.org/publications/southafrica/iro594.html (accessed 20 June 2004).

79. See Klaus A. Sahlgren, "Scenes from my UN Journey," in *Finns in the United Nations*, ed. Kimmo Kiljunen (Helsinki: The Finnish United Nations Association, 1996), 196–214.

80. As noted in Chapter 4, this image was a by-product of the 1971–1974 events surrounding the creation of the UNCTC and the commission.

81. See U.S. Department of State, "Multinational Corporations," *GIST: A Quick Reference Aid on U.S. Foreign Relations*, pamphlet (Washington, D.C.: Bureau of Public Affairs, U.S. Department of State, 1986).

82. To the U.S. government, the term "state-owned enterprises" was synonymous with Soviet-bloc companies.

6. From New York to Geneva

1. See UNCTAD, *Beyond Conventional Wisdom in Development Policy: An Intellectual History of UNCTAD, 1964–2004* (Geneva: UN, 2004). Available online at http://www.unctad.org/en/docs//edm20044_en.pdf.

2. Ibid., xii.

3. Ibid., xi.

4. As with other international organizations, UNCTAD's foray onto the Internet was gradual. It began in the late 1990s and slowly expanded as more publications were uploaded onto its Web site. By 2004, as many publications became available on the Web, that medium surpassed print as a method of distribution. Some events were broadcast on the Web, including the annual launch of the World Investment Reports.

5. See Hansen's preface to *Transnational Corporations in World Development: Trends and Prospects* (New York: UNCTC, 1988), i. The fourth in the series that began with the 1973 report, *Multinational Corporations in World Development*, which set the stage for the creation of the UNCTC, metamorphosed into the annual World Investment Report.

6. The phrase "race to the bottom" connotes competitive bidding by host countries to attract FDI by lowering barriers and increasing the battery of incentives—the inverse of competitive devaluation and beggar-thy-neighbor policies of the Great Depression of the 1930s.

7. "Washington Consensus," a phrase coined by John Williamson in 1989, encapsulated the notion of economic liberalism along the lines advocated by the United States and its Treasury Department, the World Bank, and the International Monetary Fund. Consensus among them produced ten remedies for developing countries' economic woes: 1) fiscal discipline; 2) reordering of public expenditures in developing countries; 3) tax reform; 4) financial liberalization; 5) adoption of a single com-

petitive exchange rate; 6) trade liberalization; 7) elimination of barriers to foreign direct investment on the part of developing countries; 8) privatization of state-owned enterprises; 9) deregulation of market entry and competition; and 10) ensuring secure property rights. See John Williamson, "A Short History of the Washington Consensus," paper commissioned by Fundación CIDOB for a conference titled From the Washington Consensus towards a New Global Governance, Barcelona, 24–25 September 2004. See also John Williamson, "Democracy and 'Washington Consensus,'" World Development 21, no. 8 (1993): 1329–1336.

8. As the U.S. ambassador to the United Nations in the first half of the 1980s, Jeanne Kirkpatrick was an ardent supporter of "the market solution."

9. U.S. laws and policies on equal employment opportunity (EEO) and affirmative action are analogous here. EEO-related measures are intended to create a level playing field for all, whereas affirmative actions policies are intended to right wrongs due to injustice in the past.

10. The Kennedy Round of GATT negotiations did not satisfy the more radical developing countries, who felt that liberalizing their trade regimes was not in their interest.

11. See Rubens Ricupero, "Nine Years at UNCTAD: A Personal Testimony," in UNCTAD, Beyond Conventional Wisdom in Development Policy, x, available at http://www.unctad.org/en/docs//edm20044_en.pdf.

12. There was turbulence on many university campuses in the United States and Europe, the most infamous being the deaths of Vietnam War protesters at Kent State University in Ohio.

13. The term is borrowed from Rubens Ricupero, "Nine Years at UNCTAD: A Personal Testimony."

14. These have been in Geneva, 1964; New Delhi, 1968; Santiago, 1972; Nairobi, 1976; Manila, 1979; Belgrade, 1983, Geneva, 1987; Cartagena, 1992; Midran (South Africa), 1996; Bangkok, 2000; and São Paolo, 2004.

15. See Howard V. Perlmutter and Tagi Sagafi-nejad, International Technology Transfer: Guidelines, Codes and a Muffled Quadrilogue (New York: Pergamon Press, 1981); Surendra J. Patel, Pedro Roffe, and Abdulghawi Yusuf, eds., International Technology Transfer: The Origins and Aftermath of the United Nations Negotiations on a Draft Code of Conduct (The Hague: Kluwer Law International, 2000); and Tagi Sagafi-nejad and Howard V. Perlmutter, "Perception Gaps and Mistrust as Obstacles to Multilateral Solutions: Some Empirical Evidence from Technology Transfer Codes," in Patel, Roffe, and Yusuf, International Transfer of Technology, 247–256.

16. These initiatives soon lost their luster as OPEC's success, which commodity-exporting developing countries were trying to emulate, fizzled.

17. See UNCTAD, "Voluntary Peer Review on Competition Policy: Kenya," UN document TD/RBP/CONF.6/8, 2005. A similar peer review was conducted for Jamaica.

18. See UNCTAD, "Report of the Fifth United Nations Conference to Review All Aspects of the Set of Multilaterally Agreed Equitable Principles and Rules for the Control of Restrictive Business Practices," UN document TD/RBP/CONF.6/15, 2006.

19. In interviews with the author, Donald Guertin, an executive from Exxon Corporation who participated in these advisory groups, recalled working amicably with

the UNCTC during those days and finding the work productive. Interview with the author, Washington, D.C., 20 September 2001.

20. Peter Hansen, interview with the author, United Nations Relief and Works Agency Office, Gaza, 13 May 2001.

21. Ibid.

22. Ibid.

23. After Sauvant retired in 2005, he became officer in charge of the Division of Investment, Technology and Enterprise Development and subsequently its division chief.

24. Numerous critical editorials about and negative reporting on the work of the new division characterized this publication, whose Geneva editor, C. Raghavan, repeatedly criticized the World Investment Report for what he perceived as its biased analysis favoring TNCs and FDI. See www.sunsonline.org.

25. Hansen claimed that his dismissal was one of Boutros-Ghali's first acts as Secretary-General in late 1991 and early 1992. Hansen was not sure whether the Secretary-General had been asked to kill the UNCTC. He stated, "I do know for sure that the Americans had made the Centre a *bête noire*. The Americans seemed to need a lot of assurances from prospective Secretary-Generals that they would do certain things. . . . This is the nature of a position like that. So certainly there is a strong circumstantial case for it but I don't have the knowledge for sure to say this was demanded." The Secretary-General asked Hansen to return three months later, but by this time, the reorganization was already under way. So "[my being fired] was not personal," added Hansen. Hansen, interview with the author, United Nations Relief and Works Agency Office, Gaza, 13 May 2001.

26. According to the Global Policy Forum, a Web-based NGO specializing in matters related to the United Nations, "UN Secretary-General Boutros Boutros-Ghali undertook a number of reforms at the beginning of his term in 1992, including reorganizing the Secretariat. Many of his structural reforms were concessions to Washington and to influential conservative think-tanks such as the Heritage Foundation. Boutros-Ghali's reorganization notably eliminated the Center on Transnational Corporations, a pioneering office that most companies disliked but many NGOs admired for its excellent research into TNCs and its proposals for a TNC 'code of conduct.'" Quoted in "Secretary-General Boutros Boutros-Ghali's Reform Agenda—1992–1996," available at http://www.globalpolicy.org/reform/initiatives/1992.htm.

27. Hansen noted: "Given that nowadays the growth of foreign direct investment has outpaced trade by a factor of 3 or 4, one could venture to say that CTC might have evolved into the bigger brother and UNCTAD the smaller one. But at the time UNCTAD had the history, the building, and everything. That made it sensible to make the move from New York to Geneva." Peter Hansen, interview with the author, United Nations Relief and Works Agency Office, Gaza, 13 May 2001.

28. In a 2001 restatement of its original mandate, the division was to work toward an integrated framework, both "vertically" (analyzing policy, building capacity, and building consensus) and "horizontally" (investment, technology, and enterprise internationalization). See UNCTAD, *DITE Activities Report, 2001* (Geneva: UNCTAD, 2001), 5. Annual reports were made available on the Web in later years. See http://www.unctad.org/TEMPLATES/Page.asp?intItemID=3703&lang=1.

29. See John H. Dunning, *Multinational Enterprises and the Global Economy* (Addison-Wesley, 1993).

30. See UN Department of Economic and Social Affairs, *Summary of the Hearings Before the Group of Eminent Persons to Study the Impact of Multinational Corporations on Development and on International Relations* (New York: United Nations, 1974), 95–97.

31. The literature on international accounting and the related corporate issue of transfer pricing have both received intense attention, especially since the OECD published *Transfer Pricing Guidelines for Multinational Enterprises and Tax Administrations* in 2001. See John Neighbour, "Transfer Pricing: Keeping It at Arm's Length," *OECD Observer*, April 2002, available at http://www.oecdobserver.org/news/printpage. php/aid/670/Transfer_pricing:_Keeping_it_at_arms_length.html (accessed 29 June 2006).

32. From 1973 to 1999, the organization was known as the International Accounting Standards Committee. It was reconstituted as the International Accounting Standards Board in 2000. See http://www.iasplus.com/restruct/restruct.htm#board.

33. The Financial Accounting Standards Board participates with the International Accounting Standards Board and national standard setters to increase the international comparability and quality of standards used by its domestic constituents, who benefit from the board's compilation of comparable information across national borders. See www.fasb.org.

34. See UNCTAD Division of Investment, Technology and Enterprise Development, *Impact Review of DITE Activities 2000–2001*, DITE/OD/IR.04.02 (Geneva: UNCTAD, 2002).

35. Many of these treaties among developed countries as well as between developed countries and other countries are still in force. See U.S. Department of State, *Treaties in Force 2007*, available at http://www.state.gov/s/l/treaty/treaties/2007/index. htm (accessed 20 June 2007). Yet the spaghetti bowl of crisscrossing bilateral agreements, each different in some minute detail, seems to do little more than obfuscate. Although bilateral investment treaties may or may not do much to promote FDI, they do provide some protection to investors and probably do little harm.

36. See Kenichi Ohmae, *The Next Global Stage* (Philadelphia, Pa.: The Wharton School Press, 2005). See also Lester Thurow, *Head to Head: The Coming Economic Battle among Japan, Europe and America* (New York: Murrow, 1992).

37. It appears from the tone of UNCTAD writings, however, that not enough is said about investor responsibilities. While it states that these treaties are symmetrical, UNCTAD raises the questions about whether the treaties provide "mutual benefits to both parties" in a balanced way. See UNCTAD, *Bilateral Investment Treaties in the Mid-1990s* (Geneva: United Nations, 1998), 7.

38. See UNCTC, *Bilateral Investment Treaties* (New York, UN, 1988).

39. See UNCTAD, *Bilateral Investment Treaties in the Mid-1990s*, 29–104.

40. This is somewhat theological, and the debate on the merits of regulation is a long and unending one. See Tagi Sagafi-nejad, Richard Moxon, and Howard V. Perlmutter, eds., *International Technology Transfer Control Systems* (New York: Pergamon, 1981), Chapter 1, for an early discussion of these alternatives. For an extensive review of investment treaties and the role of UNCTAD, see UNCTAD *Bilateral Investment Treaties* (1988), which includes extensive references to the relevant literature.

41. The concept of "national treatment" is part of the standard language in bilateral treaties supported and promoted by the United States. The clause is to investment what the most-favored-nation clause is to trade. Adhering countries agree to extend the same rights and privileges to firms from all signatory countries, not to discriminate between firms.

42. This committee drew up the original OECD Code on multinational enterprises in 1976.

43. See OECD, "Meeting of the OECD at Ministerial Level: Communiqué," Paris, 1995, document SG/Press(95)41; Organisation for Economic Co-operation and Development, "Multilateral Agreement on Investment: Consolidated Text," OECD document DAFFE/MAI(98)8/REV 1, 22 April 1998. See also UNCTAD, *Lessons from MAI* (Geneva: UNCTAD, 1999).

44. For official OECD documents pertaining to the multilateral agreement on investments, see www.oecd.org/daf/mai. For analyses of why the agreement failed, see William A. Dymond, "MAI: A Sad and Melancholy Tale," in *A Big League Player? Canada Among Nations,* ed. Fen O. Hampson, Michael Hart, and Martin Rudner (Oxford: Oxford University Press, 1999), 25–54; Edward Montgomery Graham, "Regulatory Takings, Supranational Treatment and the Multilateral Agreement on Investment: Issues Raised by Nongovernmental Organizations," *Cornell International Law Journal* 31, no. 3 (1998): 599–614; Stephen J. Kobrin, "The MAI and the Clash of Globalizations," *Foreign Policy* 112 (Fall 1998): 97–109; Jessica Mathews, "Power Shift," *Foreign Affairs* 76, no. 1 (1997): 50–66; Sol Picciotto, "Linkages in International Investment Regulation: The Antimonies of the Draft MAI," *University of Pennsylvania Journal of International Economic Law* 19, no. 3 (1998): 731–768.

45. UNIDO had offered to co-publish the investment policy review on Tanzania with UNCTAD, since it had been involved in its preparation, but UNCTAD did not agree, causing a bit of friction between these sister organizations.

46. The association was formed to bring together government organizations charged with promoting inward FDI to coordinate and learn best practices. See www.waipa.org.

47. See UNCTAD, *DITE Activities Report,* 2001, 4.

48. For the World Association of Investment Promotion Agencies, see http://www.waipa.org/why.htm (accessed 18 May 2006).

49. See Fabrice Hatem, *International Investment: Towards the Year 2001* (New York: UN, 1997). The report was a result of collaboration between Invest in France Mission, Arthur Andersen, and UNCTAD.

50. An early publication based on this project is Rob van Tulder, Douglas van den Berghe, and Alan Muller, *The World's Largest Firms and Internationalization* (Rotterdam: Erasmus University, 2000). For a list of the Division of Investment, Technology and Enterprise Development collaborative ventures with academia, see DITE annual reports, available at. www.unctad.org/dite.

51. The search on 4 September 2006 found a total of 8,402 in 181 journals. See www.scirus.com.

52. UNCTAD, *Development Strategies in a Globalizing World* (Geneva: UN, 2003), 2.

53. See Theodore H. Moran, *Multinational Corporations: The Political Economy of Foreign Direct Investment* (Lexington, Mass.: D. C. Heath, 1985), vii.

54. The term is thought to have been coined in 1981 by Antoine W. van Agtmael of the International Finance Corporation, a World Bank affiliate.

55. See Richard Kozul-Wright, "Transnational Corporations and Nation States," in *Managing the Global Economy*, ed. Jonathan Michie and John Grieve Smith (Oxford: Oxford University Press, 1995), 135–171. See also Thurow, *Head to Head*.

56. See Gary Gereffi, "The Renegotiation of Dependency and the Limits of State Autonomy in Mexico (1975–82)," originally published in 1983 and reprinted in *Multinational Corporations: The Political Economy of Foreign Direct Investment*, ed. Theodore Moran (Lexington, Mass.: Lexington Books, 1985), 83–106.

57. Robert Wade argued for such a balance in the role of governments in *Governing the Market: Economic Theory and the Role of Government in East Asian Industrialization*, rev. and expanded ed. (1990; Princeton, N.J.: Princeton University Press, 2003).

58. See UNCTAD, *Report of the Panel of Eminent Persons: Enhancing the Development Role and Impact of UNCTAD* (Geneva: UNCTAD, June 2006).

59. This difference is reflected in the acknowledgement pages of the two flagship annual publications, where there is hardly ever an overlap. As a general rule, there are far fewer applied economists or management-oriented or public policy academics in the Trade and Development Report than there are in the World Investment Report. The latter also tends to cast a much wider net, interfacing with various strands of thinking as it prepares each report.

60. Peter Hansen, interview with the author, United Nations Relief and Works Agency Office, Gaza, 13 May 2001.

7. The World Investment Report Series

1. The World Bank has published the World Development Report since 1978.

2. In 1992, John Dunning was appointed as senior economic advisor and has since played a major advisory role in the preparation of each of the WIRs. The late Sanjaya Lall was a frequent contributor to the series and played a leading role on some occasions.

3. Many contributors willingly provided input for a modest fee or for free because of the prestige associated with working for the United Nations.

4. Guy de Jonquiere of the *Financial Times*, personal communication, 2 November 2000.

5. The *World Investment Report* 2000 was simultaneously released in over sixty countries and the WIR 2005 was simultaneously released in over seventy-five. While it is difficult to measure the ultimate impact of this public diffusion, it has served one of UNCTAD's purposes—broad dissemination of germane information, especially to developing countries. The series has become more widely used by practitioners, academics, and governments. Its annual launches are generating an increasing number of press reports around the world. Most of the press coverage is available at UNCTAD's Web site.

6. The World Trade Organization, likewise, undertakes trade policy reviews at members' request. See www.wto.org.

7. It was less than 100 pages.

8. This volume was the first to be published under UNCTAD in Geneva.

9. The term was popularized by Kenichi Ohmae in his *Triad Power: The Coming Shape of Global Competition* (New York: Free Press, 1985).

10. See UNCTAD, *World Investment Report 2002: Transnational Corporations and Export Competitiveness* (Geneva: UNCTAD, 2002), 80–81.

11. The World Competitiveness Report was originally begun as a joint venture between the World Economic Forum and the Institute of Management Development in the 1980s, but the two organizations parted ways in the mid-1990s and each began publishing its own index and report on competitiveness. See the annual reports and Web sites, respectively, of the Institute of Management Development, *World Competitiveness Yearbook* (www.imd.ch) and the World Economic Forum, *World Competitiveness Report* (www.weforum.org).

12. See UNCTAD, *Lessons from the MAI* (New York: UNCTAD, 1999), 11; and UNCTAD, *Trends in International Investment Agreements: An Overview* (New York: UN, 1999), 55–58.

13. The *World Investment Report 1996* reported that over sixty countries had introduced changes in their investment regimes, 106 of which were in the direction of more liberalization. The *World Investment Report 2007* noted, however, a somewhat cautionary countertrend: while the total number of national policy changes favoring further liberalization of FDI regimes continued to exceed—by a wide margin— changes away from liberalization, in 2005 and again in 2006 the pace of antiliberalization changes accelerated. See chapter 9 for further analysis of this trend. In addition, some two-thirds of the 1,160 bilateral investment treaties (BITs), double-taxation treaties (DTTs), and other agreements with investment provisions in effect as of mid-1996 were concluded in the 1990s. UNCTAD, *World Investment Report 2002*, 14–21.

14. See UNCTAD, *World Investment Report 1992: Transnational Corporations as Engines of Growth* (Geneva: UNCTAD, 1992), 52.

15. Examples include the Economist Intelligence Unit, Political Risk Services Group, Chase Econometrics, and Wharton Econometric Forecasting Associates. Many textbooks, too, borrow liberally from the WIR and refer to the source as "the United Nations," if they refer to a source at all.

16. This concept is akin to trade theory's acquired comparative advantage.

17. UNCTAD, *World Investment Report 1999: Foreign Direct Investment and the Challenge of Development* (Geneva: UNCTAD, 1999).

18. The most notable among these mergers and acquisitions were the $55 billion acquisition of VoiceStream Wireless by Deutsche Telekom, the $16.5 billion bid for PaineWebber Group by UBS, and the $13.5 billion bid for the investment banking firm of Donaldson, Lufkin & Jenrette by Credit Suisse First Boston.

19. Veblen coined the term "advances of backwardness" in *The Theory of the Leisure Class*. In retrospect, the term is more applicable to South Korea than to Argentina.

20. Michael E. Porter, *The Competitive Advantage of Nations* (New York: Free Press, 1990).

21. See www.unctad/wir.

22. The principal business papers, *Financial Times* and *Wall Street Journal*, for instance, report the main findings of these reports as soon as they are released.

23. *SUNS*, a Malaysia-based pro–Third World periodical has been harshly critical in its review of each new WIR. It often accuses the WIR of being too soft on TNCs.

24. Raymond Vernon, *In the Hurricane's Eye: The Troubled Prospects of Multi-national Enterprises* (Cambridge, Mass.: Harvard University Press, 1998).

25. H. Peter Gray, review of *World Investment Report 1998*, in *The International Trade Journal* 13, no. 3 (1999): 293–343.

26. See Lorraine Eden, "Review Article: World Investment Report 1995: Transnational Corporations and Competitiveness," *Transnational Corporations* (1996): 154–156.

27. See UNCTAD, *World Investment Report 2004: The Shift Towards Services* (Geneva: UNCTAD, 2004), 17, for a description of the methodology.

28. As it liberalized its policies to encourage FDI, the Chinese government kept a watchful eye on the series. A member of the Chinese government delegation at a 2000 UNCTAD meeting stated that his government routinely and carefully studied the WIRs as it developed its FDI policy.

29. See Robert Wade, *Governing the Market: Economic Theory and the Role of Government in East Asian Industrialization* (Princeton, N.J.: Princeton University Press, 2003).

30. See, in particular, UNCTAD, *World Development Report 2004: The Shift towards Services* (Geneva: UNCTAD, 2004), which, in addition to offering an extensive treatment of FDI in services, also focuses on the proper role of the government in a market economy.

31. It is UNCTAD's policy to discount the price of its publications, including WIRs, to buyers in developing countries, thus lightening the price burden.

32. Even some sister institutions within the UN system privately doubt the reliably of some of the FDI data.

33. This topic was taken up in the *World Investment Report 2006*.

8. Other Members of the UN Galaxy

1. Francis Blanchard, interview with the author, Ferney Voltaire, France, 10 May 2001.

2. See ILO, *Multinational Enterprises and Social Policy* (Geneva: ILO, 1973); see also Hans Gunter, ed., *Transnational Industrial Relations: The Impact of Multi-national Corporations and Economic Regionalism on Industrial Relations* (London: St. Martin's Press, 1972).

3. ILO, *Multinational Enterprises*, 176.

4. ILO conventions and declarations take on legal status upon ratification by member countries that ratify them.

5. Abebe Abate, interview with the author, Geneva, 16 May 2002.

6. The definition of the subject under study and its terminology became a matter of considerable debate. Various members of the ILO tripartite working groups believed that when a corporation operated in a country other than its own, it was subject to that country's laws. Therefore, because "transnational" connotes an over-reaching influence in areas other than business, it was an inaccurate term. Since a corporation operated in several countries, it had more than one nationality, and therefore "multinational" was considered a more appropriate term. Similar considerations went into choosing "enterprise" over "corporation." Trade union representatives

thought the term "enterprise" had fewer negative connotations than "corporation." In retrospect, this discussion of terminology may appear arcane, yet it reveals the differences in perspective among the stakeholders at that time.

7. ILO, *Multinational Enterprises*, 24.

8. At over 4,300 words, this was a rather lengthy document, signifying the importance the organization attached to it.

9. International Labour Office, *Information Document on Ratifications and Standards-Related Activities*, Report 3, Part 2 (Geneva: International Labour Office, 2006), 8, available at http://www.ilo.org/public/english/standards/relm/ilc/ilc95/pdf/rep-iii-2.pdf (accessed 17 December 2007).

10. See *Report of the Chairperson of the Governing Body to the Conference for the Year 2005–06* (Geneva: ILO, 2006), available at http://www.ilo.org/public/english/standards/relm/ilc/ilc95/pdf/pr-1.pdf (accessed 8 June 2006).

11. Jill Murray, *Corporate Social Responsibility: An Overview of Principles and Practices* (Geneva: Policy Integration and Statistics Department, World Commission on the Social Dimension of Globalization, ILO, May 2004), 15.

12. "The Oral History Interview of Juan Somavía, 2 October 2001," in *The Complete Oral History Transcripts from UN Voices*, CD-ROM (New York: UNIHP, 2007), 60.

13. Ibid., 65.

14. See Tagi Sagafi-nejad, "Should Global Rules Have Legal Teeth? Policing (WHO Framework on Tobacco Control) vs. Good Citizenship (UN Global Compact)," *International Journal of Business* 10, no. 4 (2005): 363–382; Henry Saffer, *Tobacco Control in Developing Countries* (Oxford: Oxford University Press, 2000); Raymond M. Jones, *Strategic Management in a Hostile Environment: Lessons from the Tobacco Industry* (New York: Quorum Books, 1997); and Y. Saloojee and Ross Hammond, "Fatal Deception: The Tobacco Industry's 'New' Global Standards for Tobacco Marketing," *Tobacco Control: WHO Tobacco Control Papers*, Paper WHO3, San Francisco, University of California, 1 October 2001, available at http://repositories.cdlib.org/context/tc/article/1103/type/pdf/viewcontent.

15. As early as 1964, a U.S. surgeon-general's report stated unequivocally that smoking causes cancer. See Neil Buckley, "Government vs. Industry—50 Years of Fraud: Washington Sues Big Tobacco for $240 bn of Alleged Ill-Gotten Gains," *Financial Times*, 8 September 2004.

16. Dr. Wigand later became the subject of *The Insider*, a movie based on his campaign against the tobacco industry, where he had worked as a scientist for many years. His personal Web site chronicles his campaign, including his testimony before the U.S. Congress and WHO's World Health Assembly; see http://www.jeffreywigand.com/index.php. See also Marie Brenner, "The Man Who Knew Too Much," *Vanity Fair*, May 1996, available at http://www.jeffreywigand.com/vanityfair.php.

17. See "The WHO Framework Convention on Tobacco Control on Track to Become Law by the End of the Year," WHO press release, 2 July 2004, available at http://www.who.int/mediacentre/news/releases/2004/pr47/en (accessed 11 September 2004).

18. The United States objected to certain of its provisions and did not endorse the draft until 10 May 2004. See WHO, "Updated Status of the WHO Framework

Convention on Tobacco Control," available at http://www.who.int/tobacco/framework/
countrylist/en/index.html. For the Framework Convention on Tobacco Control, see
http://www.who.int/tobacco/framework/en (accessed 11 September 2004).

19. Philip Morris and Japan Tobacco had a combined market share of 40.5 percent of the international cigarette market; this estimate was made by the Wall Street
firm of Solomon Smith Barney as reported by G. Fairclough and S. Branch, "Tobacco Giants Prepare New Marketing Curbs Ahead of UN Treaty," *Wall Street Journal*, 11 September 2001.

20. See Tobacco Manufacturers' Association, "Who We Are," available at
www.the-tma.org.uk.

21. According to services that monitor company performance, including Hoover,
Moody's, Dunn & Bradstreet, RMA, and Mergent, the performance of the tobacco
and beverages industry have often been above average compared with other industries. See Jones, *Strategic Management in a Hostile Environment*.

22. Quote from Sagafi-nejad, "Should Global Rules Have Legal Teeth?" 370.

23. See the Web sites of British American Tobacco and R. J. Reynolds at
www.bat.com and www.rjrt.com, respectively (accessed 1 November 2007).

24. Perhaps significantly, Japan Tobacco's international headquarters is in Geneva, home of the WHO, the same organization under whose auspices the Framework Convention on Tobacco Control and other antismoking measures were adopted.

25. See http://www.jti.co.jp/JTI/opinion/FCTC/statement_E.html.

26. See British American Tobacco, "WHO Framework Convention on Tobacco
Control," available at http://www.bat.com/group/sites/uk__3mnfen.nsf/vwPagesWebLive/
B20AD0AA3723CB62C1257314004EF6AA?opendocument&SKN=1&TMP=1 (accessed
20 October 2002).

27. Altria Group, "Disgorgement Summary," n.p., n.d., available at http://www.
altria.com/download/pdf/media_doj_disgorgement%20summary%2010_21_05.pdf (accessed 17 December 2007).

28. The company's aggressive campaigns included the 1975 publication of *Nestlé
in Developing Countries*, a 228-page book that it circulated widely to put forward its
case and deflect criticism. The cover of the book reads: "While Nestlé is not a phil-
anthropic society, facts and figures clearly prove that the nature of its activities in developing countries is self-evident as a factor that contributes to economic development. The company's constant need for local raw materials, processing and staff, and
the particular contribution it brings to local industry, support the fact that Nestlé's
presence in the Third World is based on common interests in which the progress
of one is always to the benefit of the other." The book outlined the company's work
in Mexico, Malaysia, India, the Philippines, and elsewhere to improve dairy farming and a host of other activities. Nestlé, *Nestlé in Developing Countries* (Vevey,
Switzerland: Nestlé Alimentana, S.A., 1975), cover page. See also Nestlé Infant Formula Audit Commission, *Fourth Quarterly Report* (Washington, D.C.: NIFAC, 30
June 1983); and Stephen Webbe, "The Nestle Boycott: Is It Fair?" *Christian Science
Monitor*, 18 July 1979; and Stephen Webbe, "The Nestle Boycott Kills Babies," *Wall
Street Journal*, 1 November 1979.

29. The author credits this point to Richard Jolly.

30. See The International Treaty on Plant Genetic Resources for Food and Agri-
cultures, available at www.fao.org/ag/cgrfa/itpgr.htm#text.

31. The Soviet Union tended to exert more influence over the operations and practices of this organization. In the post-Soviet era, that source of external pressure has been eliminated.

32. Walter Chudson, *The Acquisition of Technology from Multinational Corporations by Developing Countries* (New York: UNITAR, 1974).

33. See Desiree Abrahams, *Regulating Corporations: A Resource Guide* (Geneva: UNRISD, 2004).

34. See the Web site of the International Trade Centre at www.intracen.org.

35. The World Intellectual Property Organization, a UN specialized agency since 1974, dates back to the Paris Union of 1883 and the Berne Convention of 1886, when a regime to protect intellectual and artistic assets was first codified. Since that time, it has evolved to include all forms of intellectual property—patents, trademarks and trade names, inventions, industrial design, and copyrights. See www.wipo.net

36. See World Bank, *Curbing the Epidemic: Governments and the Economics of Tobacco Control* (Washington, D.C.: World Bank, 1999).

37. Responsible global capitalism is a term coined by John Dunning and explored in his edited collection *Making Globalization Good* (New York: Oxford University Press, 2003), 11–40.

38. This notion is reminiscent of the maxim appropriate to many early American Quakers who came to Philadelphia to do good but, inadvertently, also did well.

39. The ten principles of the Global Compact are detailed on its Web site, where each principle is hyperlinked to additional information and details. See www.unglobalcompact.org.

40. After some two years of negotiations, the convention was adopted by the UN in November 2003 in Merida, Mexico, where it was open to member countries for adoption. See UN, "Consensus Reached on UN Convention against Corruption," UN press release, 2 October 2003, available at http://www.un.org/News/Press/docs/2003/soccp270.doc.htm.

41. See "United Nations Global Compact" at www.unglobalcompact.org.

42. The goals were enunciated in September 2000, when the 191 members of the United Nations pledged to achieve them. Besides the office of Secretary-General, other UN bodies with a defined role in the Millennium Development Goals include the UNDP, the ILO, and UNCTAD. See www.unglobalcompact.org. For the text of the Millennium Development Goals, see www.un.org/millenniumgoals/.

43. See "Bluewashed and Boilerplated: A Breakthrough in International Corporate Diplomacy," *The Economist*, 17 July 2004.

44. See Georg Kell and John Gerard Ruggie, "Global Markets and Social Legitimacy: The Case of the 'Global Compact,'" paper presented at the conference Governing the Public Domain beyond the Era of the Washington Consensus? Redrawing the Line between the State and the Market, York University, Toronto, Canada, 4–6 November 1999.

45. Peter Utting, *Business Responsibility for Sustainable Development*, UNRISD Occasional Paper 2 (Geneva: UN Research Institute for Social Research, January 2000); Peter Utting and Ann Zammit, *Beyond Pragmatism: Appraising UN-Business Partnerships* (Geneva: UN Research Institute for Social Research, 2006). For a conceptual analysis of stakeholder theory, see R. Edward Freeman, *Strategic Management: A Stakeholder Approach* (Boston: Pitman, 1984).

46. See Tagi Sagafi-nejad, "Should Global Rules Have Legal Teeth? Policing (WHO Tobacco Control) vs. Good Citizenship (UN Global Compact)," *International Journal of Business* 10, no. 4 (2005): 363–382.

9. The Legacy and the Future

1. Rubens Ricupero, "Nine Years at UNCTAD: A Personal Testimony," in UNCTAD, *Beyond Conventional Wisdom in Development Policy* (New York: UN, 2004), x.

2. The term "born global" was first introduced my Michael W. Rennie of McKinsey and Company in 1993 and referred to firms that venture into arenas outside of their home country from the beginning. See his "Global Competitiveness: Born Global," *The McKinsey Quarterly* 4 (1993): 45–52. He was referring to small- to medium-sized Australian firms that successfully competed from inception with large established global players. Although the UN was born global, this concept has not heretofore been applied to it. See Tagi Sagafi-nejad, "United Nations Galaxy as the Ultimate Born-Global Organization: Contributions to the Study of FDI and TNCs," presented at the 7th Annual Asian Academy of Management and the 4th World Congress of Association for Global Advancement, Penang, Malaysia, 21–25 May 2007. Published in *Advances in Global Business* 4, no. 1 (2007): 401–416. This theme is explored further in a forthcoming article by Dunning and Sagafi-nejad.

3. The terms "fragile," "fertile," and "futile" encapsulate Howard V. Perlmutter's three alternative scenarios for "the first or last global civilization." Some of these ideas were presented as the keynote address at the 12th Annual Conference on Western Hemispheric Challenges, Texas A&M International University, 22 March 2007 and will be published as the inaugural essay in the TAMIU Essays on the Global Economy Series by Texas A&M International University. These themes will be further explored in his forthcoming book, *The First of Last Global Civilization: The Race*. See also Paul Kennedy, *The Parliament of Man: The Past, Present, and Future of the United Nations* (New York: Random House, 2006).

4. Louis Emmerij, Richard Jolly, and Thomas G. Weiss, *Ahead of the Curve? UN Ideas and Global Challenges* (Bloomington: Indiana University Press, 2001).

5. Most of the work is a labor of love, and champions admit that it is nearly impossible to sanction a UN employee who is unwilling to perform.

6. Evidence shows that small countries generally have taken more advantage of UN advice on matters of policy than have larger developing countries, probably because small countries have greater dexterity in seizing external opportunities, be they exports or advice from international organizations. Larger countries tend to be hamstrung by their larger bureaucracies and the conflicting demands by many competing internal stakeholders. "Small is beautiful," popularized by the late E. F. Schumacher, founder of the London-based Intermediate Technology Development Group, is relevant to this point. In 1968, Schumacher circulated a pamphlet titled "Small Is Beautiful," which led to the 1973 publication of his book *Small Is Beautiful: Economics as if People Mattered* (New York: Harper and Row, 1973), released again in 1999 by Hartley and Marks Publishers (London). He advocated small-scale technologies suited to local conditions in poor developing countries. The phrase became short-

hand for an alternative approach to development that is more suited to conditions in rural areas in developing countries.

7. These parameters of legitimacy, originally developed by Howard V. Perlmutter and Tagi Sagafi-nejad, were last applied to a comparative analysis of the World Health Organization's Framework Convention on Tobacco Control and the UN Global Compact. See Tagi Sagafi-nejad, "Should Global Rules Have Legal Teeth? Policing (WHO Framework on Tobacco Control) vs. Good Citizenship (UN Global Compact)," *International Journal of Business* 10, no. 4 (2005): 363–382.

8. Textbooks in economic development, international business, international political economy, and international relations, among others, have made extensive use of material first published in WIRs. Examples include John Daniels, *International Business* (various editions); and Gerald M. Meier and James E. Rauch, *Leading Issues in Economics of Development*, 8th ed. (Oxford: Oxford University Press, 2005).

9. Developing countries, in particular, regularly monitor the WIR to observe trends and track policy advice. This is evident from the extensive coverage the publication receives each year in these countries. See http://www.unctad.org/Templates/Page.asp?intItemID=1481&lang=1 for a list of WIR reviews.

10. See http://www.ilo.org/public/english/employment/multi/download/english.pdf. Note that multilateral conventions become binding and legally enforceable in a country when that country ratifies them. The declaration stopped short of a convention, thereby sidestepping the thorny and divisive issue of whether the instrument should be legally binding.

11. Activism on the issue of child labor pitted the ILO against Ukraine and Myanmar and other nation-states for not adhering to these principles. In the twenty-first century, the ILO is playing an important role in evaluating the contributions of TNCs to social issues.

12. See *Investing for Long-Term Value: Integrating Environmental, Social and Governance Value Drivers in Asset Management and Financial Research—A State-of-the-Art Assessment* (New York: Global Compact, 2005), available at http://www.unglobalcompact.org/Issues/financial_markets/zurich_rep.pdf.

13. It is difficult, however, to gauge how intensively the skills and knowledge have been diffused within the host countries.

14. Examples are the South Korean company Hyundai's entry into the U.S. automotive manufacturing market, the Indian steel conglomerate's acquisition of the Luxemburg-based Arcelor, a Venezuelan company's bid for a Canadian firm, and the Chinese company Lenovo's purchase of the personal computer division of IBM. UNCTAD's *World Investment Report 2006* was devoted entirely to this new breed of TNC.

15. Iran writhed in the grip of Islamic fundamentalists as President Mahmoud Ahmadi-nejad sought to lock horns with the world and sweep Israel into the sea. Venezuela's president Hugo Chavez, meanwhile, continued his anti-American rhetoric, telling Al-Jazeera television on 4 August 2006 that "the American empire is the number one enemy in the way of the kingdom of peace and justice"; quoted in Sidney Weintraub, "Energy Cooperation and Confrontation in the Western Hemisphere," *Issues in International Political Economy*, no. 80 (August 2006), available at http://www.csis.org/media/csis/pubs/issues200608.pdf. Leaders of Bolivia, Cuba, Ecua-

dor, and Argentina have embraced the Chavez rhetoric, accompanied by largesse that Venezuela's oil boom has fueled. Leftist Mexicans continued to dispute conservative Felipe Calderon's close victory in the 2006 presidential election by demonstrating in the streets, even after Mexico's court ruled in favor of Calderon. All these events portended the possible advent of another storm. See Russell Gold, "Exxon, Conoco Exit Venezuela Under Pressure," *Wall Street Journal*, 27 June 2007, A1, for one such disquieting news item.

16. The terms "right" and "left" are shorthand expressions and are used here as they are in ordinary discourse. Countries more prone to state intervention and public control over most economic activities, such as communist and socialist countries, are commonly regarded as on the "left." Those on the "right" are market-based economies where private property dominates the economic sphere.

17. These scandals are symbolized by Enron Corporation, whose misadventures and ultimate demise have been extensively reported. Casualties of corporate misdeeds continued to mount as executives were found out, disgraced, and fired. In another example, Heinrich von Pierer, chairman of the board of the German giant Siemens and an advisor to two former German chancellors, was forced to resign in April 2007, the victim of a series scandals that enveloped that company. See Richard Milne, "Von Pierer Is First Scalp in Siemens Scandals," *Financial Times*, 20 April 2007.

18. These questions were addressed in Sagafi-nejad, "Should Global Rules Have Legal Teeth?" and in Chapter 8.

19. Nearly all UN agencies were either under scrutiny or were the subject of reports that called for structural reform. The UNIHP series of which this book is a part contains several references to ideas for reform, including the inaugural volume in this series, *Ahead of the Curve? UN Ideas and Global Challenges*, by Louis Emmerij, Richard Jolly, and Thomas G. Weiss. At the request of its newly anointed Secretary-General, UNCTAD received a report of the Panel of Eminent Persons in June 2006. See *Report of the Panel of Eminent Persons: Enhancing the Development Role and Impact of UNCTAD* (Geneva: UNCTAD, June 2006), available at http://www.unctad.org/sections/edm_dir/docs/osg20061_en.pdf. Earlier, UNIDO underwent major restructuring in response to similar calls for reform.

20. The Texas Republican Party platform in 2006 included a proposition that the United States withdraw from the United Nations.

21. A seemingly trivial but symbolically significant example is the persistent use, over several decades, of different terminologies; the enterprise uses the term "transnational corporations" while the ILO uses "multinational enterprises." Therefore, these recent recommendations for consolidation and partnerships may not be easily accomplished.

22. This was the case when UNCTAD and UNIDO cooperated in producing Tanzania's investment policy review; they could not agree to publish it under joint sponsorship.

23. Many firms try to list their stock on the world's major exchanges. Many of these exchanges have stringent disclosure requirements. The enterprise uses the information in these disclosures.

24. These discussions sought to recalculate IMF and World Bank quotas and thus the share of power new global players such as Europe, Japan, India, and China

wielded. None of these countries were taken seriously enough when the UN and the Bretton Woods institutions were being created. Now "the times are a-changing." See Colin Bradford and Johannes Linn, *Global Governance Reform—Breaking the Stalemate* (Washington, D.C.: Brookings Institution, 2007).

25. See, for instance, WTO, *Trade Policy Review: Separate Customs Territory of Taiwan, Penghu, Kinmen, and Matsu (Chinese Taipei)*, WTO document WT/TPR/S/165, 16 May 2006.

26. The OECD has been working on matters related to TNCs for three decades. Its "Guidelines for Multinational Enterprises," initially agreed upon in 1976 and revised periodically, constitute its most visible product. It is a group of wealthy countries (with an addition in the last decade of two formerly developing countries, South Korea and Mexico) and is not a member of the UN family. However, the OECD's work on MNEs is monitored by the UN, as the UN's work is by the OECD. Its quest to develop the Multilateral Agreement on Investment came to naught, but its convention on bribery met with modest success.

27. The literature on strategic alliances can provide insights. See Farok J. Contractor and Peter Lorange, *Cooperative Strategies in International Business* (Lexington, Mass.: D. C. Heath, 1988).

28. See Rubens Ricupero, "Nine Years at UNCTAD: A Personal Testimony," in UNCTAD, *Beyond Conventional Wisdom in Development Policy: An Intellectual History of UNCTAD* (New York: UN, 2004), xv. Available at http://www.unctad.org/en/docs//edm20044_en.pdf.

29. For a discussion of centripetal and centrifugal forces impacting globalization, see Tagi Sagafi-nejad, "Globalization and Regionalism: Contending Forces in the Integration of the Americas," Business Association for Latin American Studies (BALAS) annual meeting, Boston, 17–20 April 1991. These terms have been used more recently in the scholarly literature on globalization. See, for instance, Paul Krugman, *Pop Internationalism* (Boston: MIT Press, 1995).

30. See Howard V. Perlmutter, "On the Rocky Road to the Global Civilization," *Human Relations* 44, no. 9 (1991): 897–920; and "The First or Last Global Civilization: Three Scenarios," keynote address at the 12th Annual Western Hemispheric Conference, Texas A&M International University, Loredo, Texas, 22 March 2007.

31. See Sagafi-nejad, "Globalization and Regionalism."

32. See James Coleman, "Social Capital in the Creation of Human Capital," *American Journal of Sociology* 94, supplement (1988): S-95-S120.

33. See Joseph Siglitz, "Towards a New Paradigm for Development," in *Making Globalization Good: The Moral Challenges of Global Capitalism*, ed. John H. Dunning (Oxford: Oxford University Press, 2003), 77–107. See also Joseph E. Stiglitz, *Making Globalization Work* (New York: Norton, 2006).

34. See Ellen Laipson, "The United Nations in 2015: Some Alternative Futures— A Workshop Summary," The Henry L. Stimpson Center, Washington, D.C., 2006.

Appendix 1: Organizational Diagram of UNCTC at Its Inception, 1974

Executive Director
Assistant Secretary General   Klaus A. Sahlgren

Office of the Executive Director

Associate Director in Charge   Gustave Feissel

Special Assistant to the Executive Director
and Chief of the Administrative Unit   Sylvanus Tiewut

Administrative Officer   Jacinto de Vera

Personal Assistant to the Executive Director Carolyn Scott

Special Advisor   Sidney Dell

Chief Advisor on
Legal Matters   Samuel Asante

Information Analysis Division

— Undertakes systematic collection and analysis of information relative to TNCs at the aggregate and enterprise levels, relevant national legislation and policies as well as bibliographical data

— Disseminates the above information on a continuing basis through publications and reports and other means as may be requested by governments

Policy Analysis Division

— Determines research and policy analysis on economic, legal, social, and political matters related to transnational corporations

— Conducts studies and carries out other work on the preparation of a code of conduct and of international arrangements and agreements concerning transnational corporations

Advisory Services

— Helps requesting governments
    — formulate policies related to foreign direct investment
    — acquire technology
    — review the economic, financial, legal, and operational provisions of contracts being negotiated with TNCs
    — prepare for negotiations, including drafting contracts

Director	Rana K. N. Singh	Officer-in-Charge	Itsuo Kawamura
Assistant Director	Ralph Tsvilev	Assistant Director	Gerhard Rambow
Senior Transnational Corporations Affairs Officer	E. H. Wong	Senior Transnational Corporations Affairs Officers	Mohamed Al-Ali Maurice Odle Hans-Fredrik Samuelsson
Transnational Corporations Affairs Officers	Ian Kinniburgh Sok-Chun Tang Edith Ward Slawomir Borowy Fahri Boumechal Harris Gleckman Charles Kirudja	Transnational Corporations Affairs Officers	Mohamed Fayache Ahmed Rhazaoul Karl P. Sauvant Michael Mimicopoulos Nickolay Zaitsev Anne Muroux

—Organizes and conducts training workshops on matters related to regulating and negotiating with TNCs aimed at strengthening the skills of officials of developing countries

—Helps institutions of higher learning develop and conduct ongoing programs of training in matters related to TNCs

Associate Director in Charge	Gustave Feissel
Senior Transnational Corporations Affairs Officer	Benny Widyono
Transnational Corporations Affairs Officers	Felix Mosha Boris Velk Ellen Seidensticker Donald De Vivo Charles Kim

Joint Units of UNCTC with the Regional Economic Commissions

Africa (ECA)	Asia and Pacific (ESCAP)	Europe (ECE)	Latin America and the Caribbean (ECLAC)	Western Asia (ECWA)
Chief of Unit	Chief of Unit	Chief of Unit	Chief of Unit	Chief of Unit
Bingu Wa Mutharika	Tyn Myint-U	Jean-Michel Collete	A. Nuñez del Prado	———

Appendix 2. From New York (UNCTC) to Geneva (DITE): Leadership

1975–82	Klaus Sahlgren
1983–84	Sidney Dell (retired December 1984)
1985–92	Peter Hansen
1992–93	Transition from "UNCTC" to "Transnational Corporations and Management Division," the United Nations Department of Economic and Social Affairs
1993	Moved to UNCTAD, Geneva as its Division of Investment, Technology and Enterprise Development (DITE), Roger Lawrence (Director, Globalization Division), Officer-in-Charge
1994–2001	Lyn Mytelka, Division Chief, DITE
2001	Karl P. Sauvant, Acting Division Chief, DITE
2002–2005	Karl P. Sauvant, Division Chief, DITE
2005–	Khalil Hamdani, Division Chief, DITE

Index

Page numbers in italics indicate illustrations.